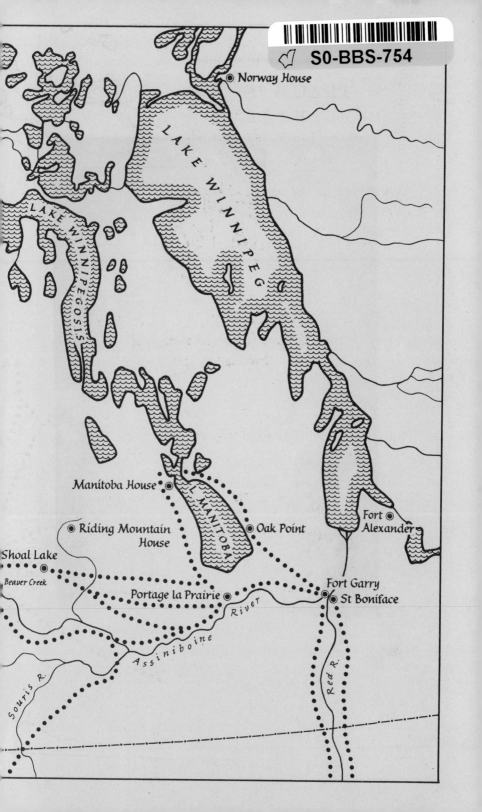

Norway House

LAKE WINNIPEG

LAKE WINNIPEGOSIS

Manitoba House

L. MANITOBA

Riding Mountain House

Oak Point

Fort Alexander

Shoal Lake

Beaver Creek

Portage la Prairie

Assiniboine River

Fort Garry
St Boniface

Souris R.

Red R.

# IN RUPERT'S LAND
*Memoirs of Walter Traill*

# IN RUPERT'S LAND

*Memoirs of Walter Traill*

---

*Edited by*

**MAE ATWOOD**

McCLELLAND AND STEWART LIMITED

*Toronto/Montreal*

*The Canadian Publishers*
McClelland and Stewart Limited
25 Hollinger Road, Toronto 374

*Printed and bound in England by*
Billing & Sons Limited, Guildford and London

# CONTENTS

# FOREWORD

In the centre of what is now Canada a stone gateway faced to the
North-West across thousands of miles of prairies and mountains
to the far Yukon, south to Vancouver Island, and north to the
Mackenzie River Basin. What remains of this north entrance to the
headquarters of this vast area now stands in Fort Garry Park a
few blocks from the Union Station in Winnipeg. No one was near
to disturb the solitude on a frosty December day in 1968 when I
stood beside this silent monument to the men who for two
hundred years travelled the broad spaces before it. A hundred
years ago an uprising bespoke the birthpangs of the Province of
Manitoba. It is of the years immediately preceding this event that
Mr. Traill writes.

For many years my husband's great-uncle, Walter Traill,
intended to write the story of his life in the West. Finally he enlisted my aid in assembling the wealth of material he had written.
After his death in 1932 I continued to work with the large collection of papers he left in my charge, endeavouring to do justice to
his style of narration while arranging its substance to make it
more readable. This is the result. The writing is almost entirely his
own. A minimum of words have been added to achieve continuity,
while the greatest care has been taken to preserve in entirety the
facts he has related.

It is with gratitude and admiration that I acknowledge my
debt to the National and Provincial Archives of Canada for their
painstaking preservation of our country's national literature, and
for their assistance in gaining access to it. The late John Hosie of
the Provincial Archives of British Columbia in Victoria was the
first to impress upon me the importance of preserving Mr. Traill's
writings while his successors, Willard Ireland and Dr. Dorothy

Blakey Smith, have assisted with advice and relevant information. Dr. C. Bruce Ferguson, in charge of the Public Archives of Nova Scotia at Dalhousie University in Halifax, on reading a manuscript of Walter Traill's, reassured me that it was of interest to all Canadians. In Winnipeg Provincial Archivist H. W. L. Bowsfield, M.A. and his staff accorded my inquiries a responsive warmth that was reminiscent of Mr. Traill's attachment to his old friends there. To Mr. Robin Farr, former Editor of McGill University Press, who gave unstintingly of his time in reading and evaluating the author's writings, I am grateful for his valuable advice and encouragement towards publication.

MAE ATWOOD

# INTRODUCTION

WALTER TRAILL came striding across the valley on his first visit
to us in the early years of our marriage. A tall figure, spare from
the activity which greatly belied his eighty years, he wore with an
air of distinction his black tam, a silver thistle cresting the front
of its tartan band. The aquiline features of a long face lost their
sharpness beneath the light of his blue eyes, eyes so like those that
smile from the portrait of his mother, Catherine Parr Traill, on the
frontispiece of a recent edition of her book, *Backwoods of Canada*.
That he would stride across two generations of Canadian history,
decade by decade and year by year, as he had passed orchards of
blossoming trees, row by row, that morning, was to be revealed to
me during many subsequent visits.

My husband, Clinton Atwood, was a favourite nephew, and I
was delighted when the old world courtesy of Uncle Walter's
warm greeting enveloped me in this happy relationship. As he
followed me to the kitchen his comments of current affairs
sparkled with mention of people and places he had known. One
name was disquieting – surely Lord Strathcona had been dead
some fourteen years. Two miles was a long walk, thought I, and
the day was warm. Uncle Walter would be better after lunch.

It was then that conversation flowed easily as he held me
enchanted by his extensive vocabulary and graceful phrases,
interspersed with the stately discourse of a Hudson's Bay
Company officer and spoken in the cultured accents of a gentleman
of an age gone past. Suddenly my mind flew open – of course, he
had lived and worked in the centre of Canada from the beginning
of Confederation. The names I heard were those of real people
who had shared in the events of the growing West during his
vigorous young manhood. Here was its history, alive and exciting,

A*                                                              9 resurrected for me from the desiccated residue of history lessons.

It was not long before his quick mind perceived that after each visit I was recording much of what he had told me. Letters were exchanged when visits were not possible. Sometimes he enclosed freshly written stories, "knowing," as he once wrote, "that you have a ravenous appetite for such." At other times a package would arrive with a note: "I am sending you another bunch of copy." This might be stories he had written some time ago.

Probably it was a letter he received in May, 1930, from his old friend Mrs. John Archibald McDonald that did most to kindle his desire to publish a book:

*Dear Mr. Traill:*

*Can you be so good as to give me a few details of the trip my mother, my brother Glenlyon and myself made from Fort Pelly in 1870? . . . The person in charge of the expedition . . . I always thought it was you . . . the point at which we parted from our "Company's escort" has always been unknown to me.*

*With kindest regards,*
*Yours most sincerely,*
*Elleonora C. McDonald*

There is an unfinished letter in reply written by Walter Traill with his left hand as his right hand, which had once been frozen, now gave him trouble. He wished to send her a more detailed account than one he had written some time ago. This he brought to me to type. Mrs. McDonald was the younger daughter of Chief Factor Robert Campbell, the Hudson's Bay Company officer in charge of the Swan River District with headquarters in Fort Pelly in 1870. She had been a little girl of four years when Mr. Campbell entrusted his family to the care of his Junior Clerk.

We, too, delighted in all that Walter Traill would tell us of his former life, but it was hard to get him to talk about himself. His interests were chiefly in others and in what was happening around him, and he preferred to speak of important men and events. A gentleman of the old school, he abhorred anything in the form of boasting and in his writings any reference to himself may be a profound understatement.

Walter's parents, Catherine and Thomas Traill, arrived in
Canada in 1832 and settled near Catherine's brother, Samuel
Strickland, where Lakefield is now. While Thomas cleared the
land and built the house, his bride found a warm welcome under
the hospitable roof of Mrs. Stewart at Peterborough. The Traills
lived near Lakefield for seven years, then moved with their four
small children to the village of Ashburnham, which was to
become a suburb of Peterborough. Another seven years passed,
during which four more children were born, although only two
survived, before they moved north to a second forest home in the
vicinity of Rice Lake. A year later, on August 9, 1847, Walter
John Strickland Traill was born.* His mother was forty-five and
his father nine years older when their ninth child arrived. Although their home during Walter's infancy was at some distance
from Peterborough, this youngest son seems to have had a
special place in the warm heart of Mrs. Stewart. Years later he
still returned affectionate messages to the "friend I value highly."

The first ten years of Walter's life were spent by Rice Lake
amid the scenes of two of his mother's books, *Afar in the Forest*
and *Canadian Crusoes or Lost in the Backwoods*. The eager, alert
mind of the child found in his woodland surroundings a wealth of
interest enhanced by his mother's keen eye and lively knowledge
of its plants and animals that endear her stories to all children.

His parents were unused and ill-suited to the hard labour of
pioneer life and much of their very limited means had to go for
wages. They had great respect, however, for honest toil and their
sons and daughters became resourceful and adept in doing what
was required. Probably it was Katie, the oldest daughter, who
helped with household tasks while Annie took charge of the
smallest boy, Walter. A deep and abiding affection, one for the
other, lasted throughout their long lives until Annie's death one
year before his own.

* According to the Certificate of Death received from the Division of Vital
Statistics, Victoria, B.C., Walter Traill was born at Gore's Landing, Rice
Lake. However, a niece informed me that his birthplace was Ashburnham.
It may be that Mrs. Traill returned to the home of her great friend, Mrs.
Stewart, for the confinement.

While her husband struggled to do his best with work that never became easy for him, Catherine Parr Traill contributed articles to periodicals. Their four sons and three daughters had few opportunities for schooling, but were endowed with the benefits of close association with cultured, well-educated parents who found time to teach them. "Oaklands" was a rustic abode of logs hewn from the forest about them, but it was a home of gracious manners and enlightening conversation whereby the children escaped the narrow prejudices of ignorance. They grew up in an atmosphere of understanding and tolerance of differing religious beliefs and varying political viewpoints.

Walter's parents shared with his Uncle Samuel Strickland a high regard for the intelligence of the Indians, believing them to be endowed with minds as fully capable of education as many of their white brothers. Thus was moulded the rich heritage of high-thinking and sound character that Walter Traill found of inestimable value as a youth newly arrived in Rupert's Land.

In the home of his childhood there were long winter evenings when stories were read aloud by the fireside. A love of reading remained with him throughout life with stress upon the importance of retaining what was read. Letter-writing was a part of the education of all children of courteous, literate parents and the "Thank-you" letters to generous relatives must be rewritten if necessary until there were no blots, cross-outs, or misspelled words.

There must have been laughter and gaiety to relieve the inevitable stresses and tedium in the pioneer home of Walter's boyhood which gained him the refreshing sense of humour I found so entertaining in his later years. Certainly there were strong bonds of affection between brothers and sisters, children and parents, that remained with them always. If the older members of the family were indulgent to the youngest child they found so clever and interesting, Walter did not become selfish, but was more inclined, as a man, to send generous gifts of money to his mother and sisters. An enterprising spirit was evident when he was quite a small boy. His mother encouraged him in the great originality inherited from her family, for to her "the spirit of inquiry highly developed" was a child's natural way to knowledge.

His Grandfather Strickland's ventures in the commerce of his day may not have been always entirely successful, but there can be little doubt as to the major triumph he achieved in the education of his six gifted daughters at a time when it was considered unbecoming for young ladies to be intellectual. Five girls attained literary distinction, of whom the two younger, Catherine Parr Traill and Susanna Moodie, came to Canada. Of those who remained in England the second oldest, Agnes Strickland, is the most famous. Visitors who wish to see what is of most historic interest in the charming seaside town of Southwold, Suffolk, are directed to the churchyard of St. Edmund's where a marble monument marks her grave. A few miles away is "Reydon Hall," the Strickland home of the happy childhood of Walter's mother.

Agnes Strickland sustained her family's tradition of originality by instituting her own novel approach to the recording of history in the six volumes of *Lives of the Queens of England*. Her nephew, Walter Traill, persisted all his life in disclaiming the literary talent to which he was heir and which he might have developed had not his abundant energies been directed into other channels. He too was undeterred by conventions of his day in many a venture. If a thing had never been done before, then it was high time it was undertaken.

Walter was barely four years old when his awakening mind was attracted to the home of Grandmother Strickland far across the ocean. In 1851 Samuel Strickland, whose wife had died the previous year, came to visit the Traills with his eldest daughter, Maria, before leaving for England to visit his aged mother and sisters at "Reydon Hall."

Although Walter Traill was never a robust child, from all accounts, he was a lively boy, full of fun and mischief but willing to do his share of work and to accompany the older children on fishing expeditions to restock the family larder. Year by year his growing mind was searching farther afield from the world he saw about him, extended by the daily conversation of well-informed parents and the reading provided by books they had brought to Canada for the library that grew along the living-room walls.

Suddenly, on August 26, 1857, the Traills suffered a dreadful calamity. Their home was burned to the ground. The family barely escaped the flames that consumed everything they had. Relatives and friends rallied to their aid, and Samuel Strickland offered hospitality in the commodious "Old Homestead" in Lakefield.

For Walter, an impressionable lad of tender years, the months that followed were an expansion of former horizons. In the enlarged family circle he began to form life-long friendships with his cousins. At one time during an acute illness death threatened the life of the ten-year-old boy. Uncle Samuel hastily summoned a doctor who declared the child could not possibly last until morning. Fortunately he underestimated the amazing powers of recuperation latent in the Strickland constitution.

On May 5, 1858, Walter's beloved sister Annie married a clergyman's son who had come to Canada to farm. Forty-two guests sat down to the wedding breakfast in the "Old Homestead." The bride of nineteen years went with her husband, James Parr Clinton Atwood, to live at Rice Lake.

Thomas Traill never recovered from the shock and sorrow of losing his home and all his possessions and, when their friend Mrs. Stewart placed her "Park Cottage" at their disposal, Mr. and Mrs. Traill moved there to live until his death in June of 1859.

Thomas Traill had spent his boyhood on the estate of his father, the Reverend Walter Traill, at Kirkwall in the Orkney Islands. "Westove" had been the seat of considerable wealth with an annuity of eighteen to thirty thousand pounds derived chiefly from kelp, but when it was discovered that straw could be used successfully in the making of glass the price of kelp declined to almost nothing. The property became so heavily mortgaged that Walter's father, whose tastes were largely literary, entrusted it to his lawyers until the creditors should be paid. It never returned to him or his heirs.

After the death of his father, Walter Traill spent much of his time with Annie at Rice Lake where he became affectionately attached to her husband and their young children. Clinton Atwood seems to have enjoyed the energetic nature and the pranks of his young brother-in-law. One day a gentleman came to dine, and just as he was seating himself at the table, Walter popped a sponge full of water on his chair.

No doubt Annie and her husband encouraged the lad's interest in their farm and indulged his precocity in the business affairs of their property, which sloped to the southern shore of Rice Lake. He once became the owner of a hen which he traded so successfully that by making one wonderful bargain after another he found himself the proud possessor of a horse that had reached an age of retirement from heavier work than transporting Walter's light frame about the countryside. On another occasion Mr. Atwood let a friend have a half-acre on which to grow peas, and when these had been sown and Walter observed that they were coming up well, he persuaded the grower to trade his crop for a nice calf, then harvested the peas and sold them.

During his early youth little, if anything, took place within his reach that escaped the attention and understanding of his active, intelligent mind. Keenly observant and eager to assist with the farm animals, he acquired considerable knowledge and skill in their care. It was a family tragedy when a valuable cow was lost as she was due to freshen. Walter asked if he might have the skin, and not only did he skin the cow, but he removed the unborn calf and skinned it also.

It was probably during his family's sojourn with Aunt and Uncle Strickland at Lakefield that Walter's lively imagination was first filled with projects afoot in their environs. For many years it had been hoped that an inland waterway would be created by constructing canals, locks, and dams along the chain of lakes and rivers whose waters finally reach Lake Ontario through the Trent River flowing out of Rice Lake. When Walter left for Fort Garry eight years later, little had been accomplished of the undertaking that eventually linked Georgian Bay with Lake Ontario, but he took with him ideas and dreams of commercial transportation that might be used on the Assiniboine and Red Rivers.

The lumbering industry in the Trent Valley and to the north of Peterborough was at its height while the American Civil War brought about a thriving trade with Canada where horses, cattle, grain, and food were purchased for the Northern Army. Walter was barely eighteen when he was entrusted with his brother's grain-laden boats across Lake Ontario to the United States ports of Oswego and Rochester. He was in the latter city when victory over the South was being celebrated. In a few days the rejoicing was clouded by the assassination of President Lincoln.

The following winter Walter was in the hills north of Lakefield working for the logging company of which his Uncle Samuel was a partner, scaling timber, keeping accounts, and ordering supplies. In spring, swollen lakes and rivers floated to the Atlantic seaboard the timbers destined for Great Britain where they were used in the construction of wooden ships. Rafts of squared logs were manned by four men and a pilot with long oars and sweeps and accompanied by a crew in flat-bottomed *batteaux* to overcome obstruction. At night the men, who lived in little cabins on the rafts, sat around the fires over which, suspended by a crane, hung the iron pots in which their food was cooked.

The constellation of floating hearths reflected on the water was an enchanting sight from the front veranda of "Westove" on the shore of Lake Katchawanooka, one of the lovely Kawartha Lakes. Here Catherine Parr Traill lived for many years in the home named after the one her husband had left in the Orkney Islands. Here of an evening her youngest son and his sisters came to sit with her while they enjoyed the picturesque view created by the industry that employed him. Nearby was the Otonabee River, the outlet of the lake, with Samuel Strickland's mill a little distance down its banks.

At that time there were few good openings for young men of limited means and little education, and the Hudson's Bay Company was thought of most highly as a flourishing concern with a promising future. It was considered necessary that Walter Traill, who had suffered scarlet and rheumatic fevers in addition to the usual illnesses of childhood, should live an outdoor life. The prospect of healthy activity and the measure of education afforded by the Company's service were attractive when weighed together with the promise of an adventurous career in a newly developing country.

A cousin of Thomas Traill's had married Mr. James J. Hargrave, secretary to Governor Mactavish and an officer in the Hudson's Bay Company. When he offered to find a place for Walter's older brother William it was a most welcome opportunity; and he must have served his employers well, for subsequently his sponsor wrote to the Governor: "If Mrs. Traill has a dozen more sons like William tell her to send them along."

The only unmarried son was Walter and he was attracted, as were many of his contemporaries, by prospects of making a fortune in the United States. On the other hand, letters had been coming from William for three years which, added to all he had heard and read of the great Company, weighted his decision to be off at once to join him.

That he fully justified what was expected of one of his family came to light years later when Norman Kittson of St. Paul, Minnesota, told of a conversation with Governor Donald A. Smith regarding Walter Traill's appointment to Fort Ellice in 1870. When it was proposed that year at the Annual Council at Norway House that Walter Traill, an Apprentice Clerk, should be appointed to the charge of Fort Ellice there was opposition from the older clerks, this being about the most important outpost in the Swan River District and he, with one exception, the junior clerk. Governor Smith had spoken in favour of the appointment:

*Mr. Traill has served under Mr. MacKay, now succeeding to the charge of the District. He is responsible for the officers under him and is the proper person to say who shall be put in charge of the outposts. As to age and length of service, these must not matter. It is efficiency that regulates the Company's business.*

It was Norman Kittson who had befriended Walter Traill when he first arrived in St. Paul in June of 1866. Mr. Kittson was a Canadian by birth who came from Quebec in 1843 to the Red River Valley where he traded in competition with the Hudson's Bay Company, though he later became their agent. Seasoned in the ways of the West, he knew the five-hundred-mile trip from St. Paul to Fort Garry in mid-summer by rail, stage, and horseback would tax the wiry strength of the youth, then not very tall and not over 120 pounds in weight. The alert, well-mannered young man with the questing eyes won the heart of the older man, a heart already with his fellow officers in the service of the Company to which Walter Traill now belonged.

While waiting to join a brigade going north he rode daily about St. Paul, delighting in the associations of Lake Nokomis and the Falls of Minnehaha or Laughing Waters with Longfellow's poem *Hiawatha*. In his letters to his mother he shared with her this inherited love of poetry and his interest in the flora and fauna of a new country. Catherine Parr Traill was then preparing *Canadian Wild Flowers* for its publication in 1869.

The long journey north was enlivened by the added charm of landmarks of history he had read. The travellers paused halfway at Fort Abercrombie, four long days of riding from their camp on the site of old Fort Daer in a bend of the Pembina River. Two days later the waning afternoon brought them within view of the settlement at the mouth of the Assiniboine River. Walter Traill forded its waters and rode up its dusty bank to find himself facing the south wall of Fort Garry not over a quarter of a mile away. Nearer on the east the Red River flowed to Hudson Bay. Before him, midway between stone bastions at either end of the wall was an arched gate. Thither Walter Traill directed his way to enter a new life. There he must be left to tell his story in letters to his mother, sisters, and brother-in-law, in his later writings, and his recollections.

By 1874, eight years after his first journey west, Walter Traill was in charge of five posts of the Hudson's Bay Company in the United States, four on the Red River at Georgetown, Frog Point,

Caledonia, and Grand Forks, and the fifth at the Red Lake Indian Agency. Railways had been pushing steel lines across the prairies, settlers were pouring in and towns mushroomed along the right-of-way. Walter Traill's energetic management had kept apace of the growing demands of the retail trade centred at his Company's stores. He had also built hotels and warehouses while developing adjacent farms and a boat-building industry.

He was now a full-fledged clerk with a salary in accordance which was further augmented by a hundred pounds a year due to serving outside Canada. He had been investing his savings in land that was increasing rapidly in value. At twenty-seven years of age he might well envision a rosy future.

Finally, in December of 1874, the long-awaited visit to his family became a reality. The high-spirited young lady who had helped her friends to welcome him to his makeshift room at Frog Point, Miss Emily McTavish, had returned to Ontario, taking with her his heart and his ring. He hoped their engagement would be announced and that his fiancée would visit Lakefield and Rice Lake. Alas! He had not been home a week when he received a telegram regarding his Company's affairs in the United States. He hurried back to Grand Forks by way of Yankton, the capital of Dakota Territory.

The previous June Donald A. Smith had resigned as Chief Commissioner to become the Head of the Hudson's Bay Company's Land Department. With the new Governor, James A. Grahame, came a change in policy: he wished to withdraw from the retail trade in the United States and to confine the Company's business to the fur trade, which was a small part of the many responsibilities that had come under Walter Traill's management as Officer-in-Charge.

The few days at home had not fulfilled his highest hopes. The gay, lovable boy, so willing to do an errand for his elders, had not returned. In his place came a man of stature, pleasant and courteous withal, but unmistakably accustomed to being served and obeyed. To his relatives his use of telegrams seemed an unwarranted extravagance. The scenes of earlier days held little

19

nostalgic charm for him but displayed a disappointing lack of growth in keeping with the small progress that had been made in the building of the Trent River Canal.

During the next two years he reduced the stock at the Hudson's Bay Company stores and sold their buildings and property. It was a heartbreaking undoing of all that he had worked so hard to develop. There was little left by the end of 1876. His health too was gone, for to forge ahead was life itself to his progressive spirit. He was granted a year's leave of absence to recuperate.

The winter in Florida was a pleasant one among new friends and new scenes, but he was still far from well by spring and decided to go to the Hot Springs in Arkansas. April was spent for the most part undergoing treatment at Little Rock. Notwithstanding, he managed to enjoy a week's excursion with friends to shoot wild turkeys. The return trip of thirteen days by river boats on the Arkansas and Mississippi Rivers from Fort Smith to St. Louis was a gay one with a string band and dances every night. Planters came aboard and rode all night just for the trip.

From St. Louis he went west to spend a week with the 20th United States Infantry stationed at Fort Yuma.

*From Fort Yuma* [*he wrote,*] *I made a trip on the Rio Grande River, which divides Old Mexico from the United States, travelling through Texas, New Mexico and Indian Territory to Gunnison on the Continental Divide in Colorado 11,600 feet above sea level. The Mexicans taught me the mysteries of the Diamond Hitch which is all there is to packing. We started with horses at sea level and when we got 10,000 feet up our horses could not stand the altitude and we had to get burros.*

He visited Santa Fé and Reno, Nevada, before staging back through Colorado with a party of English tourists. One day a lady was alarmed to see him driving.

"Don't be afraid," he called back, "I am an old hand at this."

That evening he overheard her indignant remark: "Passing himself off as a gentleman when he is only a common stage-driver."

He might have reinstated himself in her regard by explaining that it was due to the kindness of the Earl of Dunraven, the Vice-Chairman of the Hudson's Bay Company, that he was there. He had twice been host on hunting trips to the Earl who had arranged his leave of absence. He preferred, however, the humour of the situation and the select society of the men who drove the stage-coaches safely over the famous trails. Skilful with reins of six horses, expert shots, and fast on the draw, they must also understand and know how to provide for the comforts of their passengers. They were the élite of the road.

Summer passed pleasantly with friends in Iowa, Illinois, and Wisconsin, though in July he wrote to his brother that he was still rather shaky. By September he was back in St. Paul where he met Donald A. Smith, George Stephen, and R. B. Angus and accompanied them on a tour of inspection of the St. Paul and Pacific Railway lines.

He intended to return to work and reported to Mr. Grahame at Fort Garry who offered him a post on the coast of Labrador, where the only communication was a ship from England once a year. Mr. Traill resigned from the Hudson's Bay Company and returned to St. Paul to take charge of an elevator company. It was mid-September of 1877 when he began to buy and ship grain with such success that he quickly built up an extensive business. His own holdings of farm lands and other property had been increasing over the years.

They were long years, however, of working and waiting which never brought marriage. Possibly both lovers were burdened already with family responsibilities. Certainly Mr. Traill was concerned that Annie's children at Rice Lake should receive the education of which he had been deprived. Another sister, Mary, six years older than he, had been left a widow with two little children, and he sought to establish her son in a career. Here we have some measure of the generous, forward-looking spirit of the man who would give to the next generation what he had not received.

In July of 1878 he went east again, travelling by boat from

Duluth to Collingwood and down the Hudson from Albany to
New York. There, in the office of the Treasurer of the Northern
Pacific Railroad Company hung a large mounted trophy which
Mr. Traill had sent. This head had been much admired by a
friend of the Treasurer's, who said he wanted to meet the man who
shot that elk. The friend was Theodore Roosevelt, and his wish
was granted when he met Mr. Traill at the office and asked him all
sorts of questions about the West he planned to visit shortly.

Returning to Canada across Lake Ontario fron Rochester to
Port Hope, Walter went to his old home in Lakefield. Catherine
Parr Traill took her son up to her summer home on the island of
Minnewawa in Stony Lake. It was an idyllic holiday with a much
loved parent, young-hearted at seventy-five, and a visit all too
soon cut short by an early harvest in the Red River valley. There
were only a few days to spend with his sister Annie. He reached
her home after a pleasant trip down on the boat.

"I was very much struck with the beauty of the lake," he writes,
"and also with my little nieces, especially Annie."

From Rice Lake he took the stage to Coburg. On the train to
Toronto he met his friend Donald Smith who would have persuaded him to travel to Red River with him, but that Walter had
business in the city and relatives to see.

"I called on Aunt Moodie and found her very well," he wrote to
his mother on his return to Grand Forks in North Dakota. "I
think she would like to go to Lakefield again." There was mention
of "the evenings with the Tullys . . . at the Vickers . . . a pleasant
afternoon," and that he "dined at Walter Strickland's."

It was foreign to his nature to speak of his deepest feelings, nor
was it the custom of gentlemen of his day to discuss very personal
affairs with even a sympathetic listener. Only once did he speak
to me of his love for Emily McTavish, but it was enough to give me
a flash of insight into a rare sensitivity and the depth of his
sorrow over their broken engagement. Not long after the lovers
parted he wrote to a close friend in a letter of June 22, 1879:

*I need not tell you how grieved I was to hear of your loss in the death of your children. I know it must be a hard parting but there is a parting that is worse than death. This I have experienced and no one knows what I have suffered.*

In 1881 Walter Traill was married at West Lynne to Mary Gilbert, a widow with two children, Cora and Hardisty. He built a home on his farm at Pembina where they lived until the following year when they moved to St. Paul. A second home was built on Summit Avenue where a son was born who died in 1883. Only once did our great-uncle speak of this tragedy to me and I saw how deep was the grief within him.

The Traills moved to Kalispell, Montana, in 1890, where they lived for the next twenty years. His office and their home were in the town a few miles from his ranch. Eventually the climate proved too severe for Mr. Traill, whose lungs were affected. He came west to the Kettle Valley at Grand Forks in British Columbia where his nephew, Annie's elder son lived. This nephew, Clinton Arthur Strickland Atwood, was my husband's father.

Mr. Traill bought a farm just north of the international boundary and four miles west of the growing smelter town where he engaged in fruit farming with all the zest of his ardent nature. He made an unsuccessful attempt to ship apples by the carload as he had shipped grain from the Red River valley. Discouraged by lack of cooperation, he returned to the United States to grow fruit in the Okanogan Valley and to write his memoirs. Before he could establish himself he was overtaken by the depression of the twenties and came back to the Kettle Valley at the end of 1927.

Adverse fortune did not dismay him. By spring he had pruned acres of orchard and had become the owner of "Pine Bluff Ranch." His amazing vigour continued four more years, sustained as ever by his indomitable spirit and his keen interest in the progress of men and their affairs. He took an active interest in developing his property with plans well laid for many years ahead. His spring work had been accomplished when he died, in his eighty-fifth year, on June 20, 1932.

On June 25, 1967, a monument "in lasting tribute to Walter

J. S. Traill" was dedicated by Clarence Anderson, Registrar of Deeds, Traill County, North Dakota. Erected by the Old Settlers' Memorial Association, it can be seen from far across the prairie where it stands within a mile of Belmont, the former Frog Point, on the old stage road he so often travelled.

# WALTER TRAILL'S INTRODUCTION*

*In the Battle of Life, as we march along,*
*There's many a word and many a song,*
*That lighten our thoughts in after life*
*As we fight, as we must if we win*
*In the Battle of Life.*

W. S. TRAILL

THE pioneers of Minnesota, Dakota, and Prince Rupert's Land fought bravely and they won a great victory. They conquered a wilderness; they blazed the trails from the Mississippi to the Pelly Banks; they marked the ways that the present and all future generations will follow; they built monuments by laying the foundations for the great cities that future generations will continue to build upon until the end of time; they created new States and Provinces for which they framed wise constitutions and secured large grants of land with which to endow schools and universities and to establish homes and maintenance for the unfortunate and criminal.

They grew boys and girls and filled those places of learning from which have emanated distinguished professional men, educators, statesmen, governors of States and Provinces, members of the Dominion Parliament, Congressmen, U.S. Senators and Cabinet members, brave soldiers and sailors.

The University of Minnesota stands upon ground that I saw as the camping place of the Red River cart brigades. The University of North Dakota is located on land I once fenced as a pasture for Hudson Bay Company beef cattle when I was in charge of that Company's post in the Upper Red River Valley. This University is filled with the sons and daughters of the pioneers of Dakota,

* This introduction was written by Walter Traill in 1927.

many of whom came to the great prairies in covered wagons with oxen for motive power, their only capital being brave hearts and determination.

Where the University of Manitoba now is was once the camping ground for Indians and traders from the north and west, and where officers of the Hudson Bay Company once hunted ducks and ran wolves in the winter. On one portion of these grounds I saw a party of Crees and Saulteaux massacre seventeen Sioux whom they had invited there for a treaty of peace. Here now is the great city of Winnipeg, the fourth, I think, in size in all the Dominion of Canada.

Not being endowed with the literary talent of my gifted mother or her sisters, the distinguished Mrs. Moodie and the Misses Strickland, it is only at the urgent request of the old pioneers and the Hudson Bay Company officers under whom I served, that I have undertaken a work that should be done by a more competent person, and it is only with the promise of assistance from many of my co-workers that I undertake the task.

My own part in the development of the country has been an insignificant one, but I fought in the ranks and have received a great reward – the privilege and pleasure of associating with those brave, big-hearted, broad-minded men and women of Minnesota, Dakota and Prince Rupert's Land, and with their descendants.

There are few of my early associates who have not reached the end of the long trail and crossed the last divide to the Great Unknown beyond. To them, and to their descendants I dedicate these recollections of the pioneer days and ways in Minnesota, Dakota and Prince Rupert's Land.

THE AUTHOR
(Walter J. S. Traill)

26

# ONE

---

## *Arrival at Fort Garry*

IT was on the first day of June in the year 1866 that I received notice from Governor William Mactavish of my appointment as a Junior Clerk in the service of the Hudson's Bay Company. He had been on a visit to England and had stopped in Toronto on his return to Fort Garry as the representative of the Governor and Directors in London and the head of the Company in Canada. His letter, bearing a Toronto postmark, contained instructions for me to report to the Chief Factor [E. M. Hopkins] in charge of the Montreal department at La Chine, for further directions. By official courtesy a Chief Factor is requested, a Chief Trader is directed, but a non-commissioned officer is instructed.

As a Junior, or Apprentice Clerk, I was offered a five-year contract at the usual remuneration of £20, £25, £30, £40 and £50 sterling for the successive years. In addition to the above remuneration all living expenses are provided with the privilege of receiving what clothing and other items are purchased at the wholesale price in London, with delivery free wherever one is stationed.

No time was lost in accepting the appointment by communicating with Chief Factor E. M. Hopkins in Montreal who instructed me to proceed at the earliest possible date by the Grand Trunk Railway of Canada to Detroit, Michigan, thence by the Michigan Central Railway to Chicago, Illinois, thence by Chicago and Northwestern Railway to LaCrosse, Wisconsin, on the Mississippi River. I must then take a steamer to St. Paul and report there to the Company's agent, Mr. Norman W. Kittson who would give me further instructions.

All necessary preparations were soon made and on the seventh of June I bade my beloved mother and sisters farewell before taking the stage to Peterboro, ten miles away from the home I had just left in Lakefield. My journey continued by the Midland Railway to Port Hope on Lake Ontario where I caught a train on the Grand Trunk Railway. As there was no night train I was able to spend a day in Toronto visiting aunts and cousins before starting for Detroit, a twelve hour trip, as it was from Montreal to Toronto. That night I stayed at the Biddle House, the American city's leading hotel, which I left next morning to take the Michigan Central Railway to Chicago. There I enjoyed the luxuries of Sherman House, named for the hero of the famous march from Georgia to the sea. The bustling young metropolis took much pride in the palatial quarters of its foremost hotel, but there was no time to see much of the city as the Chicago and Northwestern train left early next morning for LaCrosse.

All that day we travelled for the most part through an un-inhabited prairie with no sign of human life save large bands of horses and some herds of cattle. We dined that evening in the Wisconsin river port where we boarded the "Eagle," one of the Anchor Line of riverboats plying between St. Louis and St. Paul. These are well-appointed, even magnificent, I learned from a fellow traveller, compared to the ruder barges that preceded them. In winter, when navigation is closed, transportation is by a stage line.

The eighteen hours spent in ascending the Mississippi were full of interest to an uninitiated youth like myself. Passengers included almost every race, class and nationality of the world, speaking as many languages and travelling to the newly appreciated opportunities of the West. There was freight of every description. Rafts of lumber floated down past us. Landings on the Minnesota, or west side, were covered with sacks of wheat piled like cordwood. There were homesteads on either side of the river but long stretches of country had no sign of a human dwelling or evidence of life other than hundreds of horses and cattle grazing on the prairies.

28

Mr. Kittson had been advised of my coming by the Hudson's Bay House at La Chine and was at the wharf to meet me as I disembarked. He gave me a warm greeting and took me to the Merchant's Hotel.

"Take good care of this young man," he told John Dodge, the clerk, "and see that he gets a good room."

This was by no means easy at this time of year. It was June 12th and a Sunday when I arrived. The hotel is the headquarters for all the Red River traders and travellers who come in largest numbers during the present month and again in the early fall. The building is a combination of logs, lumber, brick and stone, a part of it having been in existence as long as the city itself, and additions made from time to time with the various materials. As summer approaches it brings visitors from the south to escape the heat and the place is full of strangers which makes good rooms scarce.

"Make yourself at home and call at the office tomorrow," Mr. Kittson told me on parting.

This I did, expecting to be put to work.

"You will have plenty of work when you reach Fort Garry so you just make yourself at home in the office and go around and enjoy yourself" were the words by which I was agreeably surprised. "I have orders to send you on to Fort Garry when I find a congenial party going north."

Mr. Kittson introduced me to visitors who came to see him and and gave me cards to the officers at Army Headquarters and to those at Fort Snelling. He gave me a list of places to visit such as Minnehaha Falls, Lake Nokomis and the old trading village of Mendota, where he established a trading post as an officer in the American Fur Company of St. Louis. He introduced me to the merchants and at a livery stable where I can always get a good saddle horse at the Company's expense.

All these instructions I immediately proceeded to carry out by exploring the surrounding country and making the acquaintance of the old residents and the guests at the hotel who have taken me out to their camps. I have ridden north of St. Paul where hundreds of Red River carts are arriving loaded with packs of furs and have visited the camps of the traders and freighters who are reloading with goods for the return trip. The tents of the Indians are scattered as far as Lake Como where, in passing to and from the village of St. Anthony, I have stopped to spend some time among them. In fact, I have been to every place within reach that would interest a youth with an investigating turn of mind and plenty of time at his disposal to indulge that "spirit of inquiry highly developed" for which I have been noted since early childhood.

Needless to say, I have met many very interesting people. Not the least attractive of the guests at my hotel is the actress Laura Keene who with her company is playing *East Lynne* at The Atheneum. She seems to take a motherly interest in me and has presented me with passes to the theatre.

The weeks sped by until one Sunday afternoon, on July 3rd, Mr. Kittson called and introduced me to Mr. A. G. B. Bannatyne, a former Hudson's Bay Company clerk but now the leading independent merchant in Winnipeg. Arrangements have been made for him to take me through to Fort Garry and we shall start tomorrow morning. I shall be sorry to leave St. Paul where I have enjoyed myself so much and have been so hospitably treated by the old families. On parting Laura Keene gave me her autographed photo which I shall keep as a valued treasure.

Mr. Kittson never loses an opportunity to arrange a pleasant journey for the Hudson's Bay people crossing the plains. He bade me farewell at the train on the morning of July 4th and I was off, with my host for the trip, on the St. Paul and Pacific Railway to the end of its line.

The railroad is in the course of construction which was suspended during the Civil War but this year has been renewed with all speed. We stopped at Elk River for lunch at a way station instituted for the purpose, and continued by train to Big Lake which is as far as rails have been laid. Passengers take the stage from there by the road on the east bank of the Mississippi to St. Cloud.

This is a prosperous young town where accommodation is limited at this time of year so that guests at the Hayward House must "double-up." Fortunately Mr. Bannatyne and I slept together. Had I been alone I might have been less fortunate. Among our stage passengers from St. Paul was Antoine Gingrass of Red River, a Canadian Frenchman of huge proportions and a very dark complexion. He was assigned to a bed in our hotel. During the night, the other beds being doubly occupied, the clerk put a Negro to share Mr. Gingrass' bed. In the morning an insurrection arose, not by Mr. Gingrass objecting to sharing his bed with the Negro but by the latter discovering, as he thought, that he had been put in bed with an Indian.

After supper we went out to view the town and found that there was dancing in the open air which prompted Mr. Bannatyne to introduce the Red River Jig whereby he became the lion of the occasion and did not lack for gay young partners.

Next morning our stage started at four o'clock and stopped at way-stations for breakfast and lunch. The road followed the Red River cart trail to west and north over land that was rather poor and sandy and would have made travelling tedious had it not been enlivened by Mr. Bannatyne's conversation.

He is now a freetrader though he came out from Scotland in the Hudson's Bay Company's service, in which he spent five years as an Apprentice Clerk. Junior clerks are not allowed to marry and when he fell in love with Miss Annie McDermott he resigned to start his own store as an independent merchant. The scenery improved as we approached Sauk Centre, a new village in a wooded setting on the Little Sauk River. Our night station was an hotel in all stages of incompletion. There is also a flour mill by the stream in course of construction, in addition to a blacksmith shop, lumber mill, store and saloon already in operation.

Next morning our road took us over rolling prairie dotted with clumps of oak and poplar trees set amid the attractive grassland until we found ourselves in a beautiful country of natural parks interspersed with pretty little lakes.

We stopped at noon for dinner by Lake Osakis, a beautiful body of water which, like all the Minnesota lakes, is a bright blue. The Sioux have given the State their name for the "blue waters" that are swarming with ducks and geese and teeming with fish. The prairie between lakes and trees is alive with prairie hens as the traveller nears the Big Woods. This timberland is a spur of the wooded country that crosses the state from east to west.

To avoid a long detour, a road was cut through to Alexander by the stage company some years ago and is very bad, being rough and full of mud holes, but from what I have been told it is much improved, since one driver, Lame Jake, is said to have replied to a passenger complaining of the slow rate of travel:

"You ought to have come through the Big Woods when the passengers had to walk behind and pack a rail to pry the coach out of the mud holes."

The entire country is practically uninhabited except for the mosquitoes that came to us in swarms and made life inside the coach almost unbearable. By making friends with the successive drivers I was able to enjoy the seat of honour outside, whereby I not only escaped these pests but I learned from the rugged guardians of our way the biography of every horse, driver, stage agent, station-keeper and stock-tender from Big Lake to Fort Abercrombie, as well as from LaCrosse to St. Paul.

Beyond Alexander, another new town where we stopped, the road is fine over the open prairie with little lakes to Pomme de Terre, a night station in a stockade of logs set on end into the ground. It was built to protect the settlers during the Sioux massacre of 1862, but the refugees are gone and the country virtually abandoned. The driver, before I alighted from beside him, advised me not to remove my clothes at night. Surely there were no Sioux lurking to attack us?

"The bugs will eat you alive," he explained.

We crossed the Ottertail River twelve miles above its junction with the Bois de Sioux to form the Red River. This was our first crossing of any size. Here the road turns west to avoid twelve miles of alkali swamp much dreaded by freighters in the spring, and reaches the banks of the Red River at Twelve-Mile Point, so named because of its distance from Fort Abercrombie. We had been travelling across a prairie bare of trees until we drove along the narrow strip of oak timber bordering the river and increasing in width towards McCauleyville, where we arrived in the evening to camp opposite the Fort.

Here Mr. Bannatyne found his men waiting for him with carts and horses [from his home]. The next day being the Sabbath we were glad to rest and make preparations for an early start on Monday morning. We received an invitation from General Custer, Commander of the Seventh Cavalry which garrisons this Fort, to dine at the officers' mess and were royally entertained by him and his staff.

From the Fort we could see the buffalo ranging on the plain to the west beyond the horses and mules belonging to the Army. It was my first sight of these animals which were left to graze undisturbed on this occasion, it being the Sabbath.

Before we left on Monday morning we were joined at the Fort by another Red River trader, Mr. Robert Tait who had ridden through from St. Paul. The ferry crossing the river to the camp at McCauleyville is the first to be encountered on the Red River Trail after the one on the Mississippi River at St. Cloud. Fort Abercrombie is halfway between Fort Garry and St. Paul and the end of public transportation. The remaining two hundred and fifty miles must be covered by saddle horse and wagons or carts.

Mr. Bannatyne assisted me in hiring two riding horses from a Hudson's Bay Company's freighter for which I paid a pound each for the trip. Our baggage and camp outfit were in a cart driven by a halfbreed. Mr. Bannatyne also had a one-horse spring wagon in which he and Mr. Tait took turns from riding on horseback. We travelled over forty miles the first day along the east side of the river and made our camp some miles above the Company's post at Georgetown, which I did not see at this time as we forded to the west bank the first thing in the morning. The bordering woods increase in width and height as one descends to the mouth of the Buffalo River flowing into the Red River from the southeast, with the Post on its north side hidden from view by the trees.

Sixty miles below this, our third day of travelling up to fifty miles a day brought us opposite the mouth of the Red Lake River where the timber, which has been getting broader continually, is a mile wide.

Between here and the Turtle River we saw a band of buffalo bulls. Mr. Tait rode after them but his horse was not fast enough for a buffalo runner, which is a very fast horse. We had no buffalo meat for our supper but the woods are a veritable hunter's paradise and we did have all the ducks and prairie chicken we could eat before reaching Pembina on our fourth day.

We made our camp on the south side of the Pembina River where we had dinner that evening. When Mr. Bannatyne called at the Post Office he told Mr. Cavalier, the postmaster, that he had a young Hudson's Bay clerk who could not drink tea straight, nor the Red River water which was muddy enough for a knife and fork! Mrs. Cavalier sent over a large chunk of ice, the nicest thing I ever had in my life. It has created a warm spot in my heart for all time and my only regret is that I did not have the pleasure of making the acquaintance of Mr. and Mrs. Cavalier at that time.

The following morning we left the picturesque setting of Pembina to cross the International Boundary and enter Rupert's Land. Our trail northward on the west side of the river ran between the poplar groves on the open prairie, which is unsettled except for an occasional home on the east bank. We made our last camp at Scratching River, about half way between Pembina and Fort Garry which we reached next day.

As we neared St. Boniface the log houses appeared more frequently east of the river and we passed homes of settlers along the near bank until we came to the Assiniboine, with farms on its south extending for miles to westward. Here we parted from Mr. Tait in whom I had found another good friend. He turned left towards his home at St. James leaving Mr. Bannatyne and myself to ford the Assiniboine River in front of Fort Garry.

At the gate to meet me is Mr. William Clarke with a warm welcome as he introduces himself and conducts me to the presence of Chief Factor James R. Clare who is in charge of this District. The senior officer receives me very kindly and presents me to other members of his staff following which he instructs a servant to prepare a room for me in the Bachelors' Quarters. There I follow to find myself before long in the large Hall among new friends.

One of these is Mr. James J. Hargrave, who is a pleasant gentleman occupying a very responsible position as the Governor's secretary. He has returned from his evening walk of two miles which, it is said, he never fails to take under any circumstances. He speaks of my older brother, William, telling me that he may be expected to come in from Fort Ellice during the summer.

# TWO

## *Life at Fort Garry*

ONE of my first duties was to call on Governor William Mactavish who occupies what is known as the Governor's House. His kindly attention won my heart for all time as he told me that I have been appointed to the Swan River District, which is in the charge of Chief Trader Robert Campbell with headquarters at Fort Pelly on the Upper Assiniboine River. The Governor said he would like to keep me at Fort Garry for a year, but explained that this is not possible:

*Mr. Campbell has asked for an additional officer and your services have been promised to him for the winter. I am sure you will find the Chief Trader and his charming wife and family very agreeable people. We are expecting them to arrive from their post in September. In the meantime I will turn you over to Mr. John McTavish, the accountant, who will put you to work in the office.*

I have become much attached to the accountant who, though he has the same name, bears no relationship to the Governor. I am happy to say the friendship appears to be mutual, for he is endeavouring to persuade our Head Officer to let me remain here, which I should like very much, as in these few days I have grown to like the quiet, simple way in which Governor Mactavish administers the duties of his office.

This he does with the aid of his Councillors who include Judge Black, two of the French natives, and two English-speaking members. Everyone is received courteously and cordially. No matter who he is or what his business, he is given a patient hearing as the Council assists the Governor in the supervision of civil

36

matters pertaining to the Red River Settlement which comes under his jurisdiction as Governor of Prince Rupert's Land.

This means he is also Governor of the fur trade of the Hudson's Bay Company, who are the traders and administrators of this vast domain. As such he is assisted by the following officers under him: Chief Factor James R. Clare, in charge of this District; Dr. William Cowan, Chief Trader and Medical Officer; Chief Trader Magnus Linklater, in charge of the Fort Garry store; and the Chief Clerks already mentioned, Mr. James Hargrave and Mr. John McTavish, also Chief Clerk John Balsillie. Other clerks are William Clarke, Alexander R. MacKenzie, store salesman, and James Anderson, in charge of the stores of furs. As this is the depot of the Red River District there are officers arriving from outlying posts. Mr. Clarke has just come in from a visit to Oak Point at the end of the portage from the Assiniboine River to Lake Manitoba.

Twenty miles farther down the Red River from Fort Garry is the Stone Fort, or Lower Fort Garry, under Chief Trader William Flett and staff composed of George Davis, a Chief Clerk, and Duncan Matheson, like myself an Apprentice Clerk. Chief Trader Hackland, at Pembina, is Captain of the Hudson's Bay schooner on Lake Winnipeg while Mr. Abel, the Chief Engineer, is stationed at the Lower Fort.

Mr. John McTavish has put me to work on the "Colonists' Accounts" which are the records of business done by the Hudson's Bay Company with the settlers, many of whom are engaged in farming. Others follow the migratory pursuits of buffalo hunting and freighting. Advances are made during the winter to be paid the following summer in produce from the farm, robes and meat from the hunt, or wages earned in transportation of goods to and from the Posts of the West and North, between Fort Garry and St. Paul, and by boat along the older route to seaboard down the Red River, across Lake Winnipeg and down the Hayes River to Fort York.

In nearly every account there is a "balance brought forward." One of these interests me greatly, being with an Indian named

Aak-Put-a-Wat, Saulteaux for "As old as the earth's oldest son."
He is recorded as being indebted to the Company for:

| | |
|---|---|
| *1 fathom of red stroud (cloth)* | *7/-* |
| *2 yards of Canadian Twist Tobacco* | *6/-* |
| *½ pint of gunpowder* | *1/6* |
| *2 lbs. of copper kettle* | *4/-* |
| *Balance brought forward* | *18/6* |
| *Total Owing* | *£1. 17/-* |

Although I have worked in a country store in Canada West I have
never sold cloth by nautical measure, tobacco by land measure, nor
ammunition by wine measure. In alluding to the delicate matter
of the "balance brought forward" our Indian customer explained
"that was before the flood."

What flood would the earth's oldest son know but the high
water that made Noah prominent as the first marine constructor
and navigator? It would not have surprised me to find an account
with that worthy gentleman for the material used in the building
of the ark and for the food with which it was provisioned. However, Mr. McTavish enlightened me by explaining that "the flood"
was that of five years ago when this valley was under water
which washed away buildings and fences, forcing the settlers
to flee with their livestock and personal belongings to the higher
ground at Stoney Mountain. The simple logic of his native mind
is that any debts concerning these were washed away with them,
and this is accepted by the Company to the extent of allowing
them to repudiate most debts contracted before the flood.

There are only six of us to do a deuce of a lot of work in this
office, which keeps us very busy as the Bank, Express Office,
Custom House, Post Office and Counting House are all in one for us
to look after. Mr. Clare never does a thing but sign bonds and bills
on London and Montreal. To a new clerk like myself who is
working all the time this seems a very lazy life for which to
receive a salary amounting to over thirteen hundred pounds
sterling besides his family's board. Governor Mactavish gets three

thousand pounds a year for being Governor of Rupert's Land, and also a Chief Factor's share of the Company's profits.

He is a very nice old fellow. Never a day passes but what he sends us in two bottles of ale and on Saturday afternoons he sends us in two bottles of champagne. Mrs. Mactavish, too, is a very nice person, who was Miss McDermott, and whose father is very rich indeed. John McTavish married a daughter of Chief Factor Rowand who, I believe, has five or six thousand pounds of her own.

My work in the office includes all sorts of clerical jobs in which my superior is instructing me, such as making up the mail which goes out from Pembina to the United States once in two weeks, and also having ready that which is sent to interior posts whenever there is a chance. I also make the regular payments to the Company's pensioners of whom there are quite a number retired and living in this District. Other duties entrusted to me are various jobs that do not require any particular talent or experience.

Altogether I find life at the Fort very pleasant, so much so that I have not become familiar with the surrounding neighbourhood, which by comparison is unattractive to a stranger like myself. Here, in the Fort, it is different, where we are a happy family though excluded from ladies' society, as the unmarried officers have rooms and a common living or reading room in the Bachelors' Hall, while those who are married live with their families in suitable quarters provided for them. The Officers' Mess, or dining-room, is in the Governor's House and, except on rare occasions, ladies are never present there. They are invited to balls and festivities in the winter but unfortunately this is summer and we seldom, if ever, see members of the fair sex whose numbers are greatly in the minority in this country.

It is only by special permission that leave is granted to a clerk but a commissioned officer is entitled to leave once in seven years. We see those from interior posts who stay with us on their way to and from Canada and England. Consequently I have enjoyed the privilege of becoming acquainted with many of the officers of the Inland Districts on furlough, which some prefer to spend with friends and relatives in the Settlement. Why, I cannot understand, for if I had the opportunity of going away for a holiday I would certainly do so.

This is not for lack of good society here. There are a great many English families though at first they seem very unfriendly. No person would think of going to another's house without a special invitation. The Settlement is larger than I expected, extending twenty miles down the river and about twelve miles up from the Forks and most of the people are very well off. Many are retired Hudson's Bay Company officers and families, all of whom are wealthy as a commissioned officer never thinks of retiring with less than eight hundred or one thousand pounds a year.

We see many young men going to and from Victoria who are finding plenty of gold beyond Edmonton on the Saskatchewan this side of the Rocky Mountains. If I had nothing to do I would go to-morrow to the Western States as that is the place for a young fellow to get on, but I would not give up my present position for any I might get in Canada or the States.

The life of a young clerk here is a good one. We have breakfast at eight o'clock and commence work at nine, continuing until one when we have an hour for lunch. We work from two until six in the afternoon and have dinner in the mess immediately afterwards. Dr. Cowan presides at the head of the table where the officers are seated according to seniority. As the youngster of the establishment I occupy the foot, which does not in any way prevent me from enjoying the food, which is not only good but is well cooked and served.

All work ceases from lunch time on Saturday until Monday morning. Some spend this week-end in shooting game or in riding, as I did on my first holiday, when Mr. Clare gave me an order on the groom for a saddle-horse and I rode down to the Lower Fort. I remained over until Sunday afternoon but was careful to leave in time to ride the twenty miles up the river and arrive punctually for Sunday dinner.

This meal is something of an occasion as the menu invariably includes roast beef, a welcome change from pemmican, which is followed by English plum pudding. Dinner is accompanied by sherry and port, or ale if any prefer it. Chief Factor Clare dines at home unless there are visitors requiring the formality of a senior officer being present, when he presides over the mess of a Sabbath if Dr. Cowan is absent. After dinner on work days we go out duck-shooting but never on Sunday.

There are about twenty-five churches in the Settlements and though there are three within walking distance I always go to St. John's Cathedral at Douglas Point about two miles north of here. The Lord Bishop of Rupert's Land, Bishop Machray, who is a splendid man, has just returned from York Factory. There is also a college under his Lordship where the gentlemen get their sons educated for forty pounds a year.

My fellow officers, according to their religious beliefs, attend either the Roman Catholic Church at St. Boniface or the Presbyterian Church at Kildonan, or Frog Plain, about five miles down the Red River and the centre of the Scottish settlement. The Catholic Cathedral is a splendid building which cost fifteen thousand pounds sterling and which has a beautiful chime of bells to be heard across the prairies. I often go over to morning service with McTavish who is a Catholic. Nearby is a large convent where the young ladies are educated and the college of St. Boniface where boys can get a splendid education for thirty pounds a year, or even less.

As the days pass I am making friends among the residents of the Settlement whom I now find exceedingly hospitable and so kind that I enjoy many a visit in their homes. Mr. Inkster's family have been especially good to me, partly because he was engaged on my Grandfather Traill's estate in the Orkney Islands before coming out with the Selkirk Settlers over fifty years ago. From him I have learned more of my father's home and early life than others could tell me, my father having died when I was not yet twelve years of age. Mr. Inkster's family consists of four sons and three daughters, two of whom are married. One is Mrs. Robert Tait, whose husband travelled with us from Fort Abercrombie, another is Mrs. Archibald McDonald, while Miss Harriet is at home. They are all well-educated, the boys at St. John's College and the girls at Miss Davis' school. The Inksters' estate, "Seven Oaks," adjoins the site of St. John's Church on the north. Below the Inksters the farms are for the most part occupied by the original Selkirk Settlers.

The land was surveyed in ten chain lots running a mile back from the river but these have been subdivided so that most of the farms are a few chains in width and extend two or three miles out on the prairie where the hay is cut. They all build their stables and keep their cattle on the bank of the river, depositing the manure on the ice to be carried out when the ice moves in spring.

Descending the river from Fort Garry to the Rapids is like being in a stable yard. The farmhouses are set back from the river by the road, their whitewashed logs roofed with shingles or thatched with prairie hay. Across the river are a few farms similar to these but most of the land there is still covered with poplar groves.

Every family has to go through the same course of illnesses peculiar to the human race: mumps, measles, whooping cough and other infant afflictions. Every new country is similarly afflicted and it is only with careful nursing and proper medical attention that it survives. The Red River Valley is no exception, suffering all the vicissitudes of Providence: grasshoppers, floods, frosts and droughts. The settlers tell me, however, that they have grown wheat on the same farm for forty years. This is true, but the only market they have is what the Hudson's Bay Company requires for its posts. The quantity that will be bought requires only a few acres on each farm and in the spring the farmer is told how many bushels the Company will take next fall. Instead of sowing wheat on land that has been cropped before, he sows on new land. Consequently, the farms that have been growing wheat for forty years have been growing only from one to five or six crops of wheat on the same land in that length of time.

Four miles below "Seven Oaks" is a brewery and nearby is the residence of Judge Black and the Presbyterian Church. About ten miles farther on the way to the Lower Fort, by the Church of St.

Andrew's and the Rapids of the same name, lives Captain William Kennedy who was in command of a party for the search of Sir John Franklin. He is native-born and his wife, an accomplished English lady and devoted church worker. They have a nice family and, like all the Red River settlers, are the souls of hospitality.

From the Rapids to the Lower Fort the road runs at some distance from the river and mostly through poplar groves. Riding homeward, after passing the Cathedral and College, which is quite an attractive place, the road crosses an open plain until it comes to the bridge across Colony Creek draining the marsh. Here is where we come of an evening to load our bags with mallard ducks. In a couple of hours we can get all we can carry home.

A little to the south is the village of Winnipeg and A. G. B. Bannatyne's store adjoining his residence on the north side of Andrew McDermott's dwelling. The Drever residence is across the road by a log store where the Hudson's Bay Company keeps exclusively American goods in charge of Dick Burdick, an American.

Mr. Drever and his family I know well; William, the only son, is a wonderful fellow. He is of a very dark complexion and at first I thought him to be a halfbreed but his father and mother came from Scotland and have endowed him with their traits and wisdom to which he has added the plain crafts of his Indian and native friends. There are two daughters in this family, which has been kind to me, and hospitable, as have the McDermotts.

The Common between the village of Winnipeg and Fort Garry is the camping ground in summer for both Traders and Indians, being occupied by hundreds of tents and bands of horses. Here is where our local tribes, the Crees and Saulteaux, collect after the spring hunting and trapping season is over. Though not speaking exactly the same language they understand one another, intermarry, and are about equally divided at most of the posts except Qu'Appelle where the Crees predominate. There the Saulteaux mostly hunt in the woods and the Crees on the Buffalo Plains to the south. Here they mix together, dance and feast on boiled dogs, fish and other country luxuries, and race their horses. Some engage to the Hudson's Bay Company as *voyageurs* and cart drivers for the Brigades. In the fall they work making hay and reaping wheat. The hay is all cut with scythes while the grain is reaped with sickles and bound by hand.

The traders from the West also congregate at Fort Garry to sell their furs and purchase supplies for the next year's campaign. They all mix together, the Indians trading fish for buffalo meat with the Plains' hunters, a carefree and friendly assembly. With the approach of fall they are departing to their respective winter hunting and trading places.

The only trouble I know of was when a party of Sioux came. Our local Indians, the Crees and Saulteaux, have been at war with them ever since they crossed the line and located in the Woody Mountain district after their massacre of the white people in Minnesota in '62. Because of the red hand he took in the uprising, Standing Buffalo had fled with his band across the Boundary where he has remained until he arrived here in August with a large number of his warriors.

Our Indians had sent a messenger to invite them to come to Fort Garry to hold a Treaty of Peace and to bury the hatchet. They were royally entertained with feasts of dog soup, fish, and all the luxuries of the season which were highly appreciated. A treaty was duly signed but this proved of short duration. The Sioux were ready to depart next day, but at daybreak the Saulteaux made a raid on their camp and scalped seventeen while the others made a hasty and disorderly retreat. This caused quite a break in the friendly relations, some of the Saulteaux having been inter-married with the Sioux.

Among the halfbreeds feeling has run high in consequence, though public sentiment is divided. The consensus of opinion seems to be that it was a very unfriendly act on the part of the Saulteaux. To confirm his conviction one François Desmarais, who is connected by marriage, or otherwise, with the Sioux Nation disembowelled one of the Saulteaux warriors in the Company's trading store while I was there.

44

The Indian came in with an antelope skin and commenced negotiating with Mr. McKenzie for a sack of vermilion paint in exchange for the skin, though he still wore red war paint and other colours on those parts of his anatomy not covered by his red blanket, breech clout and beaded mocassins. An eagle feather on his head, he had at his waist as further evidence of his bravery a scalping knife with a fresh Sioux scalp dangling beside it.

The transaction completed to his satisfaction, he was about to leave when the French halfbreed entered. Without a sound he seized the Saulteaux's knife and cut him open to the waist so swiftly that our clerk did not see what had happened until the unfortunate customer returned to trade the now useless war paint for some cloth to tie himself together.

When Mr. McKenzie did not understand, the Indian opened his blanket held tightly around him, thereby letting his whole interior fall out on the floor to be instantly covered by his body. In a few seconds his soul was with those of his late victims in the mytical hunting ground that is the destiny of all brave Indians.

His murderer was promptly put in gaol and afterwards tried before Judge Black, convicted of murder and sentenced to be hung by the neck until dead with the usual hope that the Lord would have mercy on his soul. However, a deputation of François' friends and relatives waited upon the Governor and protested against hanging, with the result that his sentence has been commuted to life imprisonment at Stewart Lake in Caledonia. The order of the Judge now reads "that he be confined in the Fort Garry gaol until the departure of the Saskatchewan Brigade of carts and then forwarded in charge of the Guide to Carlton House, the officer in charge there to be directed to forward him with the spring brigade of carts the following summer by way of Jasper House and the Yellowhead Pass." From there transportation is by means of the Company's pack train to his final destination which appears to be some sort of penal colony where undesirables are deported and where they seem to regain their liberty at a safe distance from the Settlement.

The busiest season is now over and the traders, plains hunters and trappers who came in from the North and West with the furs and provisions they had collected during the long winter are leaving their summer camping ground and the acquaintances they have renewed while supplying themselves with food, clothing, ammunition and tobacco to see them through another year.

I wish the Company would send me across the Rocky Mountains or down to York Factory. Governor Mactavish is very anxious for me to stay here for another year to get used to the office work, and I would like to do so to improve my handwriting and my knowledge of the Company's business in general, though the work here is much harder than at the outposts. While waiting for Mr. Campbell I am making the most of present opportunities in the practice of book-keeping and in acquiring useful information. We have at least seven hours work a day and not so much fun as the outsiders have.

My brother Willie is only three hundred miles from here at Fort Ellice and I have been hoping he would come in to see me as I don't think he can have much to do in the summertime. I suspect he is very happy in the society of the young ladies there, the Miss MacKays, or else surely he would have been down. Now that his busier season is commencing he is not likely to do so. I do not intend to fall in love with any young lady before seeing a good deal of this continent, which I mean to do before settling down to married life as my two oldest brothers have done.

As yet I do not know to what post I shall go, though rumour has it that I have been appointed to Qu' Appelle Lake and this my brother has written to my mother, though it cannot be other than supposition for in the minutes of the Council at Norway House, which began on July 2nd I was put down as "disposable."

Appointments and promotions are an important part of the considerations of this annual meeting of the Governor and Council which is held here or at Norway House as is convenient. No clerk is ever appointed to a post before the Council meets and "disposable" means that I could be sent anywhere in the Western Department, or in this one. I know only that I have been assigned to Mr. Campbell's District with headquarters at Fort Pelly.

I shall be sorry to leave the friends who have been so hospitable and the scenes now grown familiar. From the Fort the east view is the most attractive, where are the beautiful Church of St. Boniface with its twin towers, the Bishop's Palace, boys' school, the nunnery and Sisters' School. Here live the French halfbreeds, their farms extending along the east side of the Red River. Some of my friends are the original Selkirk Settlers and their descendants, others are retired Hudson's Bay officers and their families. I have met them in the course of their visits to the Fort and during the business which brought them to the office where I was working. They are all the finest people I have ever known. The Golden Rule is their religion and they hold strictly to it.

## THREE

# By Brigade to Fort Ellice

It is not the province of this story to give a history of the Hudson's Bay Company but a few lines regarding it may not be amiss. The correct name of the Company is: "The Governor and Company of Adventurers of England Trading into Hudson's Bay" and as such it operated under a charter granted by King Charles II in 1670. The name "Hudson's Bay Company" was doubtless adopted for convenience. The leading spirit, if not its prime mover, was Prince Rupert, a first cousin of the King, who was chosen the first Governor.

The terms of the charter gave the Company absolute control of Prince Rupert's Land which is all the territory having waters flowing into Hudson's Bay, a vast territory from the Rocky Mountains east and from the United States boundary north.

Originally the home office in London controlled all matters, but in 1821, when the Company was joined by the Northwest Fur Company, conditions made changes necessary and control was placed in the hands of the Governor of Rupert's Land and his Council composed of Chief Factors and certain Chief Traders.

The general divisions of the Company's present operations are Northern, Southern, Western and Montreal. Ours is the Northern, which entails most of the administrative work, not only because of its size, extending from the Rockies to Hudson's Bay, but because the Company is responsible for the government of the country as well as that of the fur trade. The Montreal Division coincides with what is known as Canada while adjoining it is the Southern Division extending east and south from Hudson's Bay. The Western Department lies west of the Rocky Mountains. Each

48

Division, or Department, is subdivided into Districts with Posts located on transportation routes and in fur-bearing areas.

As previously stated, my contract as a Junior or Apprentice Clerk is to serve for five years at the usual remuneration of £20, £25, £30, £40 and £50 for the successive years. If I wish to remain in the service after that I must sign a second contract for three years at a salary of £75 annually during which I shall be a full-fledged clerk. A third contract may follow, also for three years, as a Chief Clerk with £100 a year, the maximum paid to this class of officer. After twelve to fifteen years in the service there is the prospect of a Chief Trader's commission, which means that I would receive a share of the Company's profits and this varies greatly from year to year. This year it amounts to just over £600 but this is very high, though it has been up to £1,000, and a Chief Factor's is over £1,200 sterling and his expenses paid, including his family's. This is worth working for. Besides, directly a fellow gets his commission, he can retire and receive half-pay for seven years after he leaves the service.

In addition to my pay I am provided with my living expenses and can get my things at 50% advance on prime cost in London (a commissioned officer at $33\frac{1}{3}$% ditto). I am finding that these do not cost nearly so much as in Canada, with the exception of boots and soap. For the former we have to send to London but delivery is free to whatever station I may be posted. I have to buy my own bedding, room furniture, etc., as every clerk must on entering the service. We get the best Hudson's Bay blankets for £1 a pair. They are worth at least four pair of the best Canadian ones, being over a quarter of an inch thick and of the very finest wool. The Company itself manufactures them in Glasgow and we get them in all colours: red, green, black, blue, white, etc. I don't expect to feel the cold more here than in Canada and, from what I can find out, no person dresses a bit warmer but much the same as there. So far, though we are getting into fall, the weather has been very fine.

My living expenses include the following rations for a year: two hundred and forty pounds of flour, twenty of tea, one hundred and twenty of sugar, ten of raisins, the same of currants, five pounds each of coffee and cocoa, all of which food is imported. To this is added any produce obtainable in the country, also provided by the Company without cost to the recipient and delivered to him without charge no matter where he may be.

If I am required to travel I shall receive the additional allowance made to officers when absent from their Posts. Each is provided with an engaged servant to cook for him and to attend to his personal wants, while travelling and at his Post, extra rations being allowed as follows: fifty-six pounds of flour, ten of tea and thirty of sugar. Altogether the food allowance is ample and of the best quality. Most of the Posts maintain a number of cows to furnish fresh milk and butter and where this is not possible, as in the far northern stations, butter is distributed, usually from imports from England.

The Company also imports splendid liquor of all kinds, viz. brandy, rum, sherry, champagne and whiskey. My ration for the year is the same as the other clerks: two gallons of sherry, two of port, two of brandy, and the same of rum for which we may substitute Scotch whiskey if we prefer. If we want more than our given ration we pay the following prices: two shillings per bottle for wine, three shillings for brandy, while rum costs sixteen shillings per gallon, and champagne is sixteen shillings per bottle. We can also get lemon syrup, lime juice, etc., very cheaply.

In spite of these liberal supplies of liquor, the officers are very temperate in their drinking habits and we are sorry to hear of a friend who could not get his appointment to the Company's service because he is not. His widowed mother cannot afford to keep him, but this is no place for any fellow who is not steady.

At last, on September 10th, Chief Trader Robert Campbell has arrived from Fort Pelly accompanied by his wife and children and, to my surprise and joy, my brother, whom I have not seen for three years. Mr. Campbell claimed me at once. To-morrow I must leave the office in the Fort much to my regret and give all my time to the loading of the Swan River carts.

The York Boat Brigade has arrived from Hudson's Bay with the freight left there by ships crossing the Atlantic during the summer. We make up the Fall Cart Brigade which must wait for the *voyageurs* to make their way up the Red River from Lake Winnipeg every September with mail and goods for the winter trade. Thus transportation is provided for officers like myself newly assigned or returning to their posts. This is also the last regular means of despatching mail from the Settlement until the departure of the Winter Packet in November.

It has taken ten days of hard work to assemble the men and see to the loading of fifty Red River carts, each carrying about four hundred pounds and drawn by a horse. If we were to use oxen we could double our loads but we would not be able to travel as fast. There are three drivers to every ten carts and a Guide who is in charge of all the Brigade and consequently a person of no little importance.

The carts have been built for the most part in the Settlement, the wood being native oak while the leather used in the bindings and harness is raw-hide from buffalo or ox skins. There are only two wheels, seven and a half feet in diameter with hubs ten inches across and space in them for the axles bored out by hand, lined with bushings and bound on the outside with raw-hide. The rims, or fellowes, are three inches wide and made of segments of oak joined together with oak pins. The axles are fashioned from split oak so as to have the strength of a straight grain. Repairs to the wheels are made with "shaganappi," which is raw-hide.

The body of the cart is six feet long and three feet wide and is open back and front. The bottom is of inch boards and the sides of round, upright poles capped with a split pole. The trams or shafts taper in width from six to four inches but are three inches thick throughout their nine and a half feet length. The collars, too, are of raw-hide, usually buffalo, and stuffed with hay. They are attached to the trams by iron pins fastened through holes in the wood. This and the iron used in the bushings in the wheel caps is the only metal used, though formerly, I am told, the carts were made entirely of wood.

On September 20th our brigade of fifty carts forms a long file and moves across the prairie. We have left behind us a populous region of some thirteen thousand souls and are travelling on the north side of the Assiniboine where the farm lots front on the river from Fort Garry to White Horse Plains (but are not divided as along the Red River). Six miles out we saw across the river, on the south bank, the estate of James McKay and the residence of Chief Factor John Rowand. Thirty-five miles from the Forks are the Company's store and farm at White Horse Plains with Chief Trader W. D. Lane in charge. Here wheat, barley and oats are grown for the inland trade.

Since the land is prepared with a wooden plough, harvested with sickles and threshed with flails I don't think the grain will add much to the Hudson's Bay Company's dividends. Mr. Lane says that the seed is returned tenfold, or in other words, ten bushels for one seeded.

The trip promises to be a pleasant one over country new to me, and beautiful in the golden colours of autumn under a clear blue sky with mellow sunshine by day and frost by night. My camp outfit consists of the usual two saddle horses and a horse and cart for baggage, driven by an engaged servant whose duty it is to cook for me, look after the horses and perform such work as I might require. I have been given charge of some of the carts and of the men who look after them, including Sandy McLean and two live hogs he is caring for during the journey. It is hoped to raise enough of these domestic animals to furnish pork for the inland trade.

On our first night out from Fort Garry I have been surprised and not a little horrified to find that assisting my man in the preparation of our evening meal was the prisoner who murdered the Indian last summer. On demanding an explanation I was informed that the Guide has assigned François to assist my man, whereupon I interviewed the Guide. He was quick to reassure me with the utmost politeness that he promised the Governor to do his best to make my journey comfortable, that François is an efficient hand on the plains and furthermore that he is a very good young man and his own cousin.

Although my idea of what constitutes a good young man differs slightly from the Guide's, having witnessed his assassination of his enemy, I think it better not to have any difference of opinion with the cousin. Leaving François' moral character out of the question, he is proving all that the Guide has said. Although he has no gun he is keeping my mess supplied with prairie chicken, duck, rabbit and even antelope meat.

Past White Horse Plains we saw little of settlement until we came to High Bluff from where farms are comparatively frequent as far as Portage la Prairie. Here, about seventy miles from Fort Garry, the Company has a post under Mr. John Dougal MacKay.

The nights have become colder but no matter how short of fuel the other campfires are, crossing the Big Plain, François has seen to it that I have an abundant supply at my tent. One night I was awakened by a foreign and disagreeable odour penetrating within and on looking outside I found that Sandy had placed his hog cart close to my camp fire and was peacefully sleeping under the cart. For the remainder of the journey I ordered a strict quarantine to be kept at Sandy's camp which was removed to the proper distance and provided with fuel by himself.

We have been favoured with fine weather all the way and in five days we have covered the two hundred and sixty miles to Fort Ellice, the first station in the Swan River District.

A warm welcome awaited us from Mr. MacKay, the *bourgeois*[1] of the Post, and, with my brother I was enjoying the kind hospitality of his family when Mr. Campbell informed me that Mr. McDonald had requested an assistant at Fort Qu'Appelle. This and Fort Ellice are the two chief posts under Fort Pelly in the Swan River District, each having its outposts. Our Chief Trader has consented to my going on condition that Mr. McDonald sends me to Fort Pelly before winter sets in. Our pleasant visit of three days has come to an end and now, much to my disappointment, I must part with his charming wife and children, the Chief Trader and my brother, good friends of the past few weeks.

[1] *bourgeois* was the name commonly given to the superior officer to whom one was responsible.

Our brigade is being divided at Fort Ellice, part going to Carlton, except for those carts which branch west up the Qu'Appelle River, while the other main part continues north up the Assiniboine to Fort Pelly. To-morrow I shall set out again with that part of the Fall Brigade to arrive with the carts apportioned to Qu'Appelle.

A few days later on September 30th I am at home as a friend of the family that entertained me so kindly in the Settlement, for Mrs. McDonald is a daughter of the Inksters. Just why Mr. McDonald wants me I do not understand as he does not ask me to do anything. Time passes very pleasantly, however, riding about the beautiful Qu'Appelle Valley, shooting prairie chicken and ducks and at times escorting the ladies of the Fort on horseback rides throughout four weeks of our loveliest Canadian season, the Indian summer of October.

Today the final preparations have been made for the buffalo hunt that must provide us with fresh meat for the winter, and I have received permission from my *bourgeois* to accompany the brigade. The interpreter of this Post is Jerry McKay, an experienced Captain and hunter, and he must be in charge, Mr. McDonald has explained, but I may go along as a guest. My superior officer has outfitted me with a saddle horse and man to cook for me and look after my wants, also a horse and cart for our baggage and provisions.

We set forth in the first light of dawn across the sandy prairie that is broad, treeless and level from the banks of the Qu'Appelle and Assiniboine Rivers to the south and west, broken only by the gentle slopes of the Moose Mountains and farther to the west the Woody Mountains. In this region prairie fires have burned off the grass to such an extent that it was necessary to travel one hundred and sixty miles to the more distant hills before we sighted the first band of buffalo. Usually three days travel is enough to get all the meat that is needed.

Our hunters drew as near as possible to the grazing animals without disturbing them. In the time-honoured discipline of generations of plainsmen they formed a long line, keeping abreast in self-imposed silence until so close that the beasts became restive and their stolid heads began to rise here and there in the herd. At the instant they broke into a run the Captain gave the command to "Charge." Then, and not a second before, the riders descended upon them at full gallop, each man having an equal chance to approach and bring down a buffalo with his first shot.

The hunter carries his powder in a buffalo horn and with amazing dexterity reloads his flint-lock, single-barrelled shotgun by pouring a handful of powder in the muzzle, dropping on this a ball from his mouth, where he carries this ammunition during the hunt, and giving the gun a knock to settle the charge and prime the flint-pan, all the while riding at top speed. They shoot without raising the gun to aim, for their mounts are trained buffalo runners and uncannily expert in taking their riders close to the fleeing quarry with no other guidance than a slight pressure of the knees, both hands being busy with powder horn and gun.

The shooting is done at such close range that the muzzle is not far from the heart of the buffalo under fire, yet so skillful are the horses in carrying their riders into the edge of the stampeding throng that they avoid being drawn into it while escaping injury from wounded buffalo and missing the treacherous badger holes. At the end of half an hour all but the fastest runners have dropped behind the fleeing beasts and when all the huntsmen retrace the path of the chase they count over seventy-five dead animals.

Our train consists of fifty carts each of which will carry one and a half animals. The nights are getting longer and colder, which is freezing the loads of meat, and we are ready to start on the homeward journey.

Just then the weather suddenly turned warm, something never before known in the month of November. Fortunately there is an encampment of Indians near at hand and Jerry has made arrangements with these Crees to dry the meat for pemmican. When it again turns cold we shall set off on the return trip.

The work of preserving the meat is left to the women as part of their household duties. After skinning and scraping the hides they

55

cut the flesh in long strips and dry it before pounding it into small pieces which they place in oblong bags made by sewing a folded buffalo skin on both sides. As a rule pemmican is made in the spring when the hides are not of any value except dried and used as cart covers or "shaganappi," but the purpose of the Fall hunt is to get robes and fresh meat which is preserved for the winter by freezing.

In the Swan River District the centres of the trade in robes and pemmican are Fort Ellice, with an outpost at Moose Mountains, and Qu'Appelle, with outposts at Pile-of-Bones Creek and the Woody Mountains. We supply Fort Pelly and all the woods Posts, as well as the Saskatchewan District, with rations for the brigades to York House and to the northern Districts of Athabasca and McKenzie River.

The latter is often called the LaLoche Brigade because of the famous portage across the Divide of the watersheds of the rivers flowing east into Hudson's Bay and those flowing north into the Arctic Ocean. Our goods thus laboriously transported find their way to far-distant posts. The woods posts are situated in the belt of timber which extends across the prairies north of the Saskatchewan River. Red River District gets its main supply of pemmican from this and the Saskatchewan Districts and the rest from Pembina and the Moose River District.

The largest concentration of buffalo hunters is at Pembina as of old and before the arrival of the Selkirk Settlers, though Red River District was formerly the headquarters of hundreds of these plainsmen. They generally organize at Pembina under a Captain whose word is *law*. With him they plan the direction in which to move and when to start. This is as soon as the grass in spring has grown long enough to provide good grazing for their horses, and in time to trade their pemmican for the provisioning of the *voyageurs* who freight all summer between Fort York, Fort Garry and St. Paul.

Each day the motley array of men, women, children, horses and dogs moves forward until the evening camp is made in the most suitable location. When the buffalo are reached a permanent camp is made where the meat is converted into pemmican. The fall hunt is organized in the same way, but the hunters generally build log houses and pass the winter where they have wood, water and grazing for their horses. This is the origin of the village of Pembina.

Each hunter has at least one buffalo-runner and whoever is the possessor of a very fast horse enjoys a social and financial standing not awarded to others with ordinary horses. A man's wealth is computed by the number and quality of his band according to which he is said to be "rich in horses." The more horses he has, the more carts he possesses, most of the hunters being also fur traders taking out goods in spring and fall to trade for robes, furs and pemmican. Some have large outfits and trade for horses that the Indians bring over from the American Indians. These they forage from the Blackfeet and military posts across the Missouri River and call the "Spoils of War."

All the while the relentless slaughter of the still countless denizens of the Great Plains goes on by red man and white, and the once vast herds are thinning perceptibly. Our post in the Touchwood Hills was once a good one for the buffalo trade but is so no longer.

Today a courier has arrived with a letter from Mr. McDonald saying that I am wanted at Fort Pelly and must come in at once. The horses are all pretty well tired out but our Captain Jerry has offered me the use of Little Bishon, the best buffalo-runner in the brigade, and an Indian guide with two other mounts. This Cree, known as Little Wolf, is a crack buffalo hunter in spite of his lameness. He once killed seventeen buffalo in thirty minutes with a muzzle-loading flint-lock gun while on the little horse I am to ride. Little Wolf was told that he must take me to the Fort as quickly as possible.

"If we start at daylight we can camp where there is wood and water the first night," he replied, "and if the *Okimasis*[2] does not tire out we will reach the woods at the Old Fort the second night. If he plays out we have cached wood half-way where we can camp.

[2] An apprentice clerk.

Three days later I am back at home with the McDonalds. The weather had turned cold by the time we left, which was before it was really light. Our horses made good time over the frozen ground which enabled us to reach the woods the first night as Little Wolf had planned. While he was making a fire I shot a couple of rabbits which tasted especially good after living on buffalo meat for over a month. Long before daylight Little Wolf woke me and said it was "tomorrow morning." He had cooked a rabbit, made tea and brought in and saddled the horses.

We were soon under way and rode for what seemed hours before daylight. Little Bishon kept up a steady lope while Little Wolf changed from one horse to the other every few hours. Just before sunset we reached the Old Fort from where the cart trail to Qu'Appelle is plainly marked by much use. We again made camp with prairie chicken for our supper after which my guide went to sleep.

When I thought my Little Bishon was sufficiently rested I saddled him and rode off leaving the Indian asleep. The Old Fort is twenty miles from this post but the well-beaten trail from the Great Plains was well marked in the bright starry night. It was beginning to get light when I arrived here just about the same time that Little Wolf woke up and missed me. He lost no time in setting out after me by following my tracks and was here by noon.

Meanwhile I had told Mr. McDonald of the plan Little Wolf related to Jerry should the clerk play out, and when I got my *bourgeois* to remind my Guide about his thinking I might want to stop half-way, the Indian seemed pleased and asked how soon we could go on another trip. In two days and nights we rode one hundred and sixty miles over a burned prairie without seeing a track until we came to the Old Fort.

I have been out with the hunters for about six weeks and have greatly enjoyed sharing their life and the excitement of running buffalo.

When I returned I found the letter waiting for me from Mr. Campbell who wants me to come for the winter to work in the office.

We are loading whitefish in carts and when the brigade brings in the pemmican from the Woody Mountains we shall take some of these carts of meat to make up our train for Fort Pelly. Some posts in our District do not have fishing grounds and these we supply with fish from our lakes in addition to supplying all the posts except Fort Ellice with buffalo meat.

## FOUR

## *Christmas at Fort Pelly*

TODAY is January 20th and I must not let the Express go down to Red River without writing a few lines to tell about the past month here at Fort Pelly although I have not a whole sheet of paper fit to write a letter on and must ask to be excused for writing on scraps of paper. The Winter Packet is expected in about the eighth of February and I am longing for the letters from home that it will bring. There will be interesting and welcome letters from other clerks all over Rupert's Land. Though we seldom meet, unless in the same District, or in the Settlement, we keep in touch with one another by letters written throughout the long winter months.

It was a few days before Christmas when I arrived from Qu'-Appelle in charge of a train of carts laden with buffalo meat and whitefish. The trip from Qu'Appelle to Fort Pelly was another hundred and sixty miles or about the same distance as my ride in from the buffalo grounds, but we travelled more slowly with the carts. We passed the Beaver Hills which are the lower outskirts of the Touchwood Hills and thinking to arrive some hours before the carts I took two saddle horses and rode ahead.

Mr. Campbell reprimanded me for breaking the Company's rule that an officer must never travel alone, then he and Mrs. Campbell expressed their joy at seeing me again and I pleaded homesickness for them and their children, for it was over two months since I had seen them. I had become very attached to the family on our trip from Fort Garry and it was quite true that I wanted to see them again so much that I could not wait for the slow carts.

The past weeks have been pleasant ones for me as one of the

happy family living at this Post. Mr. and Mrs. Campbell are very kind and do everything possible to make me comfortable. We had a very jolly Christmas and New Year. Willie came up from Fort Ellice and spent the 24th, 25th and 26th with us. I had not seen him since I spent a few days with him at Fort Ellice. He is looking very well and seems to be very happy. The MacKays are a very nice family indeed and I think Willie would be sorry to leave that post as long as Mr. MacKay is in charge. Christmas dinner included plum puddings sent out from Scotland especially for the occasion.

There were the customary Christmas holidays for the men with feasts for the Indians and for themselves.

Every Sunday the Campbell children are dressed in their Highland costumes having the plaid of the Campbell Clan. Besides being herself a charming lady, Mrs. Campbell has four very good children, two boys and two girls. Her sister, Miss Stirling, is staying with her and is going to take the young Campbells home to school when she goes. She has just come out from Scotland.

Meantime the children are acquiring a fluent use of Indian dialects in addition to their Scottish brogue which is so thick one could "cut it with a knife." My own ineptitude in learning the languages of our Indians I regret very much. In this I resemble my mother. How I wish I had inherited the linguistic gift of my father who spoke the languages of Italy, Germany and France, the countries where most of his life was spent before he came to Canada.

My family will be glad to hear that I like this country even better than I expected. The life is one of change and adventure, of which I cannot tire. We are not expected to put our hand to anything but a gentleman's work, and are always treated as one wherever we go.

At an outpost our allowances are very good and here the officers have a general mess where we get the best of everything. We live chiefly upon meat: fresh whitefish or salmon for breakfast, beef or buffalo meat for dinner and rabbits or pheasants for tea. Our allowance of flour is not sufficient to keep us in bread, but I have got so used to doing without it that I don't care for it at all. We have an old French man-servant who lights our fires, makes the beds, cleans our boots and does anything for us that we need. Of an evening we enjoy being with the family while Mrs. Campbell reads stories of Scotland. After the children are off to bed we are served wine and Scotch shortbread.

In spite of so much kindness and comfortable quarters I find it a dull life. For six hours a day I work in the office. There are three of us: Mr. Campbell, the Officer in charge of the District, Mr. Smith, who is a senior clerk and takes all the shopwork, and myself with nothing to do but work at the accounts. I have been copying requisitions under his direction but there is now less to do as the Indians have gone out to their hunting grounds and the Chief Trader spends much of his time visiting other Posts.

When I run out of work I devote most of my time to driving with the children around the country, shooting rabbits and prairie chicken. Dog-driving is great fun, I often take the ladies out in the carriole. A good train of four will travel eighty miles a day drawing a man and his blankets, grub, etc. They keep a steady trot the whole day.

The Bishop of Rupert's Land is expected here in a few days en route to the north. There is a missionary in the village here who tells his Christian friends, (as he calls the Indians), that they are doing very well, that he has no fault to find with them and to carry on upon the old track. I am not sure how much good this does them.

There would be little if any winter travel without dog teams, carrioles and sleds. The carriole, like the Red River cart, is peculiar to this country but is a much more picturesque conveyance made of two oak boards ten feet long, ten inches wide and one inch thick. These are planed at one end and turned up so as to form a floor twenty inches wide with a front end to protect the traveller. This is covered with buffalo parchment stretched on a light frame and extending from the front to four feet back so as to form a shoe in which one can sleep. There is an upright back or heel in front of which is the opening by which the passenger

enters the bag in which he can sit comfortably with back supported when not sleeping. Behind this the floor extends two feet
in order to provide room for the driver to stand if he cares to
ride. Unless it is bitterly cold a carriole provides a delightful
way to travel.

We have twenty men employed at Fort Pelly and our interpreter, Daniels. One day an Indian came in to ask if we would
send a man to their camp for some furs and Daniels was entrusted to go, but with strict instructions from Mr. Campbell that
he must be back on the third day. Our men are Indians speaking
Cree and Saulteaux and it is the interpreter's duty to translate
whatever orders the Chief Trader gives each night for the work
next day. In the absence of Daniels I must do my best to direct
the cutting of wood, the hauling of hay, and putting up of ice
among other things.

Daniels had been severely reprimanded last spring for being
absent when Indians came to the Fort to trade and warned that in
future he must not neglect his duties to attend to his traps. Notwithstanding this reproof, he found it convenient to make a
detour to visit his trapline but managed to be back on time as
charged. However he did not dare to ask Mr. Campbell for leave to
go and dig out a fox that had got away from one of his traps. He
was sure from some fur left from its foot that it was a very fine
black or silver grey specimen. He came to tell me that he had
traced it to its hole which he had plugged up and if I would assist
him he would give me half of the value of the pelt.

At the present trading price a black or silver fox is worth from
eight to ten pounds in goods which will be paid to employees of the
Company, a welcome addition to my Junior Clerk's salary of
twenty pounds for the first year. Moreover, I have observed from
the London sales that fox furs have been sold for as high as one
thousand pounds a pair and I had implicit confidence in Daniel's
assurance that this fox was a very choice specimen, despite having
heard Mr. Campbell impress upon him that his trapline was of
relatively little importance compared to his services as an
interpreter.

63

If the Chief Trader would permit me to make a trip in the vicinity of this particular trap I might be allowed to take Daniels with me. We would share the labour and the proceeds of the pelt. I have accompanied Mr. Campbell on several occasions to a marsh about half a mile from the fox's hole to see how a large band of our horses there are wintering. He has complained to me that he has not a man except Daniels who knows the horses well enough so that when he sends for saddle horses he will not bring in cart horses.

When I suggested to Mr. Campbell that Daniels could tell me all about the horses if we spent a day with them he thought this an excellent idea. He said that I might take his dogs and carriole next day and that Daniels would drive me down.

One obstacle remained. We had to have the sapper's and miner's outfit if we were to dig out the fox and this is in the custody of Thompson Smith, my senior clerk. It was necessary to take him into our confidence and, alas, to submit to his terms, which meant giving him half my share. This I considered a hard bargain as he is a Chief Clerk receiving one hundred pounds a year but he regarded it as a purely financial arrangement.

Mrs. Campbell saw to it that I was provided with a good lunch which was of a size sufficient for both of us, and we made an early start. Mr. Smith had concealed the tools under the robes in the carriole and we soon covered the six miles, which has taken the Chief Trader and myself much longer during our trips which we made on snowshoes.

We lost no time in setting ourselves to dig out the fox. The ground was frozen hard but we picked and we dug at the hole until noon when we reached its den, only to find a little undersized gray fox worth about two shillings and sixpence. My visions of wealth faded with my good opinion of Daniels' judgement of a fur-bearer from a bit of fur from its foot.

A good lunch helped us to bear our disappointment and to raise my hopes that Daniels' knowledge of the horses was better than of the fox. We stayed until dark rounding up all of them and taking an inventory with detailed information, so carefully that I can go down any time and pick out the right ones. For this I have received many compliments from Mr. Campbell, a reward to be treasured in memory. If I were an artist I could draw each animal in retrospect from the imprint on my mind.

We have always fresh meat of all kinds: beef, buffalo, moose and red deer, also bear, beaver and whatever may fall to the huntsman's snare or gun. Much of it is sold or traded to us by the Indians, but a few years ago the Company was confronted with a serious problem. The Plain Crees, the Stonies or Assiniboines and the Wood Saulteaux held a Grand Council at Qu'Appelle to demand a revision of the prices the Company paid them for the meat it must have, not only to provision its posts, but for the transport service. The Indians agreed to insist upon the following increases:

|  | *Old Tariff* | | *New Tariff* | |
| --- | --- | --- | --- | --- |
|  | *s.* | *d.* | *s.* | *d.* |
| *fresh meat (buffalo, elk, moose, antelope)* |  | 2 |  | 3 |
| *pemmican* |  | 3 |  | 4 |
| *dried meat* |  | 1½ |  | 2 |
| *ducks, prairie chicken, per dozen* | 1 | 0 | 1 | 6 |
| *rabbits, per dozen* |  | 6 | 1 | 0 |

The following rations issued daily to employees and their families will indicate something of the quantities required as our whole subsistence is almost entirely of meat. For each man six pounds of fresh meat, including rabbits; if meat is dried, four pounds; and if pemmican, ducks or white fish, three pounds. The ration for a woman is half that for a man and a child's ration is half that issued for a woman.

Families vary in size from six to fourteen members, there being no race suicide in these parts at present. The man with a wife and six children receives only eighteen pounds of meat daily while the man blessed with fourteen children receives thirty pounds, or the corresponding number of whitefish or other meat.

Upon receiving the Indians' demands the Chief Trader invited the Chiefs by messages sent to the Post managers to hold a joint council to adjust the tariff. The delegates promptly arrived at headquarters with members of our district staff who ably assisted Mr. Campbell in entertaining the visitors with a feast provided by a superannuated bull and much tobacco, among other delicacies.

But when the Officer in Charge and his clerks had exhausted all their eloquence, and much food beside, the Indians insisted as before that the new tariff must be adopted or "no meat." Consequently the new prices went into effect forthwith, though it could not be expected that our worthy *bourgeois* would submit more than temporarily to the demands, for he is a man of infinite resource and long and varied experience in such matters.

It originated in his fertile imagination that domestic animals could be raised in Swan River and that hogs were the meat producers that multiplied most rapidly. These could be imported from England by the annual ship to Hudson Bay. The requisitions on London for what comes out by the next year's ship are made up each spring during the annual meeting of the Northern Council at Norway House. In attendance are all the commissioned officers in charge of districts for the purpose of submitting their reports for the past year and discussing plans for the future.

Accordingly, Mr. Campbell sought the approval of a requisition for ten brood sows and one hog, but his views were not shared by those officers whose districts were not as yet faced with his problem of increased meat prices. However, the officer in charge of the Peace River District intimated that if the requisition were amended to read "two hogs for Swan River District and the same for the Peace River District" he would support the measure. As he was the ranking Chief Factor and acted as watch dog for the requisitions there was no difficulty in obtaining its acceptance. Before the Council adjourned they placed the following resolution on the minutes of the Annual Meeting:

*That owing to the alarming increase of the cost of subsistence in Prairie Districts caused by the unreasonable demands made by the Indians for meat and with a view to reducing the present high cost by substituting domestic animals for the production of meat for that heretofore supplied by the Indians, it is resolved that a requisition be made on London for two pairs of hogs to be purchased in the agricultural districts of England, two males and two females to be of the most improved breed of the same variety, and that care be taken that they are not of any family connection, the same to be forwarded by the ship to York Factory, and that the officer in charge of that post be requested to forward them to Norway House by the Red River Brigade, each pair being in charge of an engaged servant to be selected from those assigned to the respective Districts, and the Officer in Charge of Norway House be directed to forward those for Swan River to Fort Garry and the other pair to the Long Portage by the Cumberland Brigade.*

All appears to have gone well until after leaving Fort York there arose friction between Sandy and Rory as to the relative beauty and other good qualities of their respective pair of hogs. Upon arrival at Norway House the hostility threatened to become a fight under the influence of the pint of Demarara rum, issued to each member of the boats' crews according to the time honoured custom of welcoming a brigade to an important post.

But better council prevailed and a pugilistic encounter was avoided by agreeing to settle the dispute with the aid of two judges, to be appointed by the Guide of the Brigade, the decision of the judges to be final. The animals were turned out in an empty store house with the result that, although the males were considered to be equal in all respects, the lady companion of Sandy's hog was credited with many more fine points and awarded the blue ribbon!

And thereby hangs a tale.

The animals were again put in crates and next day continued on their journeys to Red River and Cumberland House with Sandy and Rory each accompanying two of them to his respective destination. (This was the Sandy and the hogs which were in my charge last fall from Fort Garry to Fort Ellice and which proceeded to Fort Pelly when I went to Qu'Appelle.)

When I reached this post some weeks later I heard of the enthusiasm that greeted the arrival of the crate of the first hogs to be imported into this District. Bright visions of roast pork, sausages, bacon and ham in the near future awaited its arrival. But, alas! When the animals were removed from their travelling quarters it was discovered that, instead of being one male and one female, they were both of the masculine gender. Someone had blundered!

Although I had taken charge temporarily, Sandy had been appointed by a high official at York Factory and my responsibility ended on delivering him and his charges to that part of the Brigade destined for Fort Pelly as received at Fort Garry. Upon Sandy being examined before a court of investigation he maintained that these were the same that he had received at the ocean port, that he had faithfully watched and cared for them and, in fact, had never had them out of his sight. Remembering the odour that had invaded my tent one night I consider that had he said "his nose" he would be telling strictly the truth.

An official investigation has begun, commencing in the London Office and the correspondence might have exceeded in volume that carried on between the Secretaries of State of Great Britain and the United States for the adjustment of shipping destroyed during the Civil War and known as the Alabama Claims, had not a crewman of the Peace River Brigade turned state's evidence. He has testified that at Norway House, while Sandy and his friends were celebrating their victory over Rory McLeod, he assisted the latter to kidnap the prize sow and substitute his own male animal.

With reminiscences and tales of this land, we enjoy long winter evenings together. Mr. and Mrs. Campbell are very kind, nice people and I have become exceedingly fond of all the children. Miss Stirling is a very clever girl and Mr. Smith a jolly fellow.

Mr. Campbell spent eighteen years extending the fur trade to the borders of the Russian operations in Alaska. During his explorations in the Northwest he met and overcame many difficulties. He established the Hudson's Bay Company's first post in Alaska and when besieged by hostile Indians at his post on the Pelly River he starved out the foe by sustaining himself and his men upon their windows as food. These were of reindeer parchment and more valuable as nourishment in the emergency, enabling the beleaguered souls to withdraw with all possible speed to Fort Simpson on the Mackenzie River. From there he walked on snowshoes to Fort Garry, returning for the first time in eighteen years, and continued by snowshoe to Crow Wing on the Mississippi River, thence to Prairie la Crosse and by rail and water to Scotland.

There he claimed the hand of the one who came out to be his bride seven years later. Again he travelled from the wilderness of Athabasca to meet the sisters, Elleonora and Christine Stirling, and to marry Elleonora in a ceremony in the church in Kildonan.

The bride accompanied her husband to Athabasca where James and Christine were born. A few years ago he was transferred to Fort Pelly, since when the family has been enlarged by Glenburn and Elleonora, the adored baby whom we delight to call "Queenie." No wonder I count myself fortunate to be with this happy household and to receive my early training in the service under so distinguished an officer.

During the latter weeks of January and early in February the arrival of the Winter Packet is anticipated with much eagerness, and some anxiety, for this is a very cold winter and there is speculation as to possible mishaps and delays. All the while our mail is piling up, being official letters and private correspondence. Mr. Campbell has received word from Mr. McDonald that he would like me to go to Qu'Appelle to take charge there while he comes here to meet the Packet and also while at one of his outposts on the Plains. This is what it means to be assigned as a "disposable," namely, that any post manager who wants to take a trip can ask for my services. In three days I must set out for Qu'Appelle to be "disposed of" for a month.

---

## FIVE

# *The Winter Packet*

ON the twenty-third of January I set out with two trains of dogs, one to draw my "toha," or carriole, and the other to haul the flat sled with my luggage, the grub, etc. Mr. Campbell sent his own driver and two other men to take turns in driving the dogs with the sled and in running before to break the track. The weather was very cold, from thirty to forty degrees below zero, but we were travelling through a park country between the low crests of the Beaver and Touchwood Hills with plenty of bluffs covered with poplars that made good shelter and furnished us with fuel.

Depending on the state of the trail and the weather we were able to cover thirty miles more or less a day and to arrive at the Touchwood Hills Post comfortably on the fourth day. Mrs. Campbell, who regards me as a youngster, had made a plum pudding and had instructed the driver how to heat it, besides furnishing us with other luxuries for the trip.

Conversation along the trail was confined almost wholly to the three men who spoke a curious mixture of Cree and Saulteaux intermingled with bad English and indifferent French, due to their mixed parentage of these four peoples. As we stopped for mid-day rest and food or to make camp for the night, the theme of their discussions never varied from the horses and dogs they knew by sight or hearsay. An occasional rider or driver appeared on the menu of horse for breakfast, dog for dinner, with a rehash of horse and dog for supper followed by a desert of dog drivers. By the end of the trip I was familiar with the history of every dog, cart-horse and buffalo-runner, rider and driver from the Arctic Circle to Red River.

Our Post in the Touchwood Hills is a fine fort about two hundred miles from Fort Pelly. I waited there for two days for the Saskatchewan Express. When it arrived we sat up until three o'clock and had breakfast before starting by moonlight for Qu'Appelle. We made quite a party as Mrs. Deschambeault went down to stay with Mrs. McDonald while their respective spouses were absent. Added to my responsibilities were six more sleds, making eight in all. We travelled hard all day and until twelve o'clock that night, when we arrived at Fort Qu'Appelle to find all had gone to bed. They soon turned out when they heard that the Express had arrived. McDonald and I talked all night which meant that I did not go to bed at all for two nights. The appearance of a fellow officer, even the youngest, I have found, is an event in the quiet winter.

We enjoyed a reunion of two days before Mr. McDonald started off to meet the Express from Red River and left me alone in my glory with two married ladies to console, and one young lady to console me. But Qu'Appelle is a fine post, the best in the District next to Fort Pelly. I had a good deal to do between writing, looking after the men, sending out traders and hunters and all the supervision that is the lot of a *bourgeois* of a post. There were eighteen men to look after, most of whom I kept out on the Plains.

In seventeen days Mr. McDonald was back with the return Express and my letters. Some were written in August and had been all the way around by Norway House and Hudson's Bay. I have heard from all my friends in Canada – the first letters from them in five and a half months. They all came in a heap "like Paddy found ninepence!"

While Mr. McDonald made a trip to the Plains, where he has an outpost, I remained in charge of Qu'Appelle, and when Mr. Deschambeault, the Officer-in-Charge of Touchwood Hills, went out to the Plains I took charge of his post.

My stay at Qu'Appelle was for two months, twice as long as expected, but I was very busy and enjoyed it very much. I left Mr. and Mrs. McDonald quite well. They have had an addition to their family since Christmas and she has gone to Red River where he will go for her during the summer.

71

On the sixteenth of March I left there to come in again to Fort Pelly with dogs. The lengthening days of sunlight in the never-ending whiteness of snow-covered prairie caused me to become snow-blind. For four days I lay in my carriole and could not see my dogs. The guide and one man also got blind and were not able to keep the track. We were lost on the plains for three days without anything to eat.

At last we killed one of our dogs, but on the open prairie we could not get wood to make a fire. We cut up one of the sleds for fuel and roasted the dog which gave us all a good meal and some for each of the dogs.

We reached Fort Pelly that night where for three days I lay quite blind and with sore eyes for some days afterwards. I am afraid my sister will think I am a regular "saviah" when I say that dogs are good grub, but if anyone should be as hungry as we were and forced to try one for dinner I'll bet he would say it was splendid.

This has been a very hard winter for food owing to the great fires on the Plains last summer and fall. The buffalo remained scarce and far off. It has been a very severe winter for travelling. Many have frozen and starved to death. One of our interpreters was in charge of a brigade when overtaken by a storm on a plain two hundred miles wide. It blew and drifted so hard that they could not travel for four days. They lay under the snow and lived on raw meat as the nearest wood was a hundred miles away. On the fifth day their meat was done when the weather cleared and they started off, but the dogs were so reduced by hunger that they could not travel fast. With wood cut from a sled they boiled the netting from their snowshoes down to a glue and ate it. Pretty hard tucker!

From the fourth of December until the twenty-ninth of March when the snow began to melt a little on the sunny side of the houses, it has not thawed enough to keep the snow from drifting. It was fearfully cold all February and March. The men could not keep warm running as hard as they could leg it with thick flannel underclothes, leather coats and trousers, thick blanket overcoats and buffalo coats on top of them all. On a clear bright day you can see the air full of frost like snow, but this is nothing to the cold in the Northern District or at York Factory, for there the snow does not begin to melt until the first of June.

The Winter Packet arrived at Fort Pelly while I was at Qu'-Appelle, where I received my letters a week later. With it came the latest tales of horse and dog to the delight of my two men who eagerly added these to their hackneyed reminiscences.

Little wonder! For this picturesque group of warm-coated dogs with stalwart, dusky drivers of twelve or more sleds are the only human link for six winter months between the posts that dot the frozen lakes and rivers in the MacKenzie, Athabasca and Peace River Districts. Each sled carries about two hundred pounds, or fifty pounds to each dog, of this semi-annual mail made up of letters from one officer to another and their friends in Red River Settlement, including the Governor's official letter to each officer in charge of a post.

All await the Packet with concern for its safety and hope for mail during the months that men and dogs hold steadily forward, day after day, from grey dawn to early twilight, the dogs trotting hour after hour to the tune of the little bells attached to their gay harnesses. Each train is the pride and joy of its driver who "mushes" forward on showshoes, himself an outstanding person of trust to whom each dog is prized for what it can do. All are beautiful animals especially selected for this important journey because of superior speed and endurance. In the coldest nights men and dogs lie close together for warmth, their only shelter a tent of skins and one food to sustain all – pemmican.

As soon after November 10th as Lake Winnipeg and the rivers are frozen hard enough for ice travel, the Company despatches from Fort Garry the Winter, or Northern Packet carrying the mail that has accumulated during the summer for the officers and men at Norway House and all the Districts to the north and west. At the same time a Packet is made up at Fort Simpson with the mail from the Yukon Post, Athabasca, Peace River and Saskatchewan Districts reaching Norway House in January. When the

Packet from York House, Churchill and the surrounding District arrives, a combined Packet is despatched from Norway House by way of Water Hen River, Shoal River and Fort Pelly where it is met by the Packet from Qu'Appelle, Touchwood Hills and Egg Lake. The final Packet goes on from Fort Pelly to Fort Garry by way of Manitoba House and Lake Manitoba to Oak Point, which is an easy day's journey from its destination. As Swan River District is one of the last links in the circuit, it is late February before its outlying posts have received their mail.

It is a great honour for a man to be sent to drive the Packet and he never fails to make the best time possible. The Fort Simpson driver will deduct a few hours from his time of departure and his fame as a traveller will increase with each repetition to the succeeding driver, until by the time it is related at Norway House, the driver and his dogs have exceeded a speed that is credible. When roads are bad or the dogs are being driven faster and for longer hours they must be changed every two or three hundred miles.

If an officer is sent out with a Packet he is provided with a train of dogs and a man to drive his carriole, also a man to drive the sled and dogs with his baggage, and food required for all. On reaching a Post he is provided with fresh dogs and men, if necessary, the others being returned to the Post from which they came. This is repeated until arrival at their destination.

Mr. MacKay's men, who went down with the Packet to Fort Garry, may bring more letters from home and, I hope, better news of my mother's health than I received at Qu'Appelle, for it was very bad when the letter was written months ago. There was word too of the death of my uncle. Also I was very much shocked to hear of poor Mr. Clare's death, a dreadful blow to his wife and family. I heard too of Mr. Sinclair's death at Shoal Lake from Joseph MacKay who was there at the time he died, Shoal Lake being quite close to Fort Ellice. I am sorry that Mr. William Watt did not come up to this District as I should very much like to see him. He must know a good many of my friends and acquaintances at the Sault Ste. Marie, which he has left lately.

In due course I also received letters from Mr. Hargrave dated

December 8th and February 23rd and as the Northern Express went down in January I could not manage to have a reply ready. I hear there have been a great many balls and parties at Fort Garry during the winter which I expect everyone has enjoyed very much. There has not occurred an opportunity since the Express for letters to go down to the Settlement but meantime I shall write to friends in Fort Garry and elsewhere so that letters are ready to go by the first chance, which may not be until the furs go down in a month or less.

# SIX

---

## *The Fur Brigade*

TODAY is the twenty-third of April and I have time to write while waiting for the gentlemen who are expected in every day from the outposts. When they arrive we shall be busy until the boats leave for Norway House with the furs. It will be quite an agreeable change to have something to do again. Since my return from Qu'Appelle on March 20th I have done little but pack furs.

Here at Fort Pelly I don't get enough writing to keep my hand in and have applied through Mr. Campbell to the Governor-in-Council to be sent to York Factory for a year or two, as I wish to improve my handwriting and to learn more book-keeping than I am likely to do here. Mr. Campbell quite agrees with me that it would be greatly to my advantage to be in an office for a short time. I won't know anything for certain until after the Council is held in June, when all of us will know our fate for the next outfit, or year.

I am afraid I shall not like a Bachelors' Hall such as at Fort York or Fort Garry after my comfortable quarters here, and I shall be very sorry to leave this place as I like it so much and they are all so kind to me. I do not suppose there is another place in the country where the clerks are made so comfortable as Mr. Smith and I. Mrs. Campbell is a very nice person indeed.

Mr. Finlayson is expected in here every day from his outpost at Touchwood Hills and I believe that I am to accompany him when he goes down to York Factory in charge of the boats. If I am not appointed to York Factory, I shall return to this District. My brother goes to Touchwood Hills immediately, to replace Mr. Finlayson and will summer there.

76

We have had a beautiful spring so far. The snow has all melted and the ground is fast drying up.

The men are busy getting the boats and *batteaux* ready to start for Red River. I suppose Mr. Clarke has left his winter quarters by this time and is again in the Settlement.

In a few weeks I am going to leave this District, being appointed to take charge of the Brigades with another clerk to York Factory, the depot on Hudson's Bay where all the furs, etc., and the returns of trade, are sent every summer for exportation to England by the Company's ships which come out every summer to the mouth of the Nelson River on the Bay.

We shall have twelve boats manned by a crew of twelve men to each boat, making one hundred and forty-four in all. It is a jolly trip of six hundred miles and generally takes one hundred days. The boats used are a hundred feet long and hold from ninety to one hundred packs of ninety pounds each. The rivers are very rapid and shallow with a great many portages over which the boats and cargoes are carried, or rather the boats hauled and the cargoes carried on the men's backs. And coming up, the boats have to be hauled up the stream with ropes. So you can have a pretty good idea what goods cost by the time they get to the places where they are traded. Sugar that costs us threepence at York we sell for three shillings here and other articles in proportion. We shall leave here about the middle of next month for Lake Manitoba where the boats start from about the first of June.

The Indians were arriving here with the furs they have taken during the winter before the Packet came in and when I returned here a month ago the fur packing had commenced. Close on the heels of our Indians come the officers, with the skins received at each outpost under Fort Pelly, and their accounts of the year's business. All these furs and accounts must be carefully checked and added to the records and bales already here.

This work is new and interesting to me and it is greatly to my benefit to receive my first lessons from one so expert as Mr. Campbell, as it requires systematic care and management to sort the various skins into bales and to keep account of them all at the same time. The work will continue until all the furs are loaded on boats or *batteaux* and put in charge of an officer who will be responsible for their safe delivery with any other Company property that may be included.

The returns from Qu'Appelle and Touchwood Hills may be taken by land or down the Qu'Appelle River, as will be most convenient, to Fort Ellice, from where they may be brought in here or delivered at Fort Garry to be absorbed by the Red River fur brigade by boat to York Factory, or in some cases sent by carts to St. Paul and thence to Atlantic seaports. In these various ways the annual returns from the Swan River District are transported.

When most of the furs were coming in earlier this month I was kept busy and will be working away at my desk from time to time until all the books are in from the outposts and have been made up here. I wish very much to be at a Depot for a year to learn book-keeping thoroughly as it is a great advantage to any person in the Company and one cannot manage a good place well without it.

It is a month later. After I have been working with bales of furs and their accounts for two months, the boats have departed without me and also the Overland Brigade to Red River. With them, alas, have gone my hopes of a river voyage from here to Fort York or down the Red River from Fort Garry to Hudson's Bay. A late spring has followed the hard winter in spite of some beautiful spring weather earlier. The ice has been so slow in going out from the lakes as to delay the *batteaux*, with rivers frozen solid, but at last the furs of the past winter are on the first lap of their long journey to London and spring is coming. It is very pleasant here in the companionship of my fellow clerk, Mr. Thompson Smith, and Miss Stirling, also Mr. and Mrs. Campbell and their children.

Mr. McDonald has come on a visit and Mr. Campbell tells me that I am to return with him to take charge of Qu'Appelle for the summer while he goes to Fort Garry. My disappointment in regard to a boat trip is somewhat alleviated by this third "borrowing" which will leave summer work of an important post to my supervision.

The return trip to Qu'Appelle was more pleasant by far than the one I made from there in March and a more pleasant travelling companion than Mr. McDonald cannot be found. We soon reached the Touchwood Hills Post where we found my brother with the furs and accounts of that charge ready to take with us. We left on June 1st with the furs collected here and at Egg Lake Post and hurried the seventy-five miles to add them to those at Qu'Appelle. But no sooner had this spring brigade of furs departed by carts for Red River than some Indians came in "rich in robes."

We had, however, no transportation for them and if they could not be taken to Fort Garry in time to go out by the York boats connecting with this year's ship to England we would be obliged to keep them in Rupert's Land until next year. When I asked Mr. McDonald if it would be possible to send the robes down to Fort Ellice by river he said he did not know the water below the second lake, whereupon I rode off on my saddle horse to investigate the advisability of attempting to navigate the river. It was feared that the water was too low and the rapids too bad.

Our Fort is situated at the foot of the uppermost of a chain of three lakes formed by as many expansions of the Qu'Appelle River, with numerous similar widenings of the stream above and below these nearer bodies of water. This lake is three miles long and from a quarter of a mile to one mile in width, its outlet flowing by us in a zig-zag course through the valley for three miles before again expanding to a width of two miles to form the second lake which is eight miles long. To this outlet I now went and rode on twenty miles farther to the third lake, which is ten miles long and a mile wide. My inspection convinced me that there was plenty of water for light draught boats and Mr. McDonald was easily persuaded to have two *batteaux* built.

These craft, in keeping with the carts and carrioles which they supplement, are peculiar to this land and the fur trade which is its whole life. Each flat-bottomed boat is twenty-five feet long and five feet wide midway between the ends formed by the sides meeting at a considerably greater height than in the middle, where they are four feet high. These rude barges carry about four tons each and are better adapted to going down stream than ascending. Each of our boats was being built to carry seventy-five bales of robes with a steersman and a bowman for crew and oars for motive power.

The Qu'Appelle is a splendid stream, though the most crooked I ever saw in my life. Its course is through a deep valley from one-half to two miles in width, across which the river winds from side to side and up and down. The current moves about two miles an hour and we used the oars continually. Sometimes after an hour or two we would come back so close to where we were that we could look through the rabbit holes in the banks and see the river there. In places the current is swift and we ran some splendid rapids. On one of these we struck a rock and the boat began to leak. Having no oakum to caulk it, I had to buy an Indian's leather trousers for this purpose. It may seem strange for a redman to dispose of his only pair of indispensables, but not so, for with the approach of summer he regards these as neither useful nor ornamental and wears them only to look like a white man when working for us. On the Plains they wear nothing but a blanket, which they have been known to sell to freetraders for drink and to go in a state of nature.

We came one evening to the last of six lakes and as the wind was fair and the night clear, the men suggested that we continue on our way instead of making camp as usual. With the help of an improvised sail we moved fifteen miles down to the outlet during the short summer night. In the early dawn we saw what we thought to be a mass of drifted ice blocking the entrance to the river. As we approached it began to melt away and we perceived it to be thousands of swans feeding on a bed of weeds.

The river became more crooked and so sluggish that we had to use the oars to make any headway. Red River is a straight stream comparatively. The weather was unusually rainy, there not being a day throughout the trip without rain at some time during the twenty-four hours. All one day we had to lie up because of wind and heavy snow. The canvas tent became coated with nearly an inch of ice while frost killed trees and grass. Fortunately I had some good books to read when I was not sleeping or ready with my gun to bring down a duck or two for food.

Our provisions were low and the bluffs on either side were so high and so densely wooded that it was impossible to tell how far we had come. The Indians get plenty of fish from the barriers they place in the lakes, but now one of them set out to hunt and soon returned with an antelope, a welcome change from the whitefish, jackfish and suckers. He also brought the information that we were *Ka kat h Amek See pecs*, or some miles above Fort Ellice and Beaver Creek, which flows into the Assiniboine just below and south of the Fort.

Next day we reached the place where the cart trails from the north cross the Qu'Appelle River three miles from the Fort. Here a saddle horse was waiting for me, sent by Mr. MacKay who was anxious about us, as we had been twelve days on the river without any communication with him. The boats moved on down the longer, slower watercourse to join those on the Assiniboine from Fort Pelly waiting to take the combined cargoes to Fort Garry, while I rode ahead with the accounts of our robes. The distance by water from Fort Qu'Appelle, as nearly as I can calculate, is seven hundred miles to Fort Ellice.

Mr. and Mrs. MacKay I found in an empty house. He was working all alone, as Willie had returned to the Touchwood Hills to take charge of that Post. Mr. MacKay at once informed me that much to his regret he must send me back next day as Mr. McDonald had sent an Indian down with saddle horses and instructions for me to ride home at once. Our cart brigade had left the previous day for Qu'Appelle, and with it Mr. MacKay had sent provisions for me, and a camp outfit.

This was the brigade we despatched with our furs just before the Indians came in with the robes we had just brought down. That evening I turned to and helped make up the packing account to send Hopkins for the furs from his District in addition to our own. We sat up all night as there were public letters to be written and these I did for him, the pleasure of helping an old friend being compensation for not staying longer. His family, including Miss MacKay, are in Fort Garry for the summer.

At three o'clock in the morning I left with a man and four saddle horses. Mr. MacKay hoped that by riding hard I could catch up with the cart brigade, already two days' travel ahead. We rode all day until dark and again the next day, starting at daylight. That evening we overtook them and made our camp with them.

It was a clear night with a good moon, which decided me to leave my servant there and continue alone to Qu'Appelle in the expectation of arriving there early next day. With two fresh horses and a lunch I rode until midnight when the sky clouded over and I lost the trail. It began to rain and became so dark that I could not find my way, so laid me down on the open prairie with my saddle for a pillow and my blanket over me. At daylight I awoke to find myself wet through and very cold. It was still raining and I was on a broad plain without a compass and no sign or landmark to guide me. I could not tell from where I had come or in which direction to go. There was nothing left to eat and my gun and powder were as wet as myself. I let my horse have his head after attempting in vain to find a trail and was soon encouraged to find that I was being taken in a straight course.

Before long I was again on a trail and rode all day without anything to eat. The rain continued but less heavily and the sky cleared for the first time that day just as the sun broke through before disappearing behind the horizon in front of me. I was by an Indian camping ground where there was a grave freshly decorated with scalps of Blackfoot Indians taken in a raid on one of their camps. I now knew where I was, near the Old Fort, and was soon on the cart trail to Qu'Appelle with some twenty miles to go.

My horses were tired out, as I was myself, and without a dry thread on me, I did not wish to sleep out again. Mr. McDonald would be anxious if I did not return that night, as indeed he was when I rode up to the Post at dusk. He did not reproach me for again breaking the rule that an officer must not travel alone, perhaps because he had recently done the same and because he was pleased to be able to leave for Fort Garry. He merely commended me for having made such a quick trip.

There was a letter waiting for me with the sad news of my brother's death on April 17th. My mother wrote on May 5th that we have lost my eldest brother James, and also of the death of my uncle earlier in the year. I wish I were near to comfort her and to help her with her garden as I used to do. Now I can only send what I can spare of my first year's income.

It was late when I went to bed, intending to have a good sleep this morning but our cook called me at daylight. Why I don't know, for I generally have to call him. He said breakfast was ready so I turned out and dressed myself feeling quite miserable but hoping to have a good meal. But this was very disappointing being only a piece of boiled jackfish about two square inches, which is beastly stuff. I have not recovered from the effects of my journey and my hand shakes so that it is difficult to write.

We have been, and still are, very hard up for grub all over this District. At Fort Ellice Mr. MacKay had to kill all his cows but one to keep his men from starving. An urgent message has come from Fort Pelly to send them five cart loads of meat as they are starving but I have not an ounce to send. Mr. McDonald left this morning for Red River and I have sent the interpreter off to the Plains with most of our men to trade and hunt for provisions. I gave him three hundred pounds worth of goods loaded into fifty carts with seven oxen, and seventy-five horses, and explicit instructions not to return without plenty of dried meat and pemmican.

We are completely out of grub and I have to send the men out to hunt instead of to work which does not pay the Company. There are plenty of antelope on the Plains but they are so swift of foot that no horse can catch them and they are extremely hard to get. By mere chance I shot one not long ago. It was one chance in a hundred. Willie has nothing for his men at Touchwood Hills but dried suckers and not enough of them.

For the past few days, the weather has been too rough for us to set nets. An old man using them gets about a hundred whitefish a day which is more than we require. What we can spare I am getting dried and split to send to Fort Pelly in case our carts do not bring back enough meat to send them. The buffalo are very far off and there is not an ounce of pemmican in the District.

---

## SEVEN

## *Summer at Qu' Appelle*

In spite of all there was to do the first day I was back, and though I have had enough riding during the three days in the saddle from Fort Ellice, it was necessary to ride twelve miles down the river this afternoon to the Indian village to hire men. We employ them in farming, for the land is splendid and very easily worked, being free of stones and other obstructions. But Indians, French half-breeds and Orkney men are so little inclined to this occupation that it is almost impossible to get them to work. I, too, find it hard to put my heart into growing crops when I do not know how long I shall be here.

Our garden, however, is looking very well. We have a good lot of turnips, a field of potatoes, some carrots, onions and peas. A few vegetables are a welcome substitute to our flour ration. There is now very little for me to do but put the men to work haying and looking after horses and other stock, also I must give out the rations which means keeping our old Indian fishing with nets. A few Indians are coming in to trade, but much of my time is spent shooting ducks and prairie chicken and hunting antelope.

These animals are numerous because they can run faster than any horse and are very hard to shoot. If one can afford the time for a slow hunt it is possible to wear them down by stalking them, provided one has a horse of sufficient stamina and that the rider too has the endurance for a long hunt.

One afternoon I set out in the hope of getting an antelope. It was a bright summer day and as I rode past a field of some twelve acres of barley near the Fort I noticed that the crop was looking splendid and almost ready to harvest. Suddenly I was aware of a heavy black cloud on the western horizon which looked like an approaching storm, but the sky around me remained clear and thinking it was a prairie fire in the distance I rode on until dusk. On the way home I again passed the barley field and it was not too dark to see that it was now a blackened ruin.

"Did you have a fire?" I asked the watchman who opened the gates for me. "The barley for our saddle horses is all burned."

"We had no fire," he said, "did you not see the grasshoppers?"

Then I looked around and saw them three inches deep inside the Fort. They had devoured everything in the garden except roots, stripped the trees, and had fallen in the lake until the outlet was blocked, and they were piled up on its shores in wind-rows.

To prevent them from filling the Fort I had to keep half the men in double shifts carting them out in order to live. The ducks and prairie chicken ate grasshoppers until they were unfit for us to eat. Even the eggs tasted of them. The train dogs got fat and the cattle became poor for lack of grass. The whole valley looked like a burned-over prairie. They came in clouds like smoke and for twelve days the air was alive with them as high as one could see. They darkened the sun and lay an inch thick on the ground. The lakes and rivers stink with the dead ones. The frost has at last killed them and some of the vegetables they left. Farming here is all a delusion.

A week of August remains and surely it is very early to have cold weather. The summer season is very short. On the twenty-ninth of May our boats all stopped at Fairfield because of ice. We had little warm weather in June, with snow on the thirteenth on my boat trip to Fort Ellice. We have had a miserable, wet summer with rain that has done a great deal of damage to crops in the Red River Settlement where a large part of the French Settlement has been completely flooded and many of their houses carried away.

Fortunately there is a considerable amount of prairie hay though the grasshoppers destroyed much of it. We are busy making hay and drawing it in. Already we have three hundred loads home and we shall be done in a few days.

It is too bad that our Indians are at war with other tribes for it means that we cannot get any meat. There are eight men to feed here and fourteen families besides seventy to eighty dogs from other posts that are sent to us to feed during the summer. They keep themselves fat by hunting and I have a great deal of trouble to see that the dogs themselves are not eaten by our men, who prefer this meat to the daily ration of fish. I am having a hard time to see that the servants get one good meal a day which has been the situation for a week at a time this summer. We cannot get any pemmican for love or money. Last year we traded nine hundred bags of one hundred pounds each but this year we have obtained only forty-six bags. Moreover, Indians from among the enemy are a nuisance to us as they are great thieves. The other day they shot one of our best cows with an arrow. But a Blackfoot's scalp is sometimes found among our Indians and I have been given one for a keepsake.

Early in July as soon as I thought I could leave this place in charge of the apprentice-interpreter I took my horse and rode up the lakes alone for about sixty miles, exploring the country which is exceedingly pretty. I was able to ride along beaches all the way as there are large lakes within a few miles of each other joined by the beautiful but crooked river. There are fine groves of balsam poplar and our more common poplar along the banks and, though a long way up, I was fortunate in finding plenty for building houses and *batteaux* for next year.

My camp outfit consisted of a little tea and some ammunition in my saddle bags, with a small kettle and my gun and blanket strapped to my saddle. I shot ducks and pigeons which I roasted over a fire, except on one night when I camped by a lake where there was not a stick of wood to be had. There was not a stake to which I could tie my horse, and as he was a very wild animal, and there were plenty of horse thieves about, I had to hold on to one end of a lasso, or rope, around his neck. I had had no supper when I lay down to sleep with my head on my saddle and my blanket over me. Just as I would be dozing off there would be a jerk on the rope and by jumping about and pulling on it the horse kept me awake all night.

I wish we could get lumber here as cheaply as in Canada. The poplar or whitewood just located is all we have and the poles have to be rafted a long way down the lakes and rivers for timber to enlarge the Fort and to build boats for next spring's transport. I have been building large stores and houses for the men. We make a frame and fill in the sides with logs that have been squared by sawing them by hand with a pit saw. The roof is made of straight poles which are thatched with long prairie grass. Buffalo parchment is used for the doors and windows and is quite transparent which gives the Fort a strange appearance at night when the fires are all burning. We use nothing but fireplaces with chimneys made of mud, a cooking stove being a thing seen only in the officers' cookshop.

When I returned from looking for timber I found everyone in a state of great alarm. A Sioux raiding party had stolen three horses from our very gate the night before. They were the property of one of the men but as he was afraid to follow the Indians I helped him to track them to the edge of the Grand Couteaux where we came upon the remains of a large camp of one hundred and fifty tents. These had disappeared with the Indians and our man's horses.

There are any number of Yankee soldiers deserting from the Missouri. Eleven who deserted from Fort Union came to Fort Ellice in July. Mr. MacKay engaged them to work and sent me one, a regular good-for-nothing blackguard. I tried him at everything but found him quite useless except to keep guard at night. He cleaned out a cannon and kept watch all night. When the Company engaged more of these men I got three, two good men and a worthless devil.

The Yankees are trying to establish a mail route through from St. Paul to the gold mines at St. Helena and have made several attempts but all their men have been scalped. I hope they succeed, as the route must pass near this place. The same Indians that murder there come here to trade and do no harm. We see only one really bad tribe here, the Stonies, or Assiniboines. Their Chief once shot McDonald with an arrow. Since then we consider him rather a dangerous customer and always keep a revolver in one hand while trading with him.

Fortunately the Assiniboines seldom come to the Post. Sometimes we send traders out to them on the Plains to the west where they live along the borders of the United States. They are continually at war with the American Indians known as the Grosventres, and with the Blackfeet on the Missouri River, a tribe of which I know little, nor of the Blood Indians, though both come across to Edmonton and Rocky Mountain House where they give the Company's officers a great deal of trouble. The Hudson's Bay Indians never steal our horses or any of our property but occasionally they "go to war," as they call it, and bring over a number of American horses.

The Indians in our vicinity are mostly Plain Crees, the Crees being the chief and most numerous tribe on the prairies. They are spoken of as Wood Crees, Plain Crees, or Swampy Crees according to the character of the region they inhabit. We employ several here for farm work, hunting, and for transport. Others are now beginning to come in for fall outfits which affords me my first experience in trading with them. On the whole I find them easier to deal with than customers I served in a country store in Canada. For this and their respect for me the credit is due Mr. McDonald who enjoys their confidence and has this area entirely under his control.

At Fort Pelly the Indians are either Saulteaux or Wood Crees and loyal to us without exception, in accordance with the respect shown all Hudson's Bay Company officers by the Indians. It is believed that the Saulteaux tribes originally came from around Lake Superior, the name being derived from Sault Ste.Marie. They mix with the Crees and though not speaking exactly the same language they understand one another and intermarry. These tribes are about equally divided at most Posts. Here the Crees predominate, owing to our position farther out on the Plain, originally the home of the Cree Nation where for the most part they still hunt. The Saulteaux mostly hunt in the woods to the north. All are aborigines of Rupert's Land and, to me, the First Families of America.

My family maintain that the Indians about them in Canada are possessed of a quality of mind that would enable them to acquire and benefit by education. What I have learned of the Indians in Rupert's Land is entirely in agreement with this opinion, in which I have a supporter in the person of Father Richot. He is taking a keen interest in the education of Indian children and has accomplished a great deal in his work with them.

It would be a lonely summer for me were it not for the pleasure of seeing Father Richot, who lives at the Mission he built some three miles away. I have found that with the interpreter absent on the Plains I cannot leave the Post even for a day, but it is a few minutes ride of an evening to the Mission where I spend many a happy hour with the kindly priest. Sometimes he comes to visit me and I have learned that the gratitude of my fellow officers to the missionaries for the good work they are doing, is well deserved and especially is this true of Father Richot. All honour is due these holy men who leave the world to penetrate the wilderness, sharing its privations and loneliness while teaching the Word of God in this land.

Many of my fellow officers have gone down to Fort Garry where from all accounts they have had a very gay summer. This Post is some miles off the Carlton Trail, which branches from ours at Fort Ellice and runs to the north and east of us, and consequently I have not seen them in passing. I would have gone down with the *batteaux* if Mr. McDonald had not been obliged to go down to get his teeth extracted. He and his wife returned on the twelfth of August and left on the thirteenth for Touchwood Hills where Mrs. McDonald will stay with Mrs. Finlayson while her husband goes on to Fort Pelly. I have not seen Willie all summer though his Post is only a day's journey from mine, for neither of us can leave.

It has been a very dull and lonely summer for me and I am very tired of it. At times I would go to sleep early of an evening and finding it still light when I awoke I made a notch in the stick I keep to record each day, thus gaining a day. At other times, when not well, I have slept through one day and wakened early the following morning, thereby missing a day. In this way I gained

90

more days than I lost and did not know when it was my twentieth birthday on the 9th of August.

There has been a great deal of sickness here for the past months and now I have hardly a man fit to work, for they are all laid up with sore feet and hands swelling. As a result I am kept constantly busy making poultices and lancing their hands. I think bad living is the cause of this illness which I have suffered myself for the past few days with sore throat and mouth and bad headaches.

Fortunately I have plenty of good reading, for Mrs. Campbell sent me five large volumes of Wilson's *Tales of the Borders* soon after I came and when Mr. McDonald arrived two weeks ago he brought me lots of letters and a parcel of books. One volume written by Uncle Moodie, I found most entertaining and I hope he makes a good deal by its sale.

The parcel also contained writing paper which, like the books, was damaged by getting wet in the Buffalo River when the postman and his bags of mail were helped out of its flood waters by one of the Company's clerks, who happened to be passing on his way to St. Paul. Some of my letters may have been lost as I did not receive some I expected from my family. Another misfortune was having to pay nearly eighteen dollars in duty and delivery charges because the parcel was not bonded through the States to Pembina. Nothing is worth paying the American duty on and no one can take anything through, however small, without the risk of having it confiscated or paying about twenty-five percent duty. Consequently officers coming from Montreal cannot bring things sent to them for this purpose, but what is bonded cannot be opened until it has crossed the British lines, therefore there is no duty.

It seems strange that a small parcel costs a great deal more from St. Paul than a box, but the former has to come by Overland Express to Abercrombie at the rate of one dollar per pound, and from there to Fort Garry for as much more, while a box can be sent by the Company's agent by carts and charged to their office at five shillings per hundredweight. In this way parcels sent to the care of Norman W. Kittson in St. Paul, or of Hudson's Bay

House, London, can be sent to us at a comparatively low cost. We are able to purchase what we require for less in England than in Canada. Paper costs very little in England, and there is any quantity of it in Fort Garry though we do run out of it at times at our Posts. The Company has three large sale shops where we can purchase anything we require except boots and a few articles.

The officers order a supply of clothing annually from London including boots and these are brought out by the Company's ships the following summer. Shortly after I came to Rupert's Land I grew so much that I could not wear what I brought with me and I do not know what I would have done were it not for Mrs. McDonald's kindness and expertness in altering available garments to my increased dimensions.

It is the sixth of September and the weather is getting so cold that we shall soon have frost and snow. I have not heard where I shall winter but most likely I shall remain here. When Mr. McDonald returns from the Depot a week from now I shall know. I don't think I shall be going to Fort York. Willie has been appointed to Egg Lake, rather a nice place about fifty miles northeast from Touchwood Hills Post, which he leaves soon to assume his new charge, which is in the woods and quite out of the way of all traders.

Winter will soon begin and I too would like to settle down in my winter quarters. There are four or five new clerks who have come out this year. One has already come from Canada, a young Rae who is a nephew of the great Arctic explorer Dr. John Rae. Mr. Cowie has come out by ship to take Willie's place at Fort Ellice, unless he comes here and I go there. I should prefer an office to an inland place though I like the life very much here with little to do but look after the men and keep the Fort accounts.

It was necessary for me to write a report of my trip down to Beaver Creek with the two *batteaux* and send it to the Governor and Council to inform them of the state of the river which is a splendid stream, a regular young Mississippi. I did my best to impress on them the practicability of the route and the danger of sending a brigade down without an officer to look after the packs. As a result I have been promised that I will be sent down in charge of the *batteaux* next spring.

Mr. Campbell went down to the Council held this year at Fort Garry in the Lower Fort and has received his Chief Factorship, as we hoped, due to the death of Mr. Clare.

Mr. Campbell proceeded from the Council to Norway House to meet Finlayson. His men at Fort Pelly have all rebelled and gone down to Red River. The clerk there has been making a great deal of mischief among them as many of them are half-breeds who do not like to hear their people condemned by anyone with prejudices against them which are very foolish indeed. I have been very short of men with only six to carry on the work as all the engaged servants had to be sent down to Hudson's Bay with the boats, which leaves only temporary servants inland.

If I remain at Qu'Appelle I expect to go out again this October to the Plains to bring home green meat. I wish my friends in Canada could join me in a buffalo hunt, as they have plenty of good horses there. The Company pays very high prices for swift American or Canadian horses which we keep expressly for running buffalo and never think of putting a harness on them. A good one will fetch forty or fifty pounds sterling. We have twenty runners and one hundred carters here. The Indian horses make splendid carters but very few are swift enough to make buffalo-runners.

The Indians are fond of racing their horses to see who has the fastest. This is one of their favourite sports when they gather at Fort Garry after the spring hunting and trapping is over.

## EIGHT

---

## *The Winter of 1867*

WHEN I arrived at Fort Ellice in late September the Indians were coming in for their winter supplies and I at once pitched in to give Mr. MacKay all possible help in outfitting them. There were many letters to be written, most of which fell to my lot. We had some ready to send to Qu'Appelle when a Packet from Saskatchewan came in via there and Touchwood Hills, and these must be answered and others written to send down to Fort Garry with a Brigade that is waiting. It was daylight this morning when I laid aside my pen, having taken time for some private letters to add to the public ones, and will write what others I can before the Brigade leaves.

This is the most famous of all our Cart Brigades and is now returning from Edmonton with loads of furs that arrived there too late for the Spring Boat Brigade. There are about a hundred carts each with eight hundred pounds of freight, some of which is pemmican from the summer buffalo hunts beyond our District. It is four months since this slow caravan set out from Fort Garry about the first of June, when the grass had grown sufficiently for grazing the oxen and horses.

The long single file shrieks its way on wooden wheels over a thousand miles of prairie each way at the rate of two miles an hour covering twenty to twenty-five miles at most each day. At times oxen and carts are turned over to Posts en route and horses provided with carts for a quicker trip. This Post and Carlton are main stopping places which means that we must retain a large band of horses and another of oxen to replace those that have become lame or unfit to travel.

94

The guide and drivers form a considerable crew, there being three drivers to every ten carts grouped in threes and a four. A man leads the first ox, walking beside it, while the following animals are tied at their heads to the cart in front. Occasionally the driver can rest by riding on one of the carts. The guide is an outstanding man, a native-born carefully chosen for his dependable qualities, so important for his charge. He is paid ten pounds and is provided with saddle horses so that his remuneration compares favourably with mine during my first year. Reliable men too are the drivers, each receiving five pounds for the round trip with pemmican, tea, flour and other food provided. Other horses are for the men to use in herding the oxen which are hobbled and turned out at night to graze. There is rest mid-day for men and beasts and food for both at camping places having wood and water.

There has been so much uncertainty regarding our appointments for the winter, that I am somewhat surprised to find myself here instead of remaining with the McDonalds where I was hoping to be put in charge of a hunting party of eighty to ninety carts and one hundred horses that is to be sent to the Plains to bring in fresh buffalo meat. That is, if there are any buffalo. If not, the prospect of fish and rabbits with only two sacks of flour and no vegetables is not alluring.

When Mr. McDonald returned from Red River a week or so ago he gave me the news of my transfer and it was with genuine regret that I took my leave of this kind family so soon after his home-coming. As I rode east on a bright day in mid-September along the now familiar trail, I paused to look back upon the beautiful valley of the Qu'Appelle River winding between gleaming lakes and wondered when, if ever, I should see it again and my friends there.

The clerk I am replacing is my brother Willie who has just written to me from Touchwood Hills that he is very put out at being kept there instead of coming back to his own post here or going to Egg Lake. He and Miss MacKay seem very fond of each other and as both daughters have returned from a Ladies' School in Red River I am sure he would rather be here. I would gladly change places with him, for he was about to leave for the Plains.

This is not to say that I am not happy here. I like Mr. MacKay very much, though not better than Mr. McDonald, and the family are all very nice, there being five boys and their two sisters. Miss MacKay is a very nice, amiable girl whom I like very much. I am sure she and my brother will be very happy together though I don't know when they will get married but think it may not be for some time as Mr. Campbell is very much against his young officers marrying "in the country," as he calls it, and won't let him do so if he can help it.

My sister sends me some very good advice about getting married, or rather about not doing so, which is not necessary in my case as I feel that we are all too much of adventurers to get married until we have saved enough money or have received our commissions. Willie, however, doesn't see it in this light and I am expecting him to apply to be changed to the Saskatchewan District under Mr. Christie, a very nice man and a ruling Chief Factor.

Recently I thought I was going there, and may yet volunteer to do so, or to go to the Mackenzie River, as officers are always wanted in the North, where I won't be changed about so much. Mr. Campbell tells me I am to leave here in the spring as he moved me only for the winter because he did not think I would like to be second at Qu'Appelle after being in charge there. I wish he had not been so very considerate as I had hoped to be with Mr. McDonald.

A friend who was staying with Mrs. McDonald last winter when I was there has just written to me from a far Northern District where she is twenty-four hundred miles from the Settlement after travelling for five months. In the spring she will reach her destination three thousand miles away where letters will arrive only once a year and these must be written a year before hand. Truly a lady requires great courage to go so far out.

As a rule I spend my evenings in my own room which is large and comfortable with a fine fireplace where I write without interruption unless there is a service or gathering in the Indian hall adjoining this room. I very much wish I had something to study in my spare time. I intend to send to England next year for books and among others I shall order those written by my mother.

Her book that is currently being written is descriptive of Canadian wildflowers regarding which there is considerable interest in the Settlement. A book of mosses gathered and pressed by her own hand was forwarded by me to Mr. Hargrave who has just written to thank me and to say how beautiful they are and that the Lord Bishop declares them to be quite the best of their kind that he has seen.

Mr. John McTavish would like to see flowers preserved this way and I have asked my mother to send him a collection as a present, for he is most kind to me and the other clerks, sending us whatever we want from Fort Garry and letting us draw bills on Hopkins in Montreal instead of on London in the usual way. Nothing is too much trouble for him to do.

Mr. Hargrave also is a friend I value highly for not only is he clever but warm-hearted and kind. I am sorry to say that the mosses were slightly damaged by getting wet in the Buffalo River when our clerk saved the letters by cutting open the bags and taking them out while still partly dry, but parcels were not so fortunate. All our mail by this route this summer has been similarly damaged.

My own efforts to press prairie flowers to send to my mother are not very successful as I have not acquired the art of preserving their colour. These flowers would interest her as being different from those in Canada. At times the prairies are very beautiful with them, appearing as a sea of yellow and later in waves of blue according to the season.

Mr. Campbell stopped here for only a few hours, being in a great hurry to get back to Fort Pelly where the men have been kicking up all sorts of shines during his absence. Nor could he stop in Fort Garry more than a few days as he was late getting back there from Norway House owing to the men refusing to man the boats to Fort York. As yet we have not received our private property ordered by ship from London, but hope to have it by the Fall Brigade bringing freight from Fort York. This is the same brigade with which I came here a year ago.

There wasn't much time to talk to Mr. Campbell about getting an appointment like my own for a friend in Canada. Even a Chief Factor cannot do much here, for one must be proposed to the Committee in London by someone connected with the service. There are several new clerks coming out this year who are sons or nephews of retired officers, their names being recorded in the Minutes of Council with the list of those who recommended them. Governor Mactavish gave his support to my appointment and I hear there is a cousin of Mr. Hargrave's now at York Factory who has all our Secretary's good qualities. Mr. Cowie, who will arrive with the Brigade, is from the Shetland Islands. His father, Dr. Cowie, who died last year, was a retired Chief Trader.

The two older sons of the MacKays attend St. John's College, and the family remaining at home I see daily at mess and find them all very pleasant, but most of my evenings are taken up working in my office, which is also my bedroom. There has been some consternation regarding my rations for my first year which were allotted to Fort Pelly though I was there only five months. Sugar, flour, currants and raisins are important commodities with Christmas a little over two months away. I can offer no solution, though I silently remember the good plum puddings Mrs. Campbell provided for many a trip and many a dinner, and am thankful to learn that Mr. MacKay has insisted on having my full allowance while I am here.

When at last the Brigade arrived, our two new clerks were with it, Mr. Matheson who was at White Horse Plains when I first met him and who is now going to Egg Lake, and Mr. Cowie who takes my place at Qu'Appelle. He is a very jolly sort and stayed with me for a week; when he left I loaned him my saddle horse so that he wouldn't have to ride a carter. His man has just come in without it saying that it was so used up that it could not come all the way. I wish I had not been so obliging.

Another misfortune that has befallen me is the long awaited arrival of my private property ordered last year. The garments are all too small and the invoice sent to the Company's secretary in London has been paid by charging it against my salary. I doubt if I can sell them to anyone for half what I have paid for them.

It may be possible to pay my account if I can get away to attend to my traps. Soon after I came I caught a red fox and now have several prime ones with a few wolverines and wolf skins.

Truly our washing is our main expense for with the greatest economy I am unable to reduce the cost of it to less than a fifth of my salary though I wear flannel shirts and paper collars at all times.

Unwittingly I incurred a further loss soon after my arrival. Somewhat unwillingly I found myself giving the bride away at a ceremony in our Indian Hall when a Yankee deserter was united with the object of his affections, after a courtship carried on through an interpreter, since he cannot speak her language, nor she his. My objection was due to the bride being no other than my washerwoman who is also under contract to supply us with shoes of her own making. Foolishly I paid her in advance and might count my loss as the bridegroom's gain were it not for the nuptial festivities ending in their both getting drunk and the bride giving him the deuce of a pounding, rather a high price to pay for the doubtful benefits of free laundry and the unearned profits derived from my own. I think I shall remain a bachelor.

We see many travellers: some en route to where gold has been discovered beyond Rocky Mountain House which is attracting miners who might otherwise go to the gold mines at Helena. Some, leaving there, come this far in the hope of getting food and other supplies for which we must send them on to Fort Garry. Some are deserters from Forts Rice, Union and Benton protecting the mail route from Helena to Fort Abercrombie. We see all nationalities, riding and in covered wagons with some very fine horses bred wild on the plains of Mexico and Texas.

Mr. MacKay bought two cart horses and a very fine Arabian saddle horse for me. He would have bought more if the prices had not been so exorbitant: they want from forty to a hundred pounds sterling for runners. Mine is a splendid animal, perhaps not such a good trotter as my brother-in-law's Nellie but a very good runner. We never allow harness to be put on our riding horses. It makes them stumble and dangerous for running. Our best horses are the Indian or Arabian horses, for though the Yankee animals are just as swift, they are not as sure-footed as the Indian horses which never fall.

Due to the number of miners that have gone up around Edmonton, the buffalo have been leaving and it is feared there may not be sufficient food as they cannot depend on growing any crops. Their provisions must be brought from the Settlement and run the risk of robbery by the Crows and Blackfeet. The Company is taking the precaution of fortifying Edmonton with all speed, as the latter are becoming troublesome and are having a bad influence on our Indians.

The Blackfeet have plundered one of our own brigades near Fort Pitt. Many in the States were scalped by them and the Sioux before the Americans completed their Forts, one of which has been built at Devil's Lake, a few miles from Pembina. We employ six deserters from their army. If they suspect one of their generals is among the travellers we see them beat a hasty retreat.

The Indians here and at Touchwood Hills, from what Willie tells me, are more difficult to manage than at Qu'Appelle. The discipline is much too slack, as the half-breeds acting for the Company at the outposts and elsewhere let them have what they want without proper consideration of repayment which tends to make them unmanageable. The Egg Lake Indians are especially difficult.

Mr. McDonald has had his share of trouble though no one manages his post better. My old fisherman has shot one of the Company's men. One of the Crees with whom I had trouble last summer stabbed and killed one of their best horses while another, the Touchwood Hills' Chief, attempted to stab McDonald. A party of free traders shot two of our own oxen the other day and devoured them, but much worse was a murder committed at Touchwood Hills when two hunters fell in with a trader who supplied them with liquor which led to their quarrelling.

They now have plenty of food at Qu'Appelle but unless we can get more here we shall have to send half of our men down to Red

River for the winter. There are neither rabbits nor pheasants to be had. The former are scarce at Fort Pelly, I hear, because I shot so many last year.

The great buffalo range tributary to Fort Ellice and known as the Plains lies south of the Qu'Appelle River and west of the Assiniboine and is a treeless prairie as far as the Souris and Woody Mountains, but this year the buffalo are so far off that our hunters have returned with only two for which they had to go as far as "a little this side of sunset."

Mr. MacKay has been talking of establishing an outpost in the Woody Mountains and sending an interpreter to winter there. I know he won't earn his tucker by himself and have persuaded my *bourgeois* to send me to build it in a few weeks when I shall have all my writing done. Already I am tired of Fort life and longing for the change from its monotony that the two hundred and fifty mile trip to Woody Mountains would mean. From there I would like to go to Qu'Appelle for Christmas and round by Touchwood Hills and Fort Pelly with the winter express.

In the end it was decided that I should remain in charge here being sufficiently familiar with all our work, then believed to be diminishing as the season advanced, but since Mr. MacKay left I have seldom been in bed before one or two o'clock in the morning, then up again before daylight to call the men and give them the rations for each man and his family. After looking after the men and Indians all day I have to do my writing at night. There is hay being hauled, and wood, and lumber to get out for building and repairing boats and carts. Craftsmen and blacksmith are kept busy, the latter keeping his forge going with the prairie coal found so near the surface this side of the Rockies, and preferred by him to that formerly brought from the States.

It is important every fall to make sure that our log buildings are made warm by chinking any cracks or openings that have appeared from shrinkage during the summer heat. This must be done before it is so cold that the mixture used for filling freezes before it dries. I find myself handicapped by lack of workers for

Mr. MacKay has taken the greater part of our engaged servants with him to the Plains.

Every post has one or two hangers-on and here we have one universally known as Jack's Fool. Before departing this life his father, a retired Chief Factor, made provision for the London office to pay Jack every year for life the sum of two pounds, eighteen shillings and sixpence. His financial standing is accordingly of the best among the First Families of America but owing to his diminished mental faculties (and not to his mother being a Dog Rib Indian) his social standing is quite the reverse. Sturdily built with ample strength for work, he disdains all forms of labour as unfitting for the son and heir of a great man. He drifts from camp to camp, foraging grub from Indians on promise of rewarding them with a feast on pay-day. June the first is many months hence and his store account already equals his annuity but no financial offer will induce him to work.

Two weeks later the chinking is done with Jack's help. Knowing that the one dark spot on his happy and carefree existence was his name, I made him an alternate proposal. If he would mix mud, clay and prairie hay for plaster I would see that he was given a new name and submitted for his approval that of Leather Brains. This appealed to him as "nee sheen," or fine, and I requested our men to address our new worker by his future name.

He set to work with a will and, conscientiously trying to live up to such recognition, he introduced a new method of his own. He threw down his hoe, took off his moccasins and jumped into the mixture. By trotting back and forth he performed the task to the satisfaction of the men doing the mudding up, and is now on the top rung of the social ladder of the aforementioned aristocracy. Also my own quarters, with every convenience for work and rest, are now very comfortable.

Most of our trade is done through our outposts to which I must send supplies of imported goods to give the Indians in exchange for the furs they bring in. At Riding Mountain, sixty miles to the east, a half-breed is in charge and our trade is not as profitable as it should be. If I could get out to visit some of our Indians, I believe I could obtain more of their furs. Around Fort Ellice we have mostly Plain Crees with whom the trade is in buffalo robes but this winter a band of Saulteaux have remained about the Fort and in the woods north of us.

It has encouraged me greatly to learn that Mr. McDonald spoke well of me and my management in a public letter, especially as his opinion is one I value highly. There is an old saying in the service that one Chief Clerk is worth two Chief Traders and one Chief Trader is worth two Chief Factors. However true this may be there can be little doubt that Mr. McDonald, who has yet to receive his Commission, is a very valuable officer.

Nevertheless I have had reason to entertain doubts regarding the soundness of my judgment on a recent occasion, and for a time I feared I might have to charge the cost to experience and the amusement it afforded me.

It was a stormy day when a Saulteaux, Keech-ben-nees, came into our store to negotiate the sale of a bear skin for a blanket in trade. "A very big, black bear," he assured me it was, "worth twenty-four shillings." I went into our store house and selected a blanket valued at twenty shillings and for the other four shillings he chose a warm red shirt, but made no move to produce the bear skin. In regard to the delicate matter of payment he said he would bring it to me in four days.

"But, Big Bird (the translation of his name)," I asked in surprise, "Why do you not bring it with you now?"

In mixed Saulteaux and English he finally conveyed to me the startling information that his cash in hand was still at large, as he had not yet killed the bear. His stoical countenance portrayed not the slightest concern when he could not say exactly where the bear might be, but solemnly declared he had seen its tracks in the snow bordering Red Deer Creek. With considerable apprehension I beheld the swarthy figure before me already clad in scarlet shirt and thick green blanket.

His stolid expression gave no sign of the joy of the red man's soul when clothed in colours, and viewing the snow driving without I had not the heart to dispossess him of their much needed warmth though I had grave doubts that a bear's tracks on Red Deer Creek or anywhere else are sound collateral security on which to establish a credit of twenty-four shillings. He solemnly reassured me he would bring the bear skin in four days and went out into the storm.

To my great relief he returned on the fourth day with the skin, a beautiful specimen fully worth the value claimed for it, thereby proving that in his case a bear track when owned, or merely seen, by Big Bird is sound security for the amount of his own valuation.

Mr. MacKay has not been able to acquaint me with each Indian, especially among the Saulteaux who are not so well known to us as our own Crees, and my only way of arriving at the commercial standing of a customer is to refer to our Indian ledger in which this information is recorded. Meantime those with a debit balance previous to this fall of 1867 I must deal with on a strictly cash basis.

There has been a steady stream of other traders wanting outfits and the giving out of these supplies takes a great deal of my time and entails much care and work. It is not unlikely that Fort Ellice will be made the headquarters of this District instead of the present depot of Fort Pelly, if the Company sends a steamboat up from Red River in the spring.

We can send mail down to the Settlement by travellers returning there before winter sets in but there are few if any opportunities of receiving mail from there. Soon after the Saskatchewan Brigade went down we sent a Brigade to Portage la Prairie for flour which took letters down and should return about the first of November (we hope) with letters, if these can be sent from Fort Garry to meet our men. Clerks who accompany a Packet can see one another in this way and enjoy a brief visit which is one of our greatest pleasures. We have sent down Packet after Packet and I hoped to accompany one to Portage la Prairie via Riding Mountain outpost, but have been too busy to leave.

There have been ten to fifteen letters to write daily in the office where I spend eight hours a day. Letters to friends and family at home, and to my fellow clerks, must wait until official ones are written. We try to have them ready to send should a chance occur. Sometimes the departure of a Packet is delayed and I add news, or replies to letters it brought, by writing rapidly and crossing the written pages, if short of paper. This does not improve my writing, nor its legibility, but reduces the weight of mail. Public letters and reports to the Governor and Council must be written with due care.

Early in November we were surprised by the arrival of a large number of deserters from our own Green Lake Brigade at Carlton who were in such a hurry to reach the Settlement that they would not wait for us to finish letters. We sent what we had with the rebels and hope they are delivered safely. We are expecting a Packet from the North in a few days and this may be the last chance of sending down mail before the Winter Packet goes in February.

By the end of November winter has set in, stopping all overland communications, but to-day a Packet came in from Qu'Appelle and Touchwood Hills with long letters from Cowie and Willie and a shorter one from my friend so far away in the North. In another week the Winter Packet will leave Fort Garry to bring our mail via Hudson's Bay. It is hard to convince those in Canada that they must allow four to five weeks for their letters to reach Fort Garry in time for this Express. The Peterboro paper is most welcome and *Blackwood's Magazine* which comes monthly when possible. The prospect of six more months of winter is a dull one but fortunately I am fond of my own society and the time goes by like greased lightning.

The many boils which afflicted our men at Qu'Appelle later were suffered by myself, and the last one is now disappearing from behind my ear, though still very painful and keeping me awake at night. Probably we do not get enough good food but we are not starving. I have my full allowance of apples, rice, tea, etc., which was not always the case last year when I was moving about so much. When an officer visits Indians in their camp they insist that he accept hospitality in the form of so much food and drink that I find a great strain is put upon one's capacity and digestion.

But a worse dilemma now confronts me. Ladies in Rupert's Land as elsewhere indulge in matchmaking and have been disposing of me right and left. One even promised to work me a set of dog clothes for my wedding gift and now has actually written to say that she has commenced them. I intend to wait until I am at least a commissioned officer before I marry, even should I happen to meet a young lady foolish enough to have me, or if I had the means to marry, which I have not. The writer is a beautiful worker in beads and silk but as I cannot seriously entertain her offer, I shall refer the matter to my sister who has always foreseen that I would be a bachelor. Now is the time for the benefit of her advice in the face of such a strong inducement!

# NINE

## By River to Fort Garry

WHEN Mr. MacKay returned from the Plains my work dwindled to a few hours a week but this was soon cut short by the chance arrival of a Packet from Fort Garry and another from Fort Pelly. An invitation has come from Mr. Campbell for me to spend Christmas with them. Undoubtedly he will bring up the champagne to toast his new status as a Chief Factor. Cowie and Matheson will be there and we shall have a jolly time.

We are delighted to receive our Christmas mail from Canada and the Settlement with cartes of my mother, sisters and the children. There is a package of my own to give friends who have requested my likeness, though these were taken before I left home. Mr. MacKay is pleased to have an opportunity of sending the mail for Fort Pelly with me.

"You can make Fort Pelly in three days," he tells me, "and spend four days with the Campbells, which leaves three days for the return trip in time to be back here by New Year."

He wants me to take charge again while he visits our outpost in the Moose Mountains as soon as he can get away. He is sending me out with two of our best trains of dogs, one for my carriole and one for that carrying the mail and camping outfit. The drivers are an Indian and a halfbreed, each on snowshoes. A third man has a saddle horse to ride ahead to break trail for the dogs, as the snow is unusually deep.

The first day we covered more than a third of the distance of one hundred and twenty miles but that night there came a terrible snowstorm which continued as a blizzard all the next day.

We were forced to lie in camp throughout, and when the weather cleared the following morning we found the snow so deep that the dogs could not make more than a few miles without stopping to rest.

We all took turns going ahead and breaking the track but all that day and the next our progress was slow. It was Christmas Eve and we knew we could not reach our destination in time to spend any part of Christmas Day at Fort Pelly unless we could make more headway. Everywhere the snow lay soft and deep and our rations were nearly gone. As we struggled through the holiday we had hoped to spend with friends the temperature dropped hour by hour until it was bitterly cold when night closed about us. We were still a day's journey from Fort Pelly at the rate we were going and there was no food left for men or dogs.

We made our camp for the night in a grove of willows and when I unlaced my moccasins from my snowshoes I discovered that one of my feet was frozen. In attempting to thaw it with snow I froze my right hand. We made a good fire by which to rest until daylight and I fell soundly asleep.

Suddenly a fury of sound, and my horse was almost on the glowing logs with wolves upon its heels! Before I could aim my gun the ravenous beasts had all but disembowelled it and when I shot one of them we knew we must shoot the horse, too. This I could not do and had to get the Indian to do it for me. He boiled a kettleful of the meat for men and dogs but it was my own saddle mare and constant companion on many a hard trip and I contented myself as best I might with snow water. After supper the Indian roasted a quarter of the wolf to complete the feast.

It was late afternoon when we arrived at Fort Pelly. Mrs. Campbell's welcome was a warm homecoming with a bountiful meal soon prepared and set before me. The hardships and horror of the previous night faded, with the children around us, and everyone surprised and delighted with the first mail since the Fall Brigade in October. Unfortunately the Chief Factor and the two clerks I had hoped to see were obliged to leave that morning and this was a great disappointment. That evening the Scotch shortbread I remembered so well appeared with the choicest sherry, port wine and whiskey.

Two days passed happily with the children, their mother and Aunt Christine. Next summer Miss Stirling will take the older ones to Scotland where they will go to school, but now they are delighted to go for a ride in my carriole, flying along behind a fresh train of dogs. They begged me to stay another day when the morning of departure was alive with the loading of carrioles with provisions and the harnessing of dogs, but I remembered my promise to Mr. MacKay and hastened to return.

We would have made the trip in three days had it not been for a snow storm on New Year's Day which became so heavy that we were forced to lie in camp. We saw the New Year in wrapped in robes, looking up at the sky, now clearing and alight with all the stars of Heaven, while mile upon mile stretched the endless waste of snow, trackless save for the frail path of our making.

Nature provided Northern Lights for holiday entertainment, a wonderful illumination of the sky from zenith to horizon with all the prismatic colours of the rainbow. Prairie wolves raised their voices in wild solo and chorus to the accompaniment of answering howls from our sleigh dogs. All else was still and quiet.

Mr. MacKay was ready to set out for the Moose Mountains when I arrived next day. He took two men from the Post and several Indians and sleds to hunt elk. No hunter is better than he and this time his success provided a welcome change from pemmican, fish and buffalo meat for in ten days he was back to tell us of how he came on a band of sixty elk and was able to take them all.

The winter is a dull one for me without much change from the daily routine of the Post and not enough of that. I am alone most of the time while Mr. MacKay is away on visits to outposts, on hunting trips, and now that we are well into March he has gone to Fort Pelly.

On March 27th our long-awaited mail has arrived with letters written over two months ago by my family. Mr. MacKay has also brought letters from the Depot with instructions for me to start immediately with twelve men for Stoney la Bossa to cut cord-wood. This must be piled on the river bank for the use of the steamboat that is to come up from Fort Garry early in May. Thirty cords will be piled at intervals on the Assiniboine when the *International* comes up river on her trial trip during high water, the only time the stream may be navigable.

Before dawn I shall set out with carriole and dogs and am now writing through the night to have letters ready to go by first chance. In case I have time to write in camp I shall take my desk with me to answer letters just received from my family and fellow clerks. Mr. MacKay saw Willie at Fort Pelly and reports him to be in good health but rather low in spirits. He too seems to have had a lonely winter.

Little does one think on entering the Company's service what a clerk gives up for the chance of making money and five times out of six he makes but little. There is a clerk retiring from this District without a pound to his name after serving forty-three years. He has never been above one hundred pounds a year though he has always been a good officer but somehow or other never got his commission, and there are plenty of such cases.

Very sad news has come with Mr. MacKay from Fort Pelly. The Campbells have just lost their older daughter, a pretty little girl of seven years. Mrs. Campbell will take the others home by way of Fort Garry and Fort York in July when they will pass here. Miss Stirling's health is too delicate to stand the long trip to St. Paul, which means that my mother will not have the hoped for opportunity of meeting the friends who have been so kind to me.

We learn that grain is high in Canada and farmers there are hopeful of fair profits but here there is nothing in the shape of grub to be had in the District. In the Settlement everything is extravagantly dear. Pemmican sells wholesale for a pound sterling and flour thirty shillings per hundredweight, with other provisions in proportion.

During the winter Mr. MacKay was out on the Plains for nine-teen days in which time it cost him twenty-five pounds sterling to feed himself, two men and dogs. An Indian went out from the Post to hunt with a couple of dogs, a sled and harness I lent to him. He has returned after eating the dogs, the harness and the lashings of *shaganappi* off the sled. A party of freemen ate eleven horses where I go tomorrow. I hope they won't eat me!

Tomorrow I shall set out in a carriole with dogs but may have to return with a horse driven tandem in a cart if the snow is all off by then, but I hope to get the work well started and leave the men to complete it. This will enable me to return by carriole and look after the spring returns now coming in. My train of dogs is a fast one, being four fine large animals that Mr. MacKay gave ten pounds for the other day. Fifteen days' rations go out with the crew who have implicit directions as to how much wood to cut and where to pile it along the Assiniboine. The farthest supply will be placed fifty miles below Brandon House.

It was as I hoped and I returned to work here. A few days before, Mr. MacKay judged the wood should be all cut and piled; he provided me with a guide and saddle horse in the belief that I would arrive at the farthest pile just when it should be completed. He impressed upon me the importance of having the wood properly banked. As I had lost my own saddle mare I was permitted to ride one we have here for which the Company gave eighty pounds. He once beat the fastest race horse in the States and though not a young horse he is still a very good animal.

It was Sunday evening when I rode into camp only to find that it had been visited by a party of freetraders who persuaded our men to exchange what remained of their rations for rum. They were entirely out of food and not more than half the wood was banked. The weather had turned cold and the northward flights of ducks and geese had ceased. Consequently there was nothing to eat but what I had with me for the guide and myself, and this provided supper and breakfast for all.

On Monday morning I sent our best hunter out while I took his place with an axe. My experience in lumber camps in Canada was put to such good use that the men were forced to work their best to keep abreast of me and by night we had this last pile of wood on the river bank. Tuesday morning we started home having had no other food than a goose, the sole spoils of the day's hunt which, with a little left from what I brought, had furnished our supper the previous night. The guide and I rode all day fasting, the men following with the slower carts and horses. Just before dark we ran a young badger to his hole and managed to dig him out and boil him for our supper.

All next day we had nothing but ice water nor anything more until the following noon when we reached the Fort and were re-paid by a very good dinner. Mr. MacKay was especially pleased to know the wood was there for the boat, as we have high hopes that it will provide satisfactory transportation for the furs going out each spring. The experiment must not fail because of any neglect on our part.

During May the furs from our outposts have been coming in and these are now packed and the accounts made up. From Fort Pelly their boats have brought down their returns for the winter but we have been waiting for a week for those from Qu'Appelle, which will include what has come in there from the Touchwood Hills. It is high time for the combined cargoes to be on their way to Fort Garry if they are to arrive in time to join the Spring Brigade to Fort York.

I had hoped to be sent to Fort Garry for the summer if Mr. McDonald were taking my place here and leaving Mr. Cowie at Qu'Appelle, but was told that I am required for a home guard at one of the prairie Posts. When I asked Mr. Campbell to be allowed to go with Mr. Finlayson to Hudson Bay with the boats, I learned that another clerk would have the journey I have longed for in vain for two years. There is the prospect of another lonely summer here as the family may be away. Miss MacKay's sister goes up to Qu'Appelle to spend the summer.

The barking of dogs and sound of voices broke in upon the blues creeping over me from inactivity, anxiety and lack of anything very pleasant to anticipate in the near future. Someone had arrived whom I soon found to be Mr. McDonald, footsore and weary from walking the ten miles from where he had left his boats. He had bad news for us: the crew was out of food and the boats leaking badly. It is thirty miles by river to where they were stranded at the mouth of Scissors Creek and as I had done my best last year to promote river transport I could not but feel somewhat responsible for the present situation.

Unfortunately, the water was lower and the cargoes heavier, with the result that two of the boats were badly damaged in running the rapids which had not been a risk last year owing to the higher water. My former *bourgeois* (Mr. McDonald) planned to take food back for his men who were then mending the boats and drying the furs.

Here was my chance to justify my faith in our river highway and to prove my worth in making the best possible use of it. Perhaps my ambition to be one of the first successful navigators was due to having enjoyed Mark Twain's stories of the early days on the Mississippi, from which I learned that the pilot ranks next to the Captain in importance. As such I might hope for recognition and promotion beyond the expectations of a clerk, providing I had acquired a thorough knowledge of the river. On my first descent last spring I made a mental chart of every rapid, sand bar and obstruction on the river between Fort Qu'Appelle and Fort Ellice which I hoped would become part of an inland waterway.

Accordingly, I volunteered to go out with the food and bring the boats over the last tortuous miles of the river channel. To my joy Mr. MacKay received my offer with enthusiasm equal to my own and persuaded Mr. McDonald to remain with him. Remembering that there were no obstacles between Scissors Creek and Fort Ellice, I gave my assurance that I would have the boats here within thirty-six hours.

The worst troubles of a *voyageur's* life vanish quickly before a good meal of pemmican and strong Hudson's Bay tea. I saw to it that an extra portion of these was added to the provisions already laid out. All was loaded in ten carts with fresh drivers and horses whose brisk pace brought us to the camp in a little over an hour.

There I fed the hungry crew and when spirits and bodies were thus restored I suggested that we fall to work loading the carts with the cargo over and above what could be safely taken in the boats.

Could we reach Fort Ellice in the promised thirty-six hours? It was then early afternoon, but the men pitched into the work with such a will that the carts were soon away with loads of robes and furs and we shoved the lightened boats into the stream. By rowing hard we went downstream considerably faster than the current to arrive well within our time limit and earlier than expected.

Mr. MacKay was surprised and pleased with the success of the venture, so much so that he informed me that as I was such a good navigator he would put me in charge of the combined cargoes and I was to take the fleet down to Fort Garry. The returns from the Swan River District by this route each spring were usually entrusted to an experienced officer who was older than my twenty years.

Instead of remaining at Fort Ellice as expected I would have the longed-for river voyage and visit to the Settlement. With growing pleasure I listened to Mr. MacKay's instructions: I was to bring back the Spring Brigade for which he would forward the horses from Fort Ellice, the carts I must obtain new in the Red River District to the number of fifty. We must leave early next day.

Half of my crew were employed servants whose five-year contracts had come to an end and who were entitled to return at the Company's expense by the annual ship from Fort York. Each year there are a number of these men who have the privilege of re-engaging at Fort Garry and whether they wish to remain in Rupert's Land or to go home by the ship, all eagerly anticipate a visit at Fort Garry. Some were accompanied by their families, making about fifty persons all told for me to look after. Among the passengers were our two blacksmiths, one from Fort Pelly and one from here. Though the latter had been out only a year he had suffered much during the winter from scurvy and must be taken back to England.

The Company makes itself responsible for supplying food as

well as transportation, but as the Plains' Hunters had not come in before we left, and as what pemmican there was had been much depleted by those kept waiting during the week's delay of the Qu'Appelle boats, at least half of our rations must be made up of geese and ducks shot along the way. Fortunately the river was alive with these birds. Profiting by my unsatisfactory experience a few weeks earlier along the same route when I sent one of our woodcutters for game, I would do most of the shooting myself. By taking my position in the bow of our flagship I was able to bring down what we needed before the boats in our wake disturbed them.

This forward position was justified by reason of voyaging in one of the two York boats, the other having come down from Fort Pelly, as is the custom. These are five feet longer and two feet broader than the *batteaux* or about thirty feet in length and seven feet in width with a crew of eight to each boat. We had six *batteaux* loaded with bales of furs and robes and, coming last of all a *batteaux* serving as a hospital ship for the blacksmiths and the nurse who cared for them.

Only one mishap occurred. When I brought down a particularly large goose it fell on the head of a woman in one of the boats following, and knocked her senseless. She soon revived and claimed the goose as her especial property.

Near Portage la Prairie we came alongside Indians camping by the river from which they were taking sturgeon, and were confronted by the barricade they had built between the banks. This was a trap made by driving stakes into the riverbed where there are rapids and securing them by a mattress of willows through which the water must flow. The sturgeon land on the mattress above the water and are easily taken. I bought one of these huge fish for our next meal and to add to our rations but could not persuade the Indians to let our boats through though I offered to give them an order on the Company's store at the nearby Post for a sack of flour, five pounds of tea and five shillings' worth of tobacco. They demanded instead a pound in money for each boat.

"If you do not open the river," I said, "I will do so."

The Indians still refused to give us passage, whereupon I stood on the bow of my boat with my gun in hand and ordered my men to open the barrier. I remained thus until all the boats had passed through and my men had replaced the trap. The Indians now came to me to beg for the offered gifts but my reply was "Kah Wren," which interpreted is "not on your life."

When I called at our Post at Portage la Prairie I found the Swan River horses that Mr. MacKay had arranged to send down for our return trip and to my great joy, my own saddle horse, the successor to the one killed by wolves. The boats had come down slowly owing to the low water which had prevented all thought of sending up the steamer for which we had piled wood on the banks last March.

What a relief now from the tedious boat journey to ride across the prairie. The boats were started on their way again and a second saddle horse chosen to accompany my own, now saddled and waiting. I rode all night from early evening until dawn of the long June day and covered the sixty-five miles in time to arrive at Fort Garry for breakfast. Throughout the day, and during the two days following, I was free to visit the friends I made two years before. Then the boats came in and required all my attention.

When the cargoes were unloaded and their contents checked, I made my report to Governor Mactavish, giving into his hands the lists of fur packs and robes, of men to be re-engaged, and Mr. Campbell's requisition for goods to be brought back by the carts. There was also a verbal message from the Chief Factor given at the last minute. This I dutifully repeated to the Governor, to the effect that he would be sure to re-engage one man the Chief Factor could not do without. I shall never forget his reply:

"The Company can dispense with the services of Mr. Campbell, myself, or any man in the service."

It is hard to think of better men than those upon whom I have learned to rely, but there are many more whom I do not know and who would undoubtedly prove as worthy should occasion require.

It was over two weeks later before the carts were reloaded and ready to return to Fort Ellice in the morning. At seven o'clock I sat down to dinner in the Officers' Mess at Fort Garry and found myself next to Mr. John McTavish. He promptly delivered the message that shattered my hopes of a day for visiting the Inksters, Bannatynes and other friends. Though I had been two weeks in the Settlement, I spent scarcely two days in one place and was constantly busy.

"Dr. Cowan wants you to take the crews for the Norway House Brigade down to the Stone Fort tonight. I will have them down at the boat-landing at eight o'clock this evening and will send a team down to bring you back."

There are at the Fort a dozen officers, any one of whom might have gone and when I protested that I was being made the victim of some sort of practical joke he continued unperturbed:

"You will find the Governor's carriage pair, Polly and Pet, have been sent down. I think you are the only one he has ever allowed to drive them."

He produced a list of the names of the crew, composed of English and French halfbreeds, Scotch servants, and Indians, both Saulteaux and Crees, and we proceeded to the boat landing. He read out their names, checking them off as we found each man present. Five York boats were soon loaded and we were away, the men in all stages of intoxication.

According to long established custom the Company advances part of their wages for the voyage to Fort York before departure and I am sure the night I spent guarding those wild, drunken men will always remain a dark spot in my memory. As the gloom of evening deepened with an oncoming storm the eerie blackness seemed interminable and many of my charges more like savage beasts than human beings. When we were passing the village of Winnipeg several deserted but when we reached the Lower Fort next morning all were present but one. It was a great relief to deliver them, with the two York boats brought down the Assiniboine, to the Guide of the York Brigade. The missing man was found later and put in gaol for desertion, to be returned to Fort Garry.

Leaving the Northern Brigade to voyage by river and lake to seaboard I repaired to the Stone Fort for a few hours of sleep and a good breakfast. It was high time for me to be at the scene of our Cart Brigade where final preparations to break camp were in progress. In record time fifty carts moved out along the trail laden with supplies and goods for our winter trade. That night the Guide decided to make the first camp at Sturgeon Creek where I rode out to join my Brigade. To my surprise and delight the officers of the Fort, accompanied by Mr. Bannatyne, came out to spend the evening with me. They were eager to hear all I could tell them of the Swan River District in the two years I was there, and I no less interested in what had transpired in the Settlement during my absence. We voiced our concern for Governor Mactavish, on whom the heavy responsibilities of the changing times weighed, and wondered what the future might hold for us.

Thus passed all too quickly my brief visit of sixteen days. The return journey seemed long and tedious but I brought up my Brigade all serene. Mr. MacKay was waiting for me and ready to depart for the summer's buffalo hunt as soon as I arrived to take charge, and I am happy to be home again at Fort Ellice.

# TEN

---

## *The Summer and Autumn of 1868*

A young clerk, Duncan Matheson, who came out last fall, has been sent here to assist me. Mr. MacKay's sons are home for the summer vacation from St. John's College. Miss MacKay and her sister are here with Mrs. Finlayson and her three little daughters while Mr. Finlayson, Chief Clerk at Touchwood Hills, has gone to York Factory with the Spring Brigade. Altogether the summer promises to be a pleasant contrast to the lonely one I spent last year at Fort Qu'Appelle.

Moreover we shall be fully occupied with all that has to be done. There are new quarters to be built for the men and the Saskatchewan Brigade must be supplied with the necessary transportation. We never send ox-trains from Fort Ellice but keep enough oxen here to replace any that are lame or unfit to travel in the above Brigade. We use these animals about the Post to haul wood and hay.

As there are about a hundred oxen in the Saskatchewan Brigade going to Edmonton and this is followed at intervals by smaller brigades from Fort Garry, we require quite a number in our herd. The Company formerly sent their own ox-trains through to St. Paul when they began to use this route as an alternative to the water route to Hudson Bay, but after 1863 they contracted with native freighters to haul goods and furs. An officer usually accompanies this brigade, and always when furs are being sent out. There are officers passing through who stop with us and I must give them the courtesy of some attention.

We have a large number of horses to look after which requires much of my time during the day so that I find myself doing my office work by candlelight. My *bourgeois*, who left two days after I returned from Fort Garry, expects to be away for July and August, which leaves all the writing for me to do. Dawn comes early now and with it the sounds of our men stirring by which I was interrupted at my desk one morning whereupon I gave them their rations and orders for the day and lay down for a little sleep until the cook should have breakfast ready.

As the days go by, we are having continued rain with violent thunderstorms. On a recent night, lightning struck a cow and a bull standing by a garden fence. Both animals were killed and the pickets split to ribbons. We have had hot days too, but I do not think it nearly so warm here as in Canada where this summer seems to have been unusually hot. As to sunstroke, such a thing is never heard of here.

The summer passes tranquilly. Sometimes there are riding parties that can be arranged for the ladies but in which I am seldom able to participate. Only one incident caused some alarm as few men have been left at the Post.

One day a party of Sioux came in from the Woody Mountains to trade, with their Chief, Standing Buffalo at their head, the same warriors who came to Fort Garry during my first summer in the West, and who, with his followers, was so badly treated by the Saulteaux. His attitude to Crees and Saulteaux, never friendly, was not made less hostile by the scalping affray following the sham agreement on that occasion to bury the hatchet. Moreover, he is a well known renegade and outlaw by reason of the red hand he took in the Minnesota Massacre of 1862.

His band brought us nothing but antelope hides which they traded for gunpowder and ball shot, explaining that they were taking these back with them the same night to the mountains in the south-west from which they had just come.

All was quiet that night at the Fort when suddenly I was awakened by shots being fired and the shouting of men. I soon discovered that an attack was being made by the Sioux upon a party of Saulteaux camping just outside our Fort. The Indian's familiarity with guns, used by himself in hunting and warfare, would make our answering shots of little avail, or worse. But the white man's thunder is another matter and at once I ordered the gates opened so that I could roll out one of the old brass field-pieces with which the Company fortifies its Posts.

I loaded the cannon with ball shot and fired it into the bluffs across the river. The echoes beat against the steep bank on which Fort Ellice stands as they sounded back and forth across the Assiniboine until all was quiet once more. The cannon's roar had reached its mark in the wholesome and deep abiding fear in the hearts of the braves for the crash of its shot and we heard no more of the foes that night.

Next morning we were at breakfast when a scout returned to say he had seen the Sioux in hasty retreat for the distant plains. This was good news, especially for the ladies who had been alarmed for themselves and their children by the disturbance of the night. I am thankful to say the attackers have not been seen since.

On the whole, my second summer in the Company's service has passed very quickly. During the last two weeks of August I was very ill and when Mr. MacKay returned at the end of the month I was no better. Two more weeks passed before I was well. I think I have been overworking, for at times we became so busy that for four or five nights running I never went to bed until I had given the men their orders and then I would lie down until breakfast was ready. For nine days after Mr. MacKay came home I never moved off the sofa with a stunning headache and at last I became so weak that I could not sit on horseback.

My *bourgeois* came in from his summer campaign on the Plains with our buffalo hunters and Indians riding beside carts heaped high with dried meat and pemmican. To store it away was the work of several days, and the reason for general relief, that now we are well provisioned against the winter. Surely a mighty hunter on the Plains is MacKay and this further proof of his prowess adds to his fame among all our men and Indians, but especially those who went with him and are pleased with their share in a successful hunt.

Unfortunately for whoever may be his clerk, Mr. MacKay knows little about the work that he has to get done in the office and when I came here a year ago I had to take the whole responsibility of the accounts on my head without anyone to show me. Not only that, but the whole correspondence was left to me and although he is in charge I have been pitched into, right and left, when anything went wrong. It would be easy enough to keep things straight if I had the entire management. This explains why I nor any clerk, except Willie, ever liked Fort Ellice.

As a private individual I like MacKay very much, but as an officer in a Post like this where there is a very extensive trade, his lack of business knowledge makes it very difficult for his clerk. When the officer in charge of an inland Post looks after the business his clerk keeps the accounts under his direction, and when his work is done he is usually sent out in charge of parties. It is consequently not to be wondered at that I was eager to grasp an opportunity that occurred for a pleasant change and new work.

As soon as I began to feel better Mr. Campbell and Mr. McDonald came down to Fort Ellice to see what could be done about carrying on the trade at Riding Mountain. This is a good Post for fine furs, about eighty miles from here, which has always been in the charge of a temporary trader for want of a regular officer. Last spring it had to be abandoned before the spring trade was over on account of running out of provisions. The Indians were annoyed to find they had to take their furs so much farther to us here and burned the Post.

There is no officer disposable in Swan River, as I was during my first year, and when Mr. Campbell wrote to request that one be sent Governor Mactavish replied that none could be detached from any other District. I saw that they were at a loss as to what could be done and volunteered to take charge of Riding Mountain and to return every week or so to keep my accounts here, which is the work assigned to me and which I may not neglect. My offer was subject to one condition: that I be allowed to pick my own men.

"Take the best men, the best buffalo-runners, the best interpreters and anything else you like," said Mr. MacKay "if you can save the valuable furs that should come in to this Post from falling into the hands of freetraders."

Winter is setting in early and I must lose no time in preparing to go to Riding Mountain if I am to get a building up this autumn. Fort Ellice has already settled into its winter routine. The Indians are coming in from north of us for their winter outfits.

One day an Indian woman from the Touchwood Hills appeared wearing a blanket with my name on it. It must be the one I sold to Willie a year ago last spring when I stopped at the Post there on my way to Qu'Appelle from Fort Pelly. An Indian had died and a blanket was wanted for a shroud.

September is a month of continous arrivals and departures at Fort Ellice. A great friend of mine, Mr. W. H. Watt, spent a day with me on his way to his wintering place in the Saskatchewan. He has been visiting in Lakefield and was able to bring me all the latest news from there and of his brother, who is another good friend. The officers who went with the spring boats to York Factory have returned and departed with their wives and families for their winter quarters, leaving us to wonder when, if ever, our paths will cross.

All is now ready for an early start for Riding Mountain to-morrow, September fifteenth. Three men and a boy will go with me, taking in the supplies and the horses I have chosen. During the summer I have learned which are the best and have picked out three splendid ones for my own use, that is, a saddle horse for myself and one for my servant, the third being used as a pack horse. They are all regular howlers: Catch (a great catch), Pat and Top.

Catch is very hard to get hold of and unless I leave a long lasso on him I cannot take him without snaring him on horseback. Pat is also hard to catch and won't let anyone but myself ride him. At least, most are afraid of him. Top is a splendid buffalo-runner but was once tossed by a bull and fearfully gored, but not injured other than having the skin of his flank torn. One of the men going with me is Louis Vandall, a French halfbreed, who will cook and look after the horses.

123

Two weeks later it is the 30th of September and I find myself camped by the edge of the Little Saskatchewan River on the prairie without a stick of wood. I must wait all day, having sent my Factotum back thirty miles for a bag of shot he lost out of his cart the day before yesterday. To boil my tea I must use buffalo chips, a less vulgar expression than buffalo dung, but it is hard to keep a fire warm enough to save my fingers from the tender attentions of Jack Frost while I am writing.

A week ago I left Riding Mountain to go down to Portage la Prairie or the Settlement in order to meet Mr. McDonald and to take my outfit from his Brigade, but eight days before the appointed time I met him and was spared the trouble of going farther. For two days I travelled back with him, my greatest friend and fellow clerk. It is hard to imagine how glad we were to see each other and talk over old times (not so very old, by the by), only two years today since I saw him first when I arrived at Qu'Appelle. But white men are scarce in Hudson's Bay service and friends most valuable. He is in a hurry to reach Fort Ellice and went on after breakfast, while I have remained here, where my trail branches off for Riding Mountain and where I am waiting for my man to return with the lost bag of shot.

When on a trip I carry a small copper kettle, some tea, sugar and pemmican, if in a hurry, but if not merely tea and sugar and, depend on my gun for grub. I am quite indifferent as to how I live when out, but this morning it was a great treat to pitch into some fresh eggs Mr. McDonald brought up as he had a case full of them. His cook made the tea so strong at breakfast time that, when sugar was put in, it could be cut with a knife and fork.

I was never well until I left Fort Ellice but now, since I have been travelling about, I am as well as can be, and am happy to think of my pleasant change from Fort Ellice with which I became thoroughly disgusted. My dissatisfaction had nothing to do with the Company's service which has as great an attraction for me as ever, if not more.

Mr. McDonald brought me letters and parcels, one of which contains writing paper sent by my mother with Mr. Hamilton. I am very glad of it but at the same time sorry that she should pay double in Canada what I can get it for in England, especially as what little money I send her I intend for herself. Besides, there is the cost of sending it out and by the time I get anything of the kind from her it costs just three times what I can buy it for here. For although we are out of the world we can get clothes or any merchandise far cheaper than in Canada. For instance, good tea in London costs us one shilling per pound, sugar threepence and soap one penny and the Company bring it out *gratis*. Another parcel contains thirty-six magazines from the Bachelors' Hall Club in Red River. They will keep dull care away this winter. There still remains the difficulty of getting clothes to fit without a tailor to measure me.

Mr. McDonald likes Hamilton very much, a senior officer who is off to Cumberland House but who was at Fort Garry where Mr. McDonald met him a few days ago. News from my home in Lakefield comes through retired staff of the Hudson's Bay Company at Brockville where my mother visits and where there are at least two Chief Factors.

Among my letters are ones from my sister and her husband at Rice Lake and as I sit writing by a smouldering fire I recall the many pleasant days I spent with them and often, often wish they were not past. I hope to spend as pleasant days with them again but perhaps not so many. I am now very happy in my own society and if I am peculiar in my ideas perhaps it is just as well that I am by myself.

I have not written to my sister since the Winter Express and an earlier letter was lost when one of our Packets went astray and never reached Fort Garry. I have a whole pile of letters to write while I wait here and hope to be excused for writing with pencil as my ink is frozen. My sister and her husband are no worse treated than all the Big Little men, for I have written to Governor Mactavish and Chief Factor Campbell in the same way. I expect to spend a very quiet winter and to pass a great part of my time in study.

The weather has been unusually cold for this time of year. All the small lakes have been and are still frozen. There were eight inches of snow at Red River when Mr. McDonald left there with our carts, and while coming up his servant got one of his feet frozen very badly, but it is too early for winter, surely.

The house that I am building at Riding Mountain is pleasantly situated on this river, the Little Saskatchewan, a hundred miles further up than I am now. I changed the site from the old Fort that was burned and built on the river bank. When I left, the house was erected as far as the plates though I was there only five days with four men. By this time I expect they will have it ready to plaster. It is thirty feet by sixteen and built of large logs hewn inside and out and thatched. A store and a house for the men must be built before winter.

Directly I can spare the time we are going to hunt and salt ducks of which there are plenty, also geese; so between moose, bear and deer meat I hope that we may live well. I have three men and a couple of boys, as Mr. MacKay got one of his nephews engaged to winter with me as Apprentice Postmaster, or so I understood, but the Governor writes me: "MacKay goes up to winter with you. You will find him a good trip man as well."

When I arrived in mid-September and proceeded to build temporary quarters I did not get a very cordial reception from Little Bone Chief and his followers who came to interview me. They demanded that if they let the Company re-establish the Post it must be kept open until the spring trade is over. This is quite in accordance with my own instructions in coming up here, but a second demand presents a serious problem for they insist that there be a revision of the tariff on all goods downward and on all furs upward.

I find this very difficult as I have had no experience in arranging a tariff, nor have I foreseen any need to be equipped with this knowledge, for such matters are attended to by the officials in London and all we have to do is to accept their decrees and be governed thereby. As I have been entrusted with the management of the Post and am resolved to stay and make it pay a good profit at any cost to myself, I must frame a new tariff that will be satisfactory to the insurgents and at the same time protect the Company from paying the competitive prices of the freetraders. Until recent years the Hudson's Bay Company held its ancient monopoly as the sole fur trader of Rupert's Land but it is becoming increasingly difficult to maintain this privilege as the territory is being invaded by independent fur buyers from Red River, Canada, and from south of the International boundary.

In my new place all our furs are chiefly marten, fisher and mink and are packed only on a horse. I intend to travel about with horses until the snow gets too deep, as the Indians are all at some distance from the Post and I must go after them.

For this reason I have a guard of twenty-five horses among which is one Governor Mactavish sent up for me for a saddle horse. This is the famous Lord March that Lord March gave fifty pounds for and rode him in a buffalo hunt. In one race with the fleeing animals he killed nine of them. The Governor also sent McDonald a saddle horse to use in the Company's service in the same way that Lord March is supplied for me to ride.


Six days later, on October sixth, I am back again at Riding Mountain House though I am living in a leather tent at present. In a few days the houses will be finished, I hope, for it is exceedingly cold with deep snow though it is not too late in the year to have some fine autumn weather, which will enable me to make a trip or two round the Indian camps. Then I hope to be able to send my men to them with goods to trade for their furs.

The remainder of my outfit for this trade is at Fort Ellice and I am going back for it about the fifteenth of this month. Unless the weather changes I shall have a very cold ride across the Plains but I must do my work there, which is to make up the accounts. This will take me a week or so as there are all the outfits sent from Fort Ellice to be recorded, but Mr. MacKay will have to write his own letters.

My letters are waiting for a chance to go down. All are written in pencil as the ink here was frozen also while I was away, and is too pale to use. Some of my news is from Willie who sent me a letter recently from Egg Lake where he was well at the time of writing. I must prepare a long speech for the Grand Council the Indians will hold here on my return from Fort Ellice. I am growing quite fond of spouting to them which they do not mind, though at times I lay down the law to them at a great rate.

# ELEVEN

---

## *Two Posts in Wintertime*

It is the 15th of October and I have just arrived at Fort Ellice from Riding Mountain. The buildings there are finished and by the time I get back everything will be ready for the winter. Here everything goes on as usual, the weather is very cold with plenty of snow. Mail has come in from Touchwood Hills but no letter from Willie which means he is away from home. The outfit from Fort Pelly has not arrived and as I am obliged to wait for it I think I shall start for that place tomorrow morning to hurry it up.

Who should I find waiting here to see me but one of our best customers and hunters, Pusquaw, a Wood Cree, whose name interpreted is The Plain. He is a character worthy of note, not so much for unfailing steadfastness as for his determination to mend a disaster he has brought upon himself, regarding which I am unable to help him, much to his disappointment. In the hope of aid from me he has been waiting around here until I returned from Riding Mountain.

Earlier this fall he spent some days with us in carefully selecting an extensive fall and winter outfit. His credit is rated on our books as good for from seventy-five to a hundred pounds worth of supplies, the pound being the Hudson's Bay Company's note for this amount based on the English pound sterling. This credit, considered to be safely within his ability to repay from the proceeds of his winter work, was well nigh exhausted when he departed with numerous traps, several guns, cayuses and dogs, beside food supplies and warm clothing for himself and seven wives.

These last, but not the least, of his hunting equipment, have been carefully selected, not only for their personal attractions

E                                                                                  129 but also for their working capacity and proficiency in trapping beaver, bear, muskrat and other fur-bearing animals. From Pusquaw we have learned that his domestic establishment is spread over the entire length of his trapline in camps located at convenient intervals. He himself acts as *bourgeois* in charge of a district, supplying each outpost with the necessary equipment and directing the work thereof during frequent social and business visits, as well as collecting and bringing us the furs.

Although Pusquaw is a man of unquestioned business integrity he has one failing: he is addicted to the use of "Iskoota-wapoo," or rum. It so happened that on the occasion of his return to his hunting ground he received a visit from a freetrader whose stock in trade was largely of this commodity. Having no furs as yet to trade he disposed of a couple of his cayuses. When the rum, which had separated him from this part of his property, had been drunk and had failed to alleviate his thirst and that of his female consorts, but had rather increased it the more, he allowed the trader to separate him from the entire outfit purchased from us. I do not know what the tariff set by the trader was for rum, or would have been for furs, but a good cart horse, for which the Company would pay eight pounds in cash or trade, would be required for two quarts of rum.

His outfit being exhausted, Pusquaw was not a little dismayed to find that he had no credit with the freetrader that would enable him to proceed with his trapping operations. In his extremity he has turned to his former friend, the Company, and requests us to furnish him with another outfit. In this he is disappointed, for although Mr. MacKay has never been known to refuse an Indian food or other assistance when in want, he himself is strictly temperate and positively refuses to supply Pusquaw with goods to be exchanged for *Iskootawapoo*.

Our trapper, however, is a man of resource, and in addition to being a good hunter is a warrior of international repute among the red men. Nevertheless, he does not care to engage in a domestic civil war he knows to be inevitable if he should return to his camps without the necessary outfit and warm, bright blankets, not forgetting vermilion paint and brass wire for earrings, indispensable accessories of the well-dressed Indian matron. Knowing himself to be in the hopeless minority of seven-to-one he considers discretion the better part of valour and has decided to take a chance among a hostile band of Grosventre Indians on the American side of the line.

"The Okimaw"[1] he tells me, meaning Mr. MacKay, "thinks I cannot pay my debt, but I am going to war, and when he sees me again he will like me."

So saying he departed on foot with no military equipment other than a pair of moccasins, a scalping knife, a rawhide line and a hatchet. Since then the assembling of my own outfit for Riding Mountain has taken longer than I expected, interspersed as it has been with making up the accounts here. I cannot be sure of returning on regular trips during the winter and must take with me this time everything necessary for the successful operation of a Post. Directly the present snowstorm subsides I intend to set forth.

The flakes were still falling one day when I looked out to see the whole square filled with horses. We had not sent for any and I went out to investigate as to why the guard had brought them in. The Company keeps a large band of horses here to supply the demands made upon this Post for transportation. The horses are kept out on the range in charge of an Indian guard mounted on horseback, and when we want fresh animals to replace the travel-worn ones of a Brigade passing through we send word to the Indian who will drive as many as we want into the Fort, and return with those we give him for recuperation.

To my astonishment when the Indian dismounted and opened his blanket I discovered that it was not our guard but Pusquaw. Then I noticed that the horses were strange ones and that there were some big mules among them. Pusquaw followed me into the Indian Hall and I sent for the interpreter.

An Indian has a more gentlemanly way of begging than most white men: he tells how long it is since he has had anything to

[1] Officer.

131

eat or smoke, as the case may be. Pusquaw said he had not had anything to eat for four days. I bade the interpreter take him to the quarters where the men have their meals and fill him with pemmican and tea before bringing him back to me.

When Pusquaw reappeared, well fed and happy, he gave a full account of his war. On reaching the Missouri River he located, from a safe distance, a camp of Grosventres and their band of horses ranging not far from them. He waited until there came a snowstorm to hide all tracks, then stealthily approached the horses. Singling out one, he roped and mounted it. Putting it to the gallop, he stampeded the whole band and kept them going ahead of him to Fort Ellice. When the horse he was riding played out, he roped another, and never stopped until he reached our Post with those that had not dropped from exhaustion along the way.

He ended his narration by asking me to take from the spoils of war enough horses and mules to pay his debt. He now has secured a complete winter outfit and the next day departed for the scenes of his trapline armed with enough trinkets purchased from us to insure a peaceful and triumphant return to his camps. I question if during any of the celebrated campaigns of history any forager ever brought in single-handed an equal amount of plunder, or displayed more courage and endurance than Pusquaw.

It will require all my own resourcefulness to keep the Post at Riding Mountain open throughout the year. It has given us good returns in fur during the months it has been open but as a rule it has been abandoned before the furs are all in. The Indians here have always been a turbulent band and when this happened early last March they regarded it as an unfriendly act on the part of the Company and burned the Post in revenge. In addition to making sure I have enough provisions to last all year I must now revise the tariff as demanded by Little Bone Chief and his followers.

In the hope of framing a revision that will appeal to the Indians as much as possible without in any way increasing their profits at the Company's expense I have been studying the tariff carefully. The listed values, as decided in the head office in London, are the same for all Posts in regard to furs and the goods sent out to pay for the furs, as the same percentage of freight and overhead is added at all Posts. This is due largely to the fact that goods are furnished on our requisitions made to the London office as much as three years in advance. Different localities require different stocks of goods and herein lies my only chance.

On the Pacific Coast at Victoria is an English community of a somewhat aristocratic character where the needs of the trade include claw-hammer coats, Paris gowns, jewelry and articles of a similar nature, while the returns are largely in gold, sea otters, seal skins and canned salmon. On the other hand, from Labrador come dried codfish, seal oil, Arctic bear skins and white and blue foxes, where garments of fashion and many of the things used in highly civilized areas are quite useless.

Towards the end of October I am back again at Riding Mountain with the realization that it is one thing to revise a tariff and quite another thing to get Little Bone and his leading followers to consent to it. With this in view I have issued a general invitation to all the Riding Mountain Indians to come to a banquet. The main course of this feast will be provided by an ancient bull brought from Fort Ellice especially for the occasion, and whose toughness from age may be somewhat ameliorated by the fat accrued from a summer's grazing.

Other courses consisted of gollet made from two sacks of Red Dog flour, also especially imported, tea from two huge kettles, sugar and tobacco, all served out-of-doors and apparently much appreciated, judging from the thoroughness shown in leaving no fragments and the grunts of satisfaction that accompanied the meal.

While the braves were enjoying their after-dinner smokes, and were in an unusually happy frame of mind, I proceeded to unfold for their benefit the improvements of my revised tariff. To the best of my ability I impressed upon them the reductions I have made on cod lines, salmon fishing tackle, ladies' Paris gowns and gentlemen's dress coats, while enlarging upon the advanced prices that would be paid for sealskins, whale oil and codfish.

133

Eight-day clocks were put on the free list, and the values greatly increased to the hunter of musk-ox robes, black wolves and reindeer hides, all of which come from the barren grounds of the Mackenzie District. There is, however, a sweeping reduction on skunk skins, for my predecessor has traded for more skunk than anything else, and I want to discourage the Indians from trapping these in the hope that they will pay more attention to mink, fox, marten and beaver. In the hope of offsetting the strong opposition I anticipated to this last clause I emphasized the advances on seal skins, walrus tusks and similar items.

I doubt if ever so inexperienced a legislator introduced a measure designed to be of so little benefit to a cause supposedly in need of remedy and read it amid so little show of opposition. Not one voice rose in dissent, but when the meal had been better digested and with it the import of the tariff, I overheard some unfriendly remarks, especially as related to the reduction in the price of skunk skins. To this I explained that they, the mighty hunters of the Riding Mountains, had taken with such skill and prowess in the year before so many of these animals as to completely overstock the London market.

In the main the Indians seem satisfied with the new order of things, including the revised tariff, for they are coming in to the new Post to obtain their winter outfits and I am kept busy attending to their wants. In the intervals between their visits, my time is taken up in supervising the completion of our log buildings for our greater comfort and convenience during the remainder of the winter, which has been unusually cold and early.

Next comes the foraging for local sources of food to relieve the present demands being made on our store of pemmican. To this I am now devoting most of my time and have discovered a mountain lake teeming with jackfish. An Indian fisherman has been engaged who is taking so many that we shall have a winter's supply of fish for the train dogs. Previously they have been fed with pemmican hauled all the way from Fort Ellice. There is now an abundance of ducks and geese in this neighbourhood and these I am preserving in quantity for the men and myself by the simple process of freezing.

Since writing the above I have been south on an elk hunt. As all the hunters have been outfitted I was able to take the interpreter and another man with six horses and as many sleds, also two buffalo-runners and two other saddle horses, and to set forth in search of elk. We travelled for two days before we ran onto a big band of them.

The manner of hunting elk differs from that adopted with buffalo, for the former can outdistance the fastest horse at the beginning of pursuit but soon tire and are easily overtaken, whereas the latter have not as much speed as a horse but have greater endurance and can maintain their rate of galloping over a much longer period. Leaving the Indian in charge of the sleds and horses – excepting the two buffalo-runners on which the interpreter and I were mounted – we slowly stalked our quarry for a couple of hours until they sought refuge in some poplar bluffs. Here we surrounded them and shot ten, all we could carry home and an ample supply to save what pemmican we have left for the spring.

My undivided attention can be given to the Indian trade and my monthly visits to Fort Ellice. The winter is turning out to be one of unusually fine weather with less than the average amount of snow which aids the Indians in their hunting and makes my trips to headquarters an easy day's travel with horses or dogs, for it will be remembered that Mr. MacKay outfitted me with the very best of both animals. With genuine pleasure do I look forward to the regular visits to my *bourgeois* and his family as a welcome change from the loneliness of my isolated outpost.

The Indians, I fear, are continuing in accordance with their reputation to be a bad lot. It will be necessary to send to their camps for their furs or these will be disposed of to freetraders. It would be impossible to prevent this loss in our trade were it not for the faithful services of the men sent with me by Mr. MacKay who are proving themselves reliable and worthy of the qualities for which they have been chosen.

But the Indians here are perfect devils. These, and the Egg Lake Indians, are the worst in the District so that it is most difficult to get a native to have enough pluck to make a good

135

trader, though my men are doing very well when entrusted with commissions to the Indian camps and when left in charge during my absence each month while I am at Fort Ellice. I have an interpreter in the course of training that I am going to keep tripping for me. We are not expected to go much to the camps ourselves, though I don't mind the travelling were it not for the beastly holes we have to sleep in. I wish I could have with me a friend of my boyhood who has written to me to get him into the service if possible. I am sure he would make a good officer and trader.

This Post is some fifty miles nearer to the Settlement than Fort Ellice and with the splendid dogs in my train it will be possible to visit there occasionally. On November 15th I shall go down to Red River with the Packet. I cannot tell where I shall spend Christmas. I hope to be at Fort Pelly.

As Christmas approaches I am preparing to set off in mid-December for Fort Ellice, and am pleased to be able to report to Mr. MacKay that we have taken in twice as many furs already as were realized in the whole of last year. Moreover, our stock of provisions remains large enough to permit us to supply some of the Indian trappers who are running short. I am selling flour and pemmican to them as I made a good provision trade at Fort Ellice last summer.

We gave one shilling per pound for the pemmican we have brought here from the plains three and four hundred miles away, stuff that one wouldn't eat at first, but I am selling it at two shillings a pound. The Indians are regular devils and a fellow has to be wide awake, and must not be afraid of anything. I am getting used to this while they are learning not to try "to come Paddy over." To make matters worse I am having strong opposition from the freetraders, but I do not think they are making anything to speak of, for I am running them around pretty hard, and don't expect to have as much trouble next year.

It is now well into January and we are having a beautiful winter. I have just received word from a party of Indians outfitted by us that they want someone to come from here to get their furs and to bring more goods to trade. Their camp is a day's journey to the east of us, which means taking food for two days for men and dogs. With me will be two men and two trains of dogs.

Four days later we are back again at Riding Mountain House. When we reached the point where the Indians had camped it was to find that they had moved on toward Lake Dauphin. Next morning we followed their trail which was due north but not overtaking them before nightfall we made camp again. The following morning we discovered that all our dogs were missing and on following their trail to the crest of the hill near which we had camped we saw the Indian camp just beneath us.

As we were approaching it there came to meet us several of our own dogs packing what we thought was the leg of a moose. At their heels followed a little Indian boy who looked at us inquiringly, and by way of conversation I asked him if someone had killed a moose. He explained in a matter-of-fact manner, with the aid of the interpreter, that it was his grandmother's leg, pointing to a raised platform at some distance where it seems the old lady, who had gone to that mythical happy hunting ground of the red man, was laid to repose until rudely disturbed by our hungry dogs.

We found a gratifying number of furs awaiting us for which we traded goods we had brought with us, but we were very low on food and two days from our Post. The Indians had a lynx and this, with the small amount of pemmican we had saved for the dogs, was enough to take us back to Riding Mountain House with our sleds well loaded with furs. As to the dogs, their gruesome feast sufficed.

It was late on the second evening of our return trip when we reached Riding Mountain House and I knew the Winter Packet was expected to arrive soon at Fort Ellice. All my reports there must be completed to send by it. With a fresh train of dogs and a new man to replace the travel-worn driver of my carriole I set out immediately on the western trail. We travelled all night until at daybreak we reached the Assiniboine and crossed over on the ice to climb the steep ascent to the Fort above.

Here I found Mr. MacKay in great trouble over some Indians in the Touchwood Hills that he had supplied with a winter outfit for the whole camp. When he sent a man out for their furs they insisted they would not give them up unless the *Okimaw* came in person. Encouraged by my recent success in dealing with more or less disaffected Indians trading with my own outpost, I at once offered to go for Mr. MacKay in the hope that I would be accepted as a substitute.

The kindly officer remonstrated vigourously that I had been up all night and should go to bed, whereupon I explained that I could sleep in the carriole the next night as I had just done. By working all day in the office I could make up the reports for the Packet and be ready to start that evening after dinner. I hoped that we might reach the Indian camp the next evening and be back on the fourth day.

We started at seven o'clock with two men, and dog trains drawing sleds loaded with more goods for trading, in addition to my carriole, dogs, and driver, who was Mr. MacKay's own man. For I had asked him to let me have men who could go a long time without sleep, and he gave me three with established records of endurance. At daybreak we stopped for breakfast of tea and pemmican, fed the dogs, and rested them and ourselves for three hours. We travelled throughout the rest of the day and arrived at the Indian camp as the early dusk was falling.

The Indians were rich in furs. They had plenty to pay their debts and additional robes and furs to trade for the goods we had brought. These we proceeded to unload when, to our dismay, we found that half of them should have been sent to another outpost for which a consignment of goods was prepared at the same time as ours. Part of the two orders had been interchanged: we had a double supply of munitions of war, but blankets, cloth and the trinkets beloved by the Indian belles had gone to the braves who wanted powder, ball, shot, scalping knives and similar hardware. Fortunately I had some warning by reason of the ominous nature of the messages Mr. MacKay had received and had brought with me a generous supply of the whitefish, tea, sugar and flour which experience has taught me has a most soothing effect on disgruntled natives.

Before continuing the business of trading, we distributed our gifts of food and waited until the feast was over. When our customers were well fed they commenced to trade some of the furs left over for powder, ball, shot, flint, steel knives and guns but soon had enough of these. A considerable number of pelts remained for which they wanted just what we did not have. Being anxious to get these furs I told the interpreter to explain how the mistake occurred and to tell them that if they would give me the furs and would send one of their men back with us I would send by him whatever they wanted.

The interpreter held forth in Cree for some time, and so convincing was his argument that, to my surprise and delight, they commenced trading again and insisted on taking everything we had with us until they had given us all their furs. I was too gratified with the unexpected welcome afforded my suggestion to press for an explanation.

The goods sent by mistake to the other camp did not get such a cordial reception and it was necessary for Mr. MacKay to go in person to straighten the tangled threads. I regretted that I could not make this trip also but already I had stayed away overlong from my outpost.

Meantime the Packet has arrived and any need for sleep is forgotten in the joy of reading the long awaited letters from family and friends. This time there is a lengthy account from my mother of the events and daily happenings at "Westove", the home I have not seen for nearly three years, with numerous messages from aunts, uncles and cousins nearby, all being news of the previous fall.

In the same mail are letters from fellow officers all over the North. The re-reading and answering of these, with the final making up of the accounts of our winter's trading will occupy the long evenings at my lonely Post of Riding Mountain. The short hours of daylight are required for the urgent matter of persuading the Indians to bring to us the furs they have taken. Failing this there is no alternative but to go after them. There are also the accounts at Fort Ellice which I must complete to show all the winter's trading. During March I must make a trip to Fort Garry after which we shall soon be into our work that comes with the springtime.

# TWELVE

## *The Spring and Summer of 1869*

LEAVING Riding Mountain House late in February I made the trip to Fort Garry and back in twenty-three days. The Settlement is in a state of desperate scarcity – no crops, no buffalo, no fish and no rabbits. How very fortunate I am to have plenty of provisions. All winter I have been selling flour and pemmican to the Indians and still have enough left to feed my establishment all summer if it is decided to keep men here to work.

The trip down to Red River was made with horses and very pleasant it was but we had a bad time coming up from Portage la Prairie. My men all became ill and it was the seventh day from there before we arrived home. I sent the Brigade on to Fort Pelly and followed in my carriole, but went straight to Fort Ellice, where I met them on their return from Swan River to that Post.

It was Friday night when I arrived, for very good travelling it was with my dogs, over a good trail. We have had a beautiful, clear winter, and in the lengthening daylight towards the end of March I drove the seventy miles in eleven hours with only three stops to rest along the way.

During the Saturday and Sunday I spent with the MacKays it snowed enough to make the road miserable when I left on Monday morning and the trip back was much slower. On my return I went across the mountain to Lake Manitoba and have only just returned this morning. It is the twenty-ninth of March and I am thoroughly sick of travelling. Now I must work on the accounts and long ere I get them closed I shall be just as sick of staying home. But first I must make another trip and tomorrow I will be off again.

It has been decided to make this a permanent Post and I have been instructed to get a place built as large as I think necessary to carry on the trade. I like Riding Mountain and shall be very glad to remain here but am afraid I shall be stuck in some other place directly I get this one in order. I am going to be here again next winter, at least so I have been told, but then again there is no saying what changes may take place before then.

The contract for building the Fort I want to let to a party of miners who are wintering about fifty miles from here, and it is in order to see them that I must set out tomorrow morning.

Five days later, on April 3rd, I have my Yankees and my three men here at work building stockades, stores, etc. I have all the plans drawn out for the new Fort and hope I can get the Yankees to work all summer, for they are worth half a dozen ordinary men. When I visited their camp and learned they were builders as well as being miners I engaged them at once and left them to come in while I continued my travels.

It was necessary for me to go after some Indians who had not brought their furs in to us. It was a beastly trip for the weather has been very disagreeable since I was at Fort Ellice, one day warm and the next cold and snowing, the most miserable weather since the year One, but I suppose I must stop grumbling! Altogether I seem to have been on the rampage for the last five days.

Their camp and they themselves were the most miserable I have yet seen in this country. The women, who are the workers as a rule, did not appear to take any interest in the care of themselves or their winter home. It snowed the night I got there, which did not make our own camp more pleasant.

Coming back, the road was only just wide enough for a horse to pack through the fir trees by going under and between them. The branches were loaded with soft snow and every half-dozen yards we got an avalanche that would cover ourselves and horses. The snow would melt on the saddle and make it most disagreeable. I have made a vow not to stir out until I start for Fort Ellice on the fourteenth of this month. My trade is nearly over for the winter and next year I am not going to travel about so much.

The trade I have made here is a good one, the receipts of fur for the winter being more than three times those of last year, which has established Riding Mountain House as one of the important Posts in the Swan River District and has resulted in my being instructed to build a permanent Post. It has been a hard winter for me but not an unpleasant one, for the measure of success attendant upon my efforts promises well for the coming year when, I have been assured, I shall be kept here to enjoy living in the new Fort.

We have traded between three and four thousand pounds of pemmican at two shillings per pound and can put all the fur on one dog sled, but mink, martens and fishers are nearly worth their weight in gold. Can you imagine putting seven hundred martens in a pack two feet square? Each of these skins is worth thirty to forty shillings sterling, so that a boat cargo is a very valuable thing. All the other Posts are far behind compared to their receipts of fur for last year, except Egg Lake where Willie is.

Notwithstanding the alleged alteration in the tariff of skunk skins, I have harvested more of these than this outpost has received for many a year. The pelts are not the only source of value that the Indians derive from these furbearers for they esteem the meat a great delicacy to be preferred above all other.

Willie wrote me a long letter the other day. He is in the deuce of a fix: his men have all deserted. He also is going to build a new Fort this summer but at present is rather in the blues about his men deserting. Otherwise he is quite well and is most likely coming down to Fort Ellice in May. I hope he may stay with me a little while until I get the Saskatchewan Brigade past.

It is not only Willie who is bothered to death with bad men. Truly this is an infernal country for servants, and I often wish I had never seen it but I am no worse off than my neighbours. They are so independent that one can't get after them, for the first word that one speaks to them they inform one that they are off, and off they go. It is most provoking that, when the Company allows us to pay our men as we like, we cannot get our work done (though we can also engage whom we like).

I wish we had a few Canadians here. I get on very well with halfbreeds but one has to know how much can be expected of them and who is to be trusted. Others seem to have little desire to work and are satisfied to live like vegetables. But never mind, every dog has his day. Wait until there are plenty of people in the country and we shall be able to get our work done as we want it and when we want it.

Next year I shall require a servant to cook and look after the Fort and I am going to ask Mr. Campbell to give me a European. A green hand straight from home can be trained to make a splendid man, but if kept at York Factory a year or two before coming inland he is generally spoiled. At present I have not a single white man within a day's journey from here.

By the last mail at Fort Garry I received cartes of my sister, her husband and children which I now have beside that of my mother to remind me of home and family. I should like to visit them for a month or so when my first contract expires but I fear it will be some time before I can return to Canada nor would I like to do so while I am as poor as at present. Perhaps I may get down to St. Paul on Hudson's Bay Company business and shall certainly try to take a trip there in a couple of years in which case I could easily continue on to Canada.

At first I hated this sort of life, but now I like it and would not know what to do with myself were I to try to live at home or at Rice Lake. I am sure I have more change and see more people than they do. Even Fort Garry life would not suit me now, although I like it while there for a few days, as I do at Fort Ellice, but after that I am glad to get away.

Keeping men here with families is a great expense to the Company and a great nuisance to boot. At an established place it is hard to keep so many but at a new place, and especially a small one, I would find it too difficult. I set my men such a good example they can have no excuse for wanting to marry. If possible I am going to keep a regular bachelor establishment. I think I can manage it by paying single men higher wages and keeping a cook with this in view.

I am letting one of my best men retire on the first of June. I offered him higher wages for the next contract as a single man, but he wants to marry. By all means, but not in the service. He seemed sorry for refusing my offer but perhaps he may change his mind. If so I shall be glad, as I don't intend to change mine nor ask him again. Until I see I cannot get single men I shall not engage married men.

Mr. MacKay highly approves of my plan and said he would do the same. By way of commencement he re-engaged a man with a wife and seven children! To feed them costs the Company ten shillings sterling a day, or what I could sell for sixteen shillings. A pretty expensive servant: thirty-two pounds per annum and fed at the rate of two dollars and fifty cents per day at the least calculation.

While I have been writing, the night has passed into the morning of April 4th and ten days from now I must leave for Fort Ellice. My letters must all be written before then because I shall not have any time there until the Brigades are all off, unless I write short notes like those from Portage la Prairie which I do not like to send, though it was the best I could do last month.

This year I am going to try farming here on a small scale and if I succeed I shall make a good large farm the year following. I have every hope of grain and roots growing well. All the potatoes that I got for my mess I have kept for seed and when in Red River last month I got two bushels each of wheat and barley which I brought up. If I have a good crop from this it will supply seed for another year.

All the transport oxen from Fort Garry are to be wintered here and I must get byres made for them as this will mean a large cattle guard. It would seem that I am to have quite an important place in a year or so, although I had to live in a tent when I came last fall. I have little doubt about the grain and potatoes growing on this prairie land but the Indians are so bad that I am afraid they will steal them all. The grain may stand a better chance.

With two or three hundred loads of good building stone I would build a stone wall round my Fort, but what is required for chimneys has to be hauled with carts. I should be glad to trade a few thousand acres of beautiful prairie land in exchange for the stones my brother-in-law has removed from his farm now that he has it in such splendid order. I believe this to be an ideal place to raise cattle and horses, and also the kind of place that enables a person to show what he can do.

The Company will be obliged to fortify Fort Ellice before long and I am expecting to have a good deal of trouble with the Indians there next summer. On my last visit I sent in some of my train dogs. Mr. MacKay gave one that was too old to put in harness to an Indian for food. A dead horse had been brought in for the dogs to eat and when the Indian begged for some of it Mr. MacKay gave him one of the legs. This he put over his shoulder and picking up a piece of old tin he went off leading the dog, and singing, and beating on the old tin for joy. Poor man, he was nearly dead. Freemen and Indians are getting to be very difficult to deal with when they have too hard a struggle for what is necessary to support life.

If I am to get to Fort Ellice on the fourteenth I must stop writing and apply myself to Company's work or I shall not have my accounts ready for York Factory in time. For more than a week I have been preparing to leave here for the summer although I shall return for short visits when I can. I find it has become very hard for me to settle down to working in an office and, though I am trying to get used to it again, after a few days I feel very sick. Three or four days of writing is all I can stand and then I generally make a trip somewhere.

Whenever I study anything closely I suffer much from pain in my chest and side which, whenever I touch it, gives me great pain. I wish I did not find grinding at a desk so hard, for I would like to apply my whole time and attention to fitting myself for a government office should the Company break up. If I were stronger I would be more particular about my handwriting which I consider to be very bad. As a rule I seldom work in an office now, or outside for that matter, for my time is fully occupied in getting the men to work and in looking after them.

This not only suits me, but the Company also, at least they seem satisfied with my management. But if I were required to work in an office in a depot it would be another thing. Nor would I do for Canada for I fear I should make a poor living if obliged to work in an office out of the Hudson's Bay Company. Here we make a living much easier.

I find travelling agrees with me better than anything else, and I expect to have a good trip tomorrow. There is no prospect of the ice breaking up for some time. I wonder if there is still skating on Rice Lake? How I used to enjoy it! Here there are hundreds of lakes to skate on but I never go out. Although a great deal of my travelling is on ice and I have skates, I never put them on. This mountain is full of large lakes although miles above the level of the plains and Lake Manitoba to the east. One cannot go three miles on land at a stretch. I think it should be called the Mountain of a Thousand Lakes.

As soon as I get the books closed at Fort Ellice I shall return here for a few days before going back to take charge of that place for the summer which is not at all to my taste but it must be done. I shall leave two men here to trade and others to build, make hay, etc. I suppose I shall have a very busy summer again. Between looking after two places I shall have my hands full, but will go down to Fort Garry in the fall before coming back here for the winter and it will be worth passing a hard summer for the change which a trip to the Settlement provides.

Willie has asked leave to come down with the boats to Fort Ellice in May. If it is granted he will stay with me for a month or so until I get over the harder part of the work. I have been laying down the law to him about marrying on seventy-five pounds per annum but he doesn't seem to see it in the same light as I do. I wish someone else in my family would try their powers of persuasion. It is perfect moonshine fancying he can save anything on such wages and that is not the worst. We may be all set adrift any day without sixpence before us which will be bad for single men, but what are married men to do?

On the evening of April 15th we arrived at Fort Ellice. We brought in all our furs taken throughout the winter together with the accounts for them. Our returns and all the other furs coming in must be made up into bales and all the records of them completed in readiness for the departure of the boats for Red River. The Qu'Appelle River is icebound, but May is approaching and with it the warm spring days that will free the waters for the boats to come down, bringing with them my brother Willie.

Among the Indians who have arrived are the Crees we visited in their camp earlier this year in the Touchwood Hills. In their hands were all manners of gifts for the *Okernasses* who could "see far." It is strictly forbidden for the clerks to accept presents from the Indians, nor could I offend these faithful customers by refusing the proffered gifts. There was no alternative but to go to the Company's store for trade goods equivalent in value to the beaded moccasins, buffalo robes and furs they wanted to give us. This exchange of presents has pleased them greatly.

There must be some explanation for all this and I sought out the interpreter for an interview. What really concerned me most of all were the scalps dangling from the waists of the Crees.

Recalling the trip, I asked the interpreter if he remembered the great hurry to get back soon: how we had reached the camp on the second day from here, traded, feasted and traded again, then rested a few hours at night before starting back ahead of the dawn? We travelled all that day and just as daylight came next morning we arrived at Fort Ellice. Did he remember how surprised Mr. MacKay was to see us so soon and to see the man asleep in the carriole was the one he told me would not give out? When I thought he needed to sleep I put him in my carriole and drove in his place and so we arrived, my driver still sound asleep.

This seemed a good joke at the time and amusing to recollect, but the interpreter now realized the seriousness of what had taken place. He revealed what I believe to be the truth of what occurred during our visit and as a sequel to the trade we made in the camp of the Crees. He had not liked my plan of returning with half the

148

munitions sent by mistake for it was a heavy load to haul so many miles. He did not translate my message but told the Indians that they should buy guns and ammunition as they would see an enemy soon – the Blackfeet. He must have been convincing for the Crees resumed trading and eagerly took everything we had in exchange for all the rest of their furs.

It so happened before very long that a party of Blackfeet made a raid on their camp at the scene of our visit when, thanks to the guns and ammunition obtained from us, the Crees made a successful defence. The enemy in retreat thirsted for a trophy of victory, though thwarted, and killed and scalped an old squaw who lived alone at the mouth of a nearby canyon, thereby infuriating the Crees who drove the Blackfeet into the canyon and scalped everyone of them.

When those furs that had arrived were packed and the account of them made up, as soon as I could, I left Fort Ellice and returned to Riding Mountain. I wanted to see how the construction of the new Fort was progressing and to prepare ground for the crops I hope to grow this year.

We have managed to plough three acres and sow them with barley and wheat seed in order that we may raise our own grain for our saddle horses.

While we worked, the ducks were in flight overhead to summer to northward. The day came when the seeding was done and that afternoon I left one of our drivers to harrow the ground with our yoke of oxen while I went shooting. I returned with all the birds we could use, well satisfied with efforts rewarded. There a strange sight greeted me. My driver still harrowed our small field though he had turned the oxen loose to graze. In their places were dog trains, four of them each with three dogs, making twelve in all, hitched to the harrow.

# THIRTEEN

## *A Lonely Life*

During my last visit at Fort Ellice in April Mr. McDonald told
me as a great secret that he has received his Commission this
spring. I insisted on his bringing the champagne with him on his
return, for I knew that when I came in May from Riding Mountain
that I could then go to Fort Pelly and return to Fort Ellice in
time to be here when Mr. McDonald, now Chief Trader, arrived
fully commissioned from Fort Garry. After persuading my old
*bourgeois* that a round dozen of champagne it must be, I wrote to
the two clerks at Qu'Appelle urging them to come down at that
time.

My brother came down from Egg Lake in May, McBeath, a
clerk from Riviere la Biche, happened to arrive, and Mr. McDonald
brought up Matheson. Altogether there were eight of my fellow
officers staying at the Fort at one time so we had a jolly party.
We polished off the champagne and three gallons of port wine
besides two dozen of claret in a surprisingly short time for this
summer there are more visitors than ever.

Miss MacKay and my brother were married on June 1st, and
are spending the summer here, Will and his bride as visitors in the
MacKay's house. Mr. MacKay is absent on the Plains but the two
sons are home for the holidays from St. John's College. I get up
picnics when I can, but being the person in charge I can seldom
join them myself. At times when no one is wanting me, I go for a
ride on horseback with Harriet, my sister-in-law, and Miss
MacKay.

Mr. Matheson and I have quarters together and work in the
office until the accounts and letters are all done. Writing is a

labour for me now, for since I was snow-blind I cannot see to read or write without holding my eyes close to the book or paper. On the whole I do not see at all distinctly.

My second summer at Fort Ellice has passed so quickly that I can hardly tell what sort of a season we have had, for I have been in the office a great deal and have been sick again much of the time. Whenever I was better I had plenty of work to do to make up for lost time.

With the exception of building some additional quarters for the men, my duties have been similar to those of the preceding year. I have just received orders to send someone to meet the Brigade from York at Fort Garry and I am reminded that we are getting into another autumn.

We are all very busy making our preparations for our departures to our winter quarters and it is with genuine regret that I bid my fellow officers farewell after enjoying their companionship during their stopovers with me. Willie and his bride have gone with the Carlton Brigade and Duncan Matheson, who has been with me all summer, will take his place at Egg Lake. The Swan River staff are from near home in Canada, or have friends there, so it is a great pleasure for us to meet.

Mr. MacKay has returned with his hunters from the Plains and once again the Indians are coming in for winter outfits. The Brigade with which I came here just three years ago has this September brought our new clerk, Mr. Andy, and together we work to assist in supplying the trade goods to hunters and trappers on their way to their winter camps.

Mr. J. C. Andy is not a stranger, as we met a little over a year ago when I went to Fort Garry with the Brigade. He had just arrived from Canada and though I came two years earlier I was still comparatively a recent arrival and we found we had plenty of things to talk about. He was kind in helping me copy ladings, etc., and we became great friends. He is a Canadian and a really nice fellow. He had a situation as correspondent in the Customs Department in Ottawa but foolishly gave it up to come out here. We often talk of our own bright, happy homes so far away. He is a

Catholic but a very liberal one who goes to the English Church and a' that. Little did I think, when working with him in Red River, that we would be fellow clerks together here. I expect to be at Fort Ellice again next summer and that he will then be my clerk, a very nice prospect indeed.

It is high time for me to set about assembling my own outfit for Riding Mountain to which I am again assigned for winter duty. This year Mr. MacKay has his new clerk to work in the office and I shall not be needed for the accounts here as last winter. My supplies are loaded on the carts and I must bid the MacKays and Andy *"au revoir"* and be off with my men to my lonely Post.

On arrival there I find much to do. The storehouses and winter quarters for myself and the men were built last spring but are in need of being made tight and warm before the cold weather is upon us. The Indians are coming in for their winter outfits and the greatest care must be taken in supplying their needs without allowing more credit than it is possible for each to repay by furs he traps during the winter, at the prices we anticipate paying for them.

Most of my own Indians being supplied, I have managed to return to Fort Ellice for a short time to assist Mr. MacKay with the Indians here and to pick up more supplies for Riding Mountain House, for there is every reason to expect a better trade than ever in the coming season. Andy and I are enjoying our evenings together by the fireside in the officers' quarters where occasionally Mr. MacKay drops in to see us or to ask us to spend the evening with his family at their hearthside.

Back at Riding Mountain House once more, it is to find that a freetrader has taken advantage of my absence to establish himself quite close to my Post. His stock-in-trade is mostly rum which, no doubt, he plans to trade to the Indians for the furs they are bringing to us in payment for the outfits obtained at my Post earlier this fall.

152

Always in this locality the Indians have caused us much trouble and now they will be more independent and unmanageable than ever. But after they have been trading with freemen for two years, or at the longest four, they come back to the Company and are the truest Indians we have. They then see that they are fools to think that the freemen pay them more for their fur because at times they give more for some skins. But they sell only liquor on which they make an exorbitant profit. Somehow or other I must make sure that our furs are not diverted to pay for this forbidden luxury.

Fortunately I have nothing much to do but drive or ride about and exercise the dogs and saddle horses, all the while visiting our Indians and working for good trapping, which is more and better furs. My place of abode is very comfortable, not only for myself but for the few visitors I enjoy.

One of these is none other than the freetrader who comes to see me once in a while. Formerly he was a clerk in the Hudson's Bay Company's employ at one hundred pounds per annum. When I came out he was in charge of Pembina but he left the service because he was not getting on fast enough. I am afraid he took a step down hill. He is now trading liquor to the Indians and half-starving part of the time. He seems pleased to accept my hospitality and, though still my opponent, we now live on very friendly terms.

Last winter I worked very hard to put down free trade and am now reaping the fruits of my labour. The Indians have learned that my neighbour, and at times my guest, pays them far less than I do for their mink. He gives half a pint of alcohol for a mink while I give a large Hudson's Bay blanket for two mink. The price of one pint of alcohol is one shilling in Red River while a blanket costs eleven shillings in London.

I have great fun with some of the old Indians when I get them telling yarns. They firmly believe that Queen Victoria selects for them, and personally supervises, the sending out of all the Company's goods. Nor do they doubt that all the shirts, trousers, capotes and other articles are made by her own hands. Many a rough blessing she gets for being a bad seamstress. Were she to know how bravely I fight her battles she would certainly raise me to the peerage. Failing this, I am going on a voyage of discovery one of these days to search for a North West Passage from here to Fort Ellice which will shorten the distance materially.

Other visions of personal glory include my friend, Archy McDonald, and my brother Willie, who have taken it into their heads that a great saving of trouble and expense in the transport of goods to the Saskatchewan and Northern Districts can be made by cutting a canal through to let the water of the Saskatchewan River flow into the Qu'Appelle, which would enable us to run steamers up to Carlton.

It would undoubtedly flood the whole Settlement. If I hear that they are going to carry their project into effect I shall give the inhabitants of Red River notice to build an Ark and I shall covenant as Noah II and take into my ark two buffalo, a Chief Factor and my interpreter, "Benjamin Joyful," two parsons and numerous other specimens of humanity and animals that it would be a pity to allow to become extinct!

Mr. Andy is with me tonight and thus also do we clerks spin our yarns to one another. He has brought in the Packet from Fort Ellice and his visit is a jolly occasion for both of us before he goes on to Fort Pelly with our letters. What a lucky thing to be *"un petit commis d'argent"* and to be able to go wherever one is asked. I now would give anything to be under another, and only have to do what I am told without any responsibility on my head, but alas! those happpy days are past. While Mr. Andy sleeps through the night I am writing the answers to the letters that I have just received in the mail he has brought.

One of these is from my sister at Rice Lake and was mailed on October 31st and today is December 9th. It is a pleasure to be able to write an answer to it at a time like this when I have hours at my disposal. In summer I am kept busy writing letters from Monday until Saturday and have little inclination or opportunity to write private ones, but as a rule in winter I have plenty of time.

A letter has come from Willie also. He has gone to the Saskat-

chewan District of which Christie is in charge. I am sorry that
he has left this one but, since he is married, it is better that he
should be where he has no relations. Had I been Willie I would have
gone to Cumberland under Hamilton. He is sick of Fort Pitt
already. Harriet gives me an awful description of the place, only
what I expected. He was in charge of a good Post here and now
he is only second in command at a miserable place, not half as
good as Riding Mountain. Egg Lake is just as good a place as this
and far easier to manage. Willie writes that he has a friend up
there, Mr. Watt, a Scotch cousin of ours, who is a really good
fellow.

My sister asks if I have learned to speak Indian or French. I do
understand a little of each but cannot speak them. Oh no, we never
speak French. The tongue is never heard. It is against the rules to
use the smallest foreign word. We have no French here, only
French halfbreeds, and they mix their language so much with
Cree that unless one understands it one cannot tell what they are
talking about.

I understand more Saulteaux than anything else. It is a beastly
jargon and not at all expressive. Blue, green and red are all the
same. A letter, a newspaper, a book and a debt are all the same,
and anything in the shape of a paper is a *"mus e nac kin."* A horse
is a big dog and a boat of any kind, from an inland boat that holds
a hundred pieces to a hide canoe, is a *"che man."* This makes it a
hard language to learn. Sioux, on the other hand, is easy to learn.
They are a far more intelligent race of people and learn our language quickly. But if one wants a Saulteaux to learn anything
one must cut it out in wood.

The Crees are a different set altogether, far braver and not so
hard to teach. Last summer, when MacKay was out on the plains
trading provisions in a large camp of four hundred tents of Crees
and halfbreeds, there were two parsons, one a priest and the other
a Church missionary. One day a Cree chief came to MacKay to sell
a cart which my *bourgeois* would not buy because, as he explained
when the chief asked him why he would not buy it: "It is too
old – it is rotten."

The following Sunday after service the Chief called a Council and asked both the Catholics and the Protestants to attend, which they did. The Chief addressed the assembly at some length. He said that the Catholics had one road or "track," as he described it, and the Protestants had another but his own track was the right track. It forked off between the two, quite a new road. Their religions were too old, in fact, they were "properly rotten." He said they had used their religions far longer than he had used his cart and still the *Ketch Ucte Koo*, meaning MacKay, would not buy his cart but would listen to their old preaching.

My letters from Canada tell me how great is the interest there in all I can write of this country and of those living in it. My news gives as much pleasure as I experience on receiving home news. I have had no mail from there for three or four months, but as none has come in from Pembina for some time perhaps my letters are there. When my family will get this one I do not know, as there is no mail running between here and the outside world, but if the Rebellion* is not put down before the Northern Express arrives the Company will certainly forward it to Fort William by dogs.

Anything I could tell my family about the great disturbance in the Settlement would be stale news by the time my letter arrives, for it will surely have appeared in the newspapers. I did not go down to Red River this winter when I had the chance, as I may have to go down again at the same date as I did this spring and for this reason I declined. I could have sent a letter down by the one who took my place but was not sure whether it was safe to do so. It is written to my mother and I am keeping it in my desk meantime.

The scenes of our everyday life would shock those at home and I do not care to describe them as they are not used to such things and may fancy them worse than they are though they used to make my blood run cold at first. The ladies at our Posts see so much of savage life that they are as brave as any of us for now I am used to all sorts of adventures. Last year I had strong opposition from

* The Riel Rebellion.

traders but this year I have overcome what little there was and have comparatively little to do but sit in my office and give orders knowing that everything will go on as it should.

Traders who have failed to persuade our Indians to give them furs in exchange for their liquor will make them drunk for the sole purpose of bothering us and will put them up to evil. Such is life in Hudson's Bay and at times it is not a pleasant life. It was two days before Christmas at Fort Ellice that our Indians obtained alcohol from a freetrader and one who was half-drunk took a knife to me.

A week later, on December 30th, it was a freetrader who wanted to use his knife to an Indian to make him pay a debt of twenty-six shillings. He wanted me to help him and when I refused he turned on me with abusive language, doing his utmost to rouse me to the point of striking him. Besides myself and the trader, there were in the Hall at the time, the interpreter and three Indians, two of which were partly drunk and were just burning to use their knives on the man attempting to provoke me into attacking him. It was well for him that I kept my temper for it was with difficulty that the interpreter kept the two Indians down, else it would have been a bloody affair.

To do the trader justice, he was sorry and ashamed of his conduct directly his anger cooled, for he came to beg my pardon with a full confession of his intention to make me strike him and then he would have stabbed me in the heart. He admitted that he would not be the first to begin for then I could have taken him to law.

It was shocking to listen to him telling in cold blood of this, knowing, as I do, that he is an educated man, a son of an old Company officer. He himself was a clerk, entering the service when I was at Fort Garry. I witnessed his engagement; it was the first time I signed my name to a public document after I entered the service. He was engaged at one hundred pounds a year as a trader for three years. Unfortunately he broke his contract and was dismissed. He is now selling liquor to my Indians despite my efforts to put a stop to this traffic and has taken advantage of our

157

holiday festivities to ply his unwanted trade. Yet I would never have suspected him of so bloody a design.

If further proof were needed the above incident has shown me that the Indians will stick to me to a man. I protected one of them and they are grateful for it. It is hard for those in Canada to imagine what confidence the Indians have in the Company. They are like so many children and the Company, their father. There are many, of course, who never trade a skin with us, and others who do us harm by stealing our horses and other things but some of our Indians, who trade their furs to freemen for liquor, see when it is too late that they have been fairly dealt with by us while they have been cheating us out of their debts. They still trust us, for if they want to cache their traps, or anything else, they would not think of leaving them with a freeman but come to us with their property to be taken care of for them.

I wonder what we shall all do if the Company dissolves. I fear there will be bloodshed before there is any established government if the French and English divide, but it is a far cry from the local conflict to the Mother Country of either people and I do not think France will step in. I shall have to turn farmer if I cannot get a government situation.

Sometimes I think I would go back to Canada when my first contract is out if I had a situation at home but I fear I would not like it nor could I work as I would have to in an office. Besides, I am better off here for if I get little, I require little, and never want for anything that money will buy. Want of society is the greatest deprivation of our lives, nor can I hope to go home to Canada soon for I am not entitled to a leave of absence. Even were I to get one it will be a long time before I shall have the money to spare.

Being in charge of a Post while I am at low wages has kept me from saving anything. I must send my mother fifteen or twenty pounds when it is safe to send letters through the office to Pembina, and that will be quite all I have in the Company's hands. Next year I get fifty pounds and after that seventy-five pounds for three years and then one hundred. I must then begin to save money. My sister and her husband used to say that I had a genius for saving money but if so I have got sadly over it.

Where I shall be next summer I do not know but hope to get out of making up Fort Ellice accounts by going down to Red River for carts, or by remaining here. Mr. Campbell goes home on furlough and McDonald is expected to take his place. Mr. MacKay has also applied for a change. I could get Qu'Appelle if I said the word.

All goes on quietly here. In the fall I used any spare time I had in training young horses. While running one which was still quite wild I suffered a fall resulting in a badly sprained arm. Though quite well now it is still rather weak. The snow and cold of winter require a carriole for travelling so that my arm should be as strong as ever by the time I can again enjoy horseback riding.

There are plenty of horses here being kept for District Transport Service. Twenty-five belong to my own Post and the others to Fort Ellice. The Company is very good in allowing us to keep horses at the guard gratis and I have two of my own, a mare and a colt. When I have about ten I shall sell them and go home if I can get three months leave. Mr. Campbell told me that if I liked to give my mare into the Company I could take twenty pounds but I would rather keep them as the colt is a mare and when she is three years old will have another. By the time I want to go home I shall have quite a band.

How I wish I could take my sister for a ride in my carriole and show her how comfortable it is and how soon we can do thirteen or fourteen miles. I often drive fifteen miles and back after tea and am home before gates are closed. MacKay and Andy wrote that they wanted to run their dogs against mine so I used to race my train here every day for a fortnight. I had great fun at Fort Ellice recently when they challenged me to a race for although mine had just come from a long trip I left them far behind.

I have four splendid black dogs in my train. They travel at the rate of eight miles an hour hauling me, and quicker if the weather is cold, and I like to drive them at full speed. I keep in all three trains, or twelve dogs, and get plenty of jackfish for their grub either by angling through the ice or buying them. For large fish that weigh from two to five pounds I pay twopence each or two shillings a dozen.

Not long ago I had a splendid dog poisoned. We are constantly getting them poisoned. We lost thirty this way last year which cost us from forty to one hundred shillings each. Perhaps someone in Canada knows what to use as an antidote. I use gunpowder and cut their ears and tail but unless applied immediately it is of no use. I would give five pounds for anything that would cure them if taken fairly soon after the poison. It seems a disgusting thing to eat a dead dog but I have eaten both dogs and wolves that have been poisoned with strychnine. We boil them well and never experience the least harm.

Little does anyone at home know what our life is. The bodily privations and hardship, which they picture as so many and so great, are by far the most trifling. I would not advise any young fellow with fair prospects to give up everything to enter the service but now that I am getting used to the life and unfit for any other I would not leave the Hudson's Bay Company. Were I to choose for myself at the age of my friend who wants to join the service I would rather be a carpenter, a blacksmith, or any respectable tradesman than a clerk, for unless a clerk is well educated he is in a false position which I often think is the case with myself. There are plenty of our servants whose education is far better than mine.

On the other hand, many who crowd our Forts are wretched beings who are difficult to raise in the slightest degree without their losing the little sense they have in their degraded state. Their children grow up like Indians, only far worse, endowed with every vice that flesh is heir to. They know not God nor fear not man.

It is a shame that the native missionaries have not been able to do more for them. One has been established at Fort Ellice for eight years and with a salary of one hundred and fifty pounds a year, but has only a house with one room and a workshop, which he uses for a schoolhouse, nor is there one child that can read or write after all that time. For seven years he has been relying on the Company and using their house, and still uses the Indian Hall, or mess room, to preach in.

We supply wood and candles as a matter of course and still the missionaries abuse the Company. It seems very wrong to combine Divine worship with eating, drinking and merrymaking, for which New Year's Day is always set aside here, all in the same room as Mas done at Fort Ellice two weeks ago. In the morning the Rev. George Bruce administered the Sacrament and preached in the Indian Hall. He then joined in a game of football in the Fort and is about the best player I have ever seen. The servants danced in the Hall where service had been held, and would have continued until midnight had not Père de Corby, the priest from Qu'Appelle arrived, when we sent them to dance in their own quarters. There are no less than two Church clergymen at Fort Ellice this winter and there is no Company officer so comfortable or so well-paid as are the clergy, for in addition to their salary they use their time to make money by trading.

The state of society is not select out here nor is it likely to improve while the Settlement is in its present disturbed state. As Governor Mactavish remarked to me: "Morality is at a low ebb." The sight of so much drunkenness and immorality is enough to blunt one's feelings, but still, in the Company's service our position holds us aloof from vulgarity. Self pride is the great requisite in anyone that comes out here, for there is no society to cry down what is done amiss and if an officer does not remember that he is a gentleman others are apt to forget it also.

In writing to my mother of my life here, in answer to her requests for information, I can picture her reading my letters and saying: "I too was buried in the woods far from society when first I came from home."

But always there were white people to talk to, although not her equals in many respects, while we may live in a crowded Fort and may not have one single soul among our servants with whom we have one feeling in common. Especially is this true of the numbers of temporary servants I engage for voyaging. I have five regular servants, a cook, a horse guard and a cattle-keeper, all of whom talk to me daily of the animals that make up our world. Sometimes they bring me news of the Settlement but any that we hear is apt to be dying of old age before I get it and I never know whether to believe it or not. Unless those in the outer world know ours they cannot possibly imagine how like a vegetable a person here can become.

When at Fort Ellice I spend many, many happy hours with Mr. MacKay's family, all of whom are pleasant and kind, as are the Campbells and the McDonalds at Forts Pelly and Qu'Appelle. All are my friends, but when we meet it is only for a few hours and we are so happy that it makes our usual dull, lonely, monotonous life far more unbearable than if we saw no one.

The first winter I was out here when at Fort Pelly there was Miss Stirling just out from home, Mrs. Campbell from Red River late in the fall, Mr. Campbell from York, Thompson Smith from the North and myself, all of us the best of friends. One wouldn't think we would ever be dull but before spring we had worn out every conversable subject and were sick of the sight of each other. Yet if one of us went away for a week, when we met again it was like meeting a long lost friend.

Mrs. MacKay is as kind as ever; indeed, they are all kind to me and I should be sorry to leave this District where I have such a comfortable home to visit. But what is home without a mother? What indeed? My home is everywhere that duty calls me, wherever I pitch my tent or make my bed in winter. All are alike to me. I have become such a wandering spirit that I am just as contented sleeping by a campfire without a tent as I should be in Canada. Indeed, I am more so for I doubt if I should be content to stay any time there unless I was travelling about, for after the first novelty wore off I would be discontented.

My life has many charms and the greatest of all is the uselessness of money. How thoroughly are my own sentiments expressed by Sir Thomas Pringle in his poem:

*Over the desert I love to ride*
*Far from the busy haunts of men*
*In the wild deer's and the buffalo's glen.*

I don't mean that I care for hunting, but merely that I am happier here than I would be where I could not live as a gentleman for the want of money.

---

## FOURTEEN

## *The Riel Rebellion, 1869–1870*

FROM time to time during the last months of 1869 the Indians have come into Riding Mountain Post with scraps of information regarding the trouble in Red River, but I do not hope to know the facts until I meet the Winter Packet at Fort Ellice in January.

It is the end of the second week in January and letters have just now reached me from Fort Garry, including two from my mother written on November 12th and December 1st and I must reply at once in answer to her request that I do so, in order that, if possible, I may allay her fears regarding my safety and that of my brother and his family.

There is little time for writing before I set out for Fort Ellice and I do not know of any immediate chance of sending this letter out, or the one in my desk. The same Packet has brought a letter from Hargrave and it appears that there is some risk in sending money out of the country. He tells me they are in a miserable state in Fort Garry, there being some sixty or seventy prisoners in the Fort. Donald A. Smith, the officer in charge of the Montreal Department, is now in the Red River Settlement acting as Governor in place of Governor Mactavish.

"Will the affairs of the Company suffer by the transfer of Rupert's Land to the Canadian Government?" asks my mother. Well, that is a difficult question. Had the latter managed better, all this disturbance would not have occurred and, once the government of this country rested on them, the Hudson's Bay Company undoubtedly would be in a better position to carry on their business than while responsible for the good government of the land. But now it is hard to say what may be the end of all this.

164

In the first place the Company are at a great expense until these rebels leave the Fort. Feeding two hundred men is rather a costly arrangement, and in the interior the Company's trade may suffer very much before troops can arrive from Canada, if they are sent in.

For instance, nearly all those engaged in the Rebellion are the crews of the Portage la Loche boats which are employed every spring to take in the outfit for the Mackenzie River District. Now, this brigade starts from Fort Garry on the fourth of June and unless these boats start at the usual time they cannot reach the Portage in time for the Mackenzie River men to get to Fort Simpson before the river freezes. Should this outfit fail to arrive it would leave hundreds of Company employees totally without the means of support, for without ammunition, nets, etc., people could not exist there.

Besides the white people, there are thousands of Indians depending upon those boats for the absolute necessaries for supporting life. This being the case, the authorities at Fort Garry have to use great tact and caution not to enrage the rebels against them, which is why they submit to these beggars living upon them. To take up arms would be to leave hundreds of us without a chance of our lives, for directly the halfbreeds were driven from Fort Garry they would fly to other and weaker posts.

From the papers that have just come in I see that those who write on the subject are totally ignorant of the real state of things. It is very easy for George Brown to sit in his office in Toronto and say the Company made no resistance and that their officers apparently think the situation a good joke. I am afraid that the Canadian Cabinet will have to swallow a good many rather indigestible jokes before they have settled everything. Had they appointed Governor Mactavish instead of McDougall nothing of this sort would have occurred. They are dealing with people whose characters and natures they do not understand. Had Governor Mactavish been in good health at the beginning of this outbreak I think it would not have gone so far. I hardly think the Canadian Government can break their bargain with the Hudson's Bay

Company. If they do they ought to pull down their flag in disgrace.

It does not do for those in Canada to believe all they hear. The very fact of no communication being allowed between this and the outer world is enough to show that no one in Canada knows the whole truth. We are, as is supposed, in a dangerous situation where resistance would be useless, but we must hope that as the Company has always dealt fairly and honourably, and governed these people justly and leniently, that they will do us no harm. Should we fall into their hands I don't know that the Hudson's Bay Indians are any better than the natives of New Zealand, but for our part, we have less to fear from them than from the half-breeds.

Those in Canada cannot imagine the confidence existing between us and our Indians. I, myself, have slept in my room at Fort Ellice with the door unlocked between me and the Indian Hall where there were thirty Sioux sleeping, all armed, and some of the very same that took part in the Minnesota massacre of 1862. One woman told us of her own horrible cruelty. They are as thick as blackbirds at Fort Ellice; there are seventy Sioux women cutting wood and dressing leather at that place to gain a livelihood. They are far more industrious than any other tribe of Indians that we have seen. The daily issue of rations is something awful: five bags of pemmican at one hundred pounds per bag, three bags of flour and four hundred pounds of dried meat daily.

The late troubles on the Plains lead me to think that the Plains Indians are well-disposed towards us. So far, they have driven the halfbreeds back and have allowed only the Company to trade. With regard to the Blackfeet I can say nothing, but so far they have done no harm to us, and they are now at war with the half-breeds at Edmonton, all of which will tell against the rebels and in our favour.

With regard to the Indians attacking the outposts for the sake of plunder for what is contained in the stores, this is not to be feared. The Company's policy has always been to teach the Indians to rely upon the Company for the means of living until they could trust with safety to their own resources, and it is wonderful what an interest they take in our welfare. This they show when the Brigade is late, or if any disaster happens to it or the outfit. They look forward to its safe arrival with as much anxiety as the gentleman in charge of the Post to which they belong. They depend upon freetraders to sell them liquor, but on the Company to sell them what will support life, for although they don't get all their ammunition directly from us, they get it from those we supply, and as the Company never keeps a year's stock in advance they would gain nothing by plunder.

Fort Pitt, where my brother and his wife are, is certainly a safer place than this, being far from the seat of war, while Qu'Appelle and Fort Ellice are in no immediate danger, but as to fortifications, that is all moonshine, for none of the Company's posts are fortified. Fort Pitt may have thirty or forty old Enfield rifles, but what good are arms and ammunition with nothing but wooden walls half a foot thick? They do well enough for the purpose for which they were built: to keep Indians from stealing carts, etc., or to keep them out when drunk, but farther than that they are of no use.

Were each Post as strongly fortified as Quebec, forty men could starve us out in two or three months at longest, and few Posts could stand for a month. We are in a country the produce of which is not sufficient to support what few people there are in it, without the greatest energy of men and of horses. We would starve in no time were we not able to send to the Plains for meat or to the lakes for fish. Since the Company established its Posts in the country there has not been a shot fired in defence of a Post. Churchill is the only strong place in the Department and it could not stand against a warship. There is no need to fear; we shall not have to resort to arms in our defence. The Company always have managed the Indians with kindness, and will be able to convince them that nothing wrong has been done to them. I would rather have to deal with a hundred Indians than a single halfbreed.

They are real cabbage heads and think that the Canadian

Government will be afraid to fight them. There is not one intelligent, right-thinking, well-educated man among the French half-breeds and it is my opinion that the leaders and chief agitators are, and will remain, in the background and unknown. They are making catspaws of a lot of ignorant animals whose minds don't carry them to anything beyond three pounds of pemmican a day which they are now getting free of expense to themselves at Fort Garry.

On arriving at Fort Ellice I find that this mail, which left the Settlement in November contains the first official news that the rebels under Louis Riel have blockaded the country and turned back the new Governor, William McDougall, near the boundary line. They have taken possession of Fort Garry with all the Company's property, including fur returns from Mackenzie, Athabasca, and Peace River Districts that arrived too late for the ship sailing from Hudson's Bay last year and were sent in from Norway House to be exported this spring by way of the United States.

As the weeks pass following my return to Riding Mountain more news is received. A messenger has just arrived from Mr. MacKay with word that Mr. Campbell has written to him advising him to send me to Fort Pelly, for what purpose is not revealed but I must set out immediately. I shall leave here early tomorrow morning, February 4th.

The trail was well broken and the travelling good, which has enabled me to be this evening in Fort Ellice with the MacKays. Here I learn that a Provisional Government has been formed with Louis Riel at its head. Some Canadians have resisted and have been taken prisoners by the rebel leader.

A few days later I am with the Campbells at Fort Pelly. The Chief Factor has received copies of the speeches made by Commissioner Donald A. Smith to the distraught populace in the courtyard of

Fort Garry on January the 19th and 20th. These I read and re-read by the flickering light of an oil lamp while waiting for instructions. The words, spoken less than a month ago and several hundred miles away, are undoubtedly those of a great man. Hitherto he has been known to me as a Company's officer stationed for twenty-four years at the small trading post of Rigolet on the coast of Labrador where there is only one mail a year. In this remote spot he proved his faithfulness in whatever was trusted to his charge before he was transferred to Montreal to be the head of that Department.

It seems a wise choice that this esteemed officer and Chief Factor of the Company should be appointed by the Canadian Government at Ottawa to preside over this unnecessarily turbulent transition of Rupert's Land from the Company which has ruled it for two hundred years to the jurisdiction of the Dominion of Canada, not yet three years old. Confederation took place the first summer I was in Swan River District and meagre communications still exist between the distant Capital and Red River, with the result that the Settlement has not been appraised of the negotiations between the British and Dominion governments in regard to the purchase of the Hudson's Bay Company's rights in the land.

The Governor of Rupert's Land has sent Mr. Campbell a despatch which he read to me. The Chief Factor then told me what he wanted me to do: I must go to Fort Garry and make sure, if it is at all possible, that his reply reaches the hands of Governor Mactavish. Furthermore, I must make every effort to smuggle from the Fort the mail containing a second despatch from the Governor in answer to the one I am to take to him.

Mr. Campbell tells me that Riel has arrested leading men of the Settlement, enraged because Commissioner Smith refused to adopt his Bill of Rights and because he was outvoted in an attempt to pass a Resolution against the transfer of Rupert's Land.

It will require all the resourcefulness of which I am capable to deliver the package of despatches entrusted to me, for Riel and his followers are known to be guarding jealously the roads to and from the Fort in their hands and the centre of their insurrection.

With my man, dog teams and carriole I set out on my four hundred mile journey. No time was lost in reaching Fort Ellice where all is ready for me to continue on my way, but with added responsibilities. Mr. MacKay's sons, George and Henry, are students at St. John's College and their father is apprehensive that a civil war may develop.

He has instructed me to bring them back with me to this Post and has provided me with two extra trains of dogs and carrioles for the boys, but he has left it to me to choose the man I believe to be most suitable for fast travelling and most reliable in an emergency. I have no hesitation in saying I want to take Louis Vandall, the little halfbreed who has endured many hours of rapid progress with me from place to place, going long without sleep at times. Moreover, his loyalty is beyond question though he is of the same mixed blood as the rebels we must elude.

The first night from Fort Ellice is spent at Riding Mountain where I place the interpreter in charge during my continued absence. Two more days of rapid travel have brought us to Westbourne Mission, twelve miles from Portage la Prairie and situated on the White Mud River near the northern end of the overland portage from the Assiniboine River to Lake Manitoba. At the Mission I find Mr. John Norquay who has just arrived from the Settlement with the shocking news of the execution of Thomas Scott by Riel's order. In common with all the leading citizens of the outraged community Mr. Norquay's liberty is endangered, and he begs me not to attempt to enter the Fort.

In this place of refuge my fellow guest tells me of Major Boulton's expedition from the Portage to free the English-speaking prisoners and of Riel's treacherous imprisonment of him and fifty of his followers, though the rebel ruler, alarmed by their armed approach near to the Fort, had granted the object of their march.

Mr. Norquay gives a vivid account of the threatened execution of Major Boulton by Riel who accused him of being responsible for the first bloodshed because, while his army was encamped in the Kildonan Church, John Sutherland was accidentally shot by a half-witted youth, Parisien, who also died of wounds. Only on the earnest plea of Sutherland's mother was Boulton's life spared, but on March 4th young Scott, an Orangeman from Ontario, was shot by Riel's order.

"You will most certainly be taken prisoner unless you abandon all thoughts of visiting Governor Mactavish in the Fort," insists my friend and refugee. But I am determined to carry out the mission entrusted to me by my two superior officers and tomorrow I shall proceed to Portage la Prairie, but with the greatest caution shall I go on from there.

When I arrived next morning it was to find that the French are in possession of all the lower Posts and it would be foolish to go further, even were I able to travel. For again I have become snow-blind from the glare of the lengthening days of bright spring sunshine in early March and I cannot see a thing.

We rested that day at Portage la Prairie and when twilight began to settle over the prairie, I gave Louis Vandall two carrioles and as many trains of dogs, and bade him go with all possible care and speed to St. John's on the Red River two miles below Fort Garry. A letter which I had just written to the Bishop of Rupert's Land, (who is also headmaster of St. John's College) I added to the Chief Factor's despatches and thrust the precious package into the hands of the little French driver, urging him to make the journey each way under cover of night.

"Be sure to leave tomorrow evening in time to be back here before daylight," I warned.

In my letter to the Bishop I requested that he try to get the despatches to Governor Mactavish in Fort Garry and a return Package out and also that he keep Louis at the College until nightfall when, under cover of darkness, he be sent to me with Mr. MacKay's sons.

While two nights and a day of rest were restoring my eyesight, my faithful courier travelled steadily and rapidly to reach St. John's before daylight, where he rested throughout the day in the sanctity of Bishop Machray's shelter, which he left when it was dark enough to protect him and the boys from detection by the enemy, stationed at posts near their route. He brought his charges safely through the sixty-five miles of territory in the hands of the insurgents and drove his tired trains of dogs in here before daylight.

But we dare not stop to rest, for Riel's soldiers have taken the Post next to this which is Poplar Point and are expected here soon. We must keep right on travelling, for there is no time to lose.

It was well that we did, for I have learned that Riel's men took Portage la Prairie before we were out of sight on the prairie. Again we rested at Westbourne, but only for a few hours before continuing on our way, refreshed with food and rest. We found the trail unusually smooth and made fast time, arriving home at my own Post of Riding Mountain on the second morning after we left the Portage. By evening of the same day we were at Fort Ellice.

Mr. MacKay tells me that he will send Mr. Andy to take my place at Riding Mountain so that I may go on to Fort Pelly with the mail. This is now safely in the hands of my *bourgeois* and his two sons, thanks to the faithful man of small stature but amazing endurance whose services were indispensable to the success of our mission. Louis Vandall is worn out with long hours of hard travel and lack of sleep and will take his well-earned rest while I go on with another driver and fresh dogs.

On the third day from Fort Ellice I was at Fort Pelly and delivered to Mr. Campbell the despatch from Governor Mactavish. This was official confirmation of the news I heard from John Norquay and subsequently, including the climax in the shooting of Scott. The Chief Factor has taken a serious view of our situation in this District should the Rebellion spread inland.

Mr. Campbell has decided to send the winter's furs out by way of the United States to avoid their falling into the hands of Riel's men as would most certainly happen if they were sent down the river in the usual way. He is arranging for his family and the officers of this post to accompany this brigade to the safety of American soil. It will take an overland route to Georgetown in Minnesota from where the travellers will follow the old cart trail to St. Paul.

The senior clerk, Mr. Thompson Smith, has begged Mr. Campbell to fortify this Post, but Mr. Campbell insists that no time or energy be spared from making up the fur packs in order to have them ready some weeks earlier than usual.

Throughout the first week of April we work with haste while we watch the weather and wonder how long it may be before the rebels extend their seizures of the Company's Posts to include our own. When we last heard Fort Ellice and Fort Qu'Appelle were alright but hourly expected to be taken. Some of our Posts have already been pillaged and all will go soon. We have heard nothing from Saskatchewan nor have we received any Packet from there, by which we fear that all our Posts there have been taken long ago.

Now it is the evening of the 9th of April, 1870 and I am writing in great haste, for Mrs. Campbell and children are leaving for Canada with the Brigade that is going out in charge of Mr. Smith and I am most anxious to send with them letters that they will post for me to my family. Mr. Campbell has offered me the opportunity of accompanying them but it does not seem right for me to leave him to return to Fort Pelly alone after seeing the Brigade set off from Fort Ellice, that is, without a white officer to assist him.

For the past fortnight I have been waiting to accompany the Brigade as far as Fort Ellice and it is possible that I may go out with them on service. In any event I shall have letters written tonight and if I should go with the others to the United States I shall write again from there.

For the past year I have been much concerned regarding my mother's health, which is far from good, and have hoped that someone from here might see her and let me know if her health is improved or otherwise. Last summer Mr. Grahame very kindly took parcels to her from me but I was very sorry that he was not able to see her. I accompanied him part of the way to the Settlement as he was returning to Canada and found him to be a very pleasant companion as well as a very clever man.

From now on I shall send my mother from twenty-five to thirty pounds each year in order that there may be no necessity for her to continue writing for the press, if Willie does the same. In January I sent her a draft on Montreal enclosed in a letter to Mr. Campbell with the request that he sign it for me, though I made it payable by the Gentleman in Charge of the Office so that his absence, or Mr. Smith's, would make no difference. "There is many a slip 'twixt the cup and the lip," and I made sure of the enclosure, at the same time promising that I would send the same sum next outfit, perhaps early in the summer, so that the two hundred dollars will be something worth investing.

Mrs. Campbell intends to spend some time in Canada and I am most anxious that my mother should meet her and show her every kindness, giving her a letter of introduction to anyone who will make her visit as pleasant as possible. My family cannot do enough to repay Mrs. Campbell for all the kindness I have received from her and Mr. Campbell. But I do not know if my mother will be at home and well enough to receive a visitor or if able to meet Mrs. Campbell in Toronto or in Brockville. Nor do I like to ask either to go too far out of her way for I do not know where my mother may spend the summer.

Therefore I have written to her asking her to write to Mrs. Campbell at the latter's address which is Ridgetown, Ontario, in care of Duncan McKinley, Esq., and have asked Mrs. Campbell to write from St. Paul to my mother who will be able to send replies to both of us in care of Mr. Kittson of the Hudson's Bay Company office in that city. He will not forward letters to me if there is any danger of them being opened. I am in a great hurry but must send my mother a draft on the Hudson's Bay Company for one hundred dollars, which can be burned if the one sent previously has reached her. Our prospects for the future look black indeed. I hope my mother will write to me in answer to my question as to what chance I would have of getting a situation at home.

## FIFTEEN

---

## *The Furs Go Overland*

It was Saturday evening of April the 9th when I hurriedly wrote letters to send with Mrs. Campbell and Mr. Smith on their trip across the Plains, but more news and furs came in to change plans. It was Wednesday morning, April 13th, when I set out with Mr. and Mrs. Campbell and their two children. We headed south with our Red River carts piled high with the furs from Fort Pelly and its outposts in the north of the Swan River District. On the sixth day we arrived at Fort Ellice. Our Chief Factor's younger son, Glenlyon, rode his own pony much of the way while Elleonora, a child of four years and a general favourite, rode with her mother, Mrs. Campbell, who has her own covered wagon. The little girl, known to us as "Queenie," has many questions to ask as to where we are going and why, and why we cannot go to Red River, to all of which we assure her that Riel may be ruler of that place but the Queen of the North is herself.

With Mrs. Campbell are her maid and old Bonhomme Pluff, the cook, who has been in her service in the north for the past ten years, and an employee of the Company for altogether forty years. Four officers have come this far: the Chief Factor; Thompson Smith, who is a senior clerk returning to England; McKinley, a young Scot and Junior Clerk; and myself.

Mr. Campbell is holding council with Mr. MacKay concerning arrangements for the Brigade from here. Neither officer will accompany us but both are giving the greatest care to the supervision of all that concerns our safety. To my surprise I was summoned to their meeting and asked if I would undertake the charge of the Brigade as far as Georgetown. On inquiring as to why Mr. Smith was not going I was informed that he would be accompanying the expedition. The Senior Clerk has been the accountant in charge at Fort Pelly when the Chief Factor is absent, for as long as I have been in the service, and I voiced my misgiving that he might on occasion dispute my authority, though it has been assumed that the many hundreds of miles I have travelled with our men, carts and horses have given me the understanding of how a Brigade moves that comes only from experience.

Lest any friction arise concerning the responsibility for the expedition and bring disaster upon us, Mr. Campbell sent for Mr. Smith and explained to him that, in view of the present exigency, seniority would be disregarded temporarily and a junior clerk would be given sole authority over the Brigade. The senior clerk was told he might travel with us as a passenger if he would agree to be subject to my orders. In this he willingly acquiesced and assured all present that he quite understood the situation.

Since the above discussion took place I have received a letter which has just come in from John Dougall MacKay, in charge of Portage la Prairie and my host while there in March. He tells me that our train was still in sight when Riel's men took his Post.

A guide who has been retained at Fort Ellice for many years and who has served us well was summoned to our council.

"Can you guide Mr. Traill and his party to Georgetown with impunity?" Mr. Campbell asked him.

"I don't know that other fellow," he replied, "but I will go anywhere with Mr. Traill if I may have Little Bishon to ride." Little Bishon is the famous buffalo-runner mentioned previously.

However, on further questioning he acknowledged that he does not know the country south of the Mouse, or Souris River. Mr. MacKay then came to the rescue with the information that there is at this Fort a Chippewa Indian from Red Lake in Minnesota who knows the whole country between here and his native haunts. He has been known to us as The Cannibal since an unfortunate episode in his life a few years ago.

The snow was very deep when he was marooned in the hills with his wife and child. To avoid starvation they ate their horse and dogs. The Cannibal was the fortunate possessor of an ancient mother-in-law whose usefulness as a beast of burden, hewer of wood and drawer of water was at an end. When no food remained they ate the old girl, whereby they barely managed to reach Fort Ellice in an extremely emaciated condition. The Indians have a deep aversion to cannibalism. Consequently, "the Big Goose," or "Mis Kuk," finds that his social standing has been ruined beyond repair.

When Mr. MacKay asked him to act as our guide to George-town he was eager to seize the opportunity to return to his native jungle, requesting no other payment than a saddle horse, and a cart and horse for his family with food to be supplied for all throughout the journey, provided that when we no longer needed him on the forthcoming trip he be allowed to retain the cart and horse as his private property. This was readily agreed to and Mr. MacKay has assured me that my guide will prove reliable.

This I well believe for I have travelled with him several times. Once we ran out of food and for two days we fasted until he shot a loon which we boiled. A loon cannot be recommended as a game bird for the longer it is boiled the tougher and blacker it becomes. While we were struggling to allay the pangs of hunger with such as it was, I could not resist the temptation to ask how it compared with his mother-in-law.

"*Tapis skouch*," dolefully he mumbled, meaning "much the same," and if his taste for delicacies is reliable I can vouch for both means of subsistence being equally displeasing, judging by this unpleasant experience with the loon.

The furs from Riding Mountain House and those taken in so far at Fort Ellice are to be included in our Brigade. Mr. MacKay has instructed me to choose the men I want to take with me and the saddle horses for them and the two clerks, in addition to two horses for each cart in order that we may travel with all speed. It did not take long for me to select the men I know are best suited for the task in hand, and with their help the best animals have been brought in from the guard.

177

"How soon can you be ready to start?" asked Mr. MacKay.

"Tomorrow morning," I replied, without hesitation, for I am anxious to be off without further delay and intend to work through the night if necessary so morning will find me ready to depart. Well aware of our danger, should Riel hear of our movements, I am convinced that our safety lies in reaching the United States before he can send his men out to confiscate our furs and possibly take us all prisoners. While Mr. MacKay has supervised the final packing and loading of the furs I have made sure that we take with us enough food and necessities for at least two weeks.

It is evening of Sunday, April 24th, 1870, the first Sabbath after Easter Sunday, which was spent on the trail from Fort Pelly.

More than two weeks have come and gone since I put down my pen after writing the above. It was not yet light on the morning of April 25th when the Chief Factor viewed our assembled train of twenty-five loaded carts, a horse in the shafts of each and as many more carters for their relief, our guide, drivers and passengers in covered wagons and on saddle horses.

He bade us God-speed and we drew out along the trail on the west side of the Assiniboine River as the sky on our left grew light where it touched the prairie's rim. Big Goose was well out in front, soon breaking into the easy lope of the Indians' horses until rider and mount were small figures in the distance.

When we caught up to our guide at noon, he had made camp ready with wood and water for our mid-day meal and rest. In this he never failed, noon and evening, throughout the days he was with us. Fresh horses were hitched to the carts in the afternoon and we travelled as fast as the soggy trail and unsettled weather would permit. We followed the Assiniboine River southward until it turned toward the east when we left it to continue south-east overland to the banks of the Souris River, crossing it where it bends in a sharp angle from the direction of our route to flow north-east to join the Assiniboine. The terrain became more and more rolling until we were threading our way between water-filled hollows and marshy land.

The mists and rains that shrouded our cavalcade southeast of the Souris protected us from view and another day of travelling would see us safely across the Border. There seemed to be less chance of encountering Riel's men this far south and we believed the worst danger to lie behind us. It was our thirteenth day on the trail from Fort Ellice, which in another month or two will be drier, thereby permitting much faster travel.

It was past mid-afternoon when Big Goose rode back to tell me that he had come to a fresh trail made by iron-shod hooves crossing the way we must go. The prints of several horses clearly showed them to be on their way to the West, but as far as eye could see no horseman was in sight. We did not doubt that the horseshoes were fashioned in the forges of Fort Garry and that these men expected to pick up our trail in the belief that our route would be west of the Turtle Mountains.

We were then well to the east of the hills only dimly visible in the coming shower, when we quickened our pace, holding our course, until our broader trail crossed that of the men we believed to have been sent out from Portage la Prairie to intercept us. For two hours more we pressed on, before coming to what appeared an old river course, now dry and offering protection from view. Rain fell gently, mingled with the wisps of smoke rising from the small fires that cooked our evening meal, while our Indian drivers took turns as guards at a distance, posting themselves where the inherent training of their race would detect the earliest sight or sound of an approaching foe. For it was only the matter of a little time until the disappointed guards would turn back and find our trail, knowing that if they followed it they could overtake us unless we had reached American soil.

Big Goose had informed me that if we took to the road again after supper we could cross the International Boundary and camp in Dakota on Cart Creek by midnight.

When we halted our train I at once rode up to Mrs. Campbell's covered wagon with word of the decision to go on again after a brief stop, requesting her not to unpack for the night but to have her cook prepare a meal, after which we would go forward by moonlight. It had been a long day when even her spring wagon could not save her from the jolts of a rough trail. I was fully aware of her fatigue and though prepared to explain as best I could, I was grateful for her cheerful acceptance of the situation without question, and for her indomitable spirit in the face of what we both knew to be unavoidable.

All my time could be devoted to the general supervision of the men's supper and the care and changing of horses until in a short time we were again under way for the third time that day. We set as fast a pace as seemed wise, stopping once to change the cart horses, which were showing the strain of drawing the heavily laden carts many miles. At last our faithful guide rode back and informed me that we had "crossed the line." We were soon encamped by the stream for what remained of the night.

On Monday we continued travelling towards Georgetown making good progress on firmer, drier ground. A few days later Big Goose came to me at noon, with the interpreter to help in what promised to be a consultation of some importance. The Chipewyan words were translated to me:

"If we go on in the same direction we are now going we shall come to Georgetown in two days, but if we turn from the sun we can camp tonight on the banks of the Red River when the sun goes down."

"We shall turn from the sun," I replied.

Sure enough, as the sun was sinking behind us in the west we crossed the old cart trail between St. Paul and Fort Garry, by which I had ridden northward four years ago. Little did I think then that I would return under the adventurous circumstances of the present.

It was the evening of May 11th when we stopped for the night on the banks of the Red River twelve miles above, or south of where the Red Lake River flows into it from the east. For the last two days the mosquitoes had been increasingly bothersome. Preparations for supper and a night's rest were going forward when I saw in the distance to the south a cart and driver coming towards us, the first living soul we had encountered since leaving Fort Ellice.

This was the mail-carrier on his weekly trip from Fort Abercrombie to Pembina under his contract with the United States government to deliver mail. His arrival just then was most fortunate, affording me the opportunity to report what furs and horses we had brought into the United States from Rupert's Land. I gave him a pound sterling to compensate him for waiting an hour or two while I made out an invoice for him to give to the American Customs Officer at Pembina, with an accompanying letter saying that I would unload the cargo at Georgetown for his inspection.

By noon next day we were at Frog Point where we camped for the mid-day rest and meal before continuing south along the river trail as far as Goose River. The stream was in flood and it was raining that afternoon when we made our camp and took our dinner on its banks when carts and passengers were safely over, though we had come only twelve miles from Frog Point.

We took to the trail next morning in the belief that evening would find us at Georgetown. There was the usual stop at noon but when the time passed and I did not see the men moving to hitch up the horses I went to see what was causing the delay, and was informed by one of the drivers that Mr. Thompson Smith had told them that he wanted the Fort Pelly carts separated from the rest. To this I replied that they were to pay no attention to Mr. Smith, but that they must see to it that we were opposite Georgetown that same night.

We made our last camp opposite the mouth of the Buffalo and the Company's Post. During the evening Mr. Smith came to me and asked for the bill of lading of the carts and the invoice of their contents. I demanded of him what he meant by this, whereupon he explained that he intended to assume charge of the furs and wanted the packing account in order to send it to London.

"You will do nothing of the kind," I said, "for if Mrs. Campbell is ready on Monday I shall send all of our party up to Fort Abercrombie excepting Mr. McKinley, who will stay with me. If you are prepared to accompany them I will furnish you with a saddle horse; otherwise you may stop here as my guest."

It would not surprise me to learn that Mrs. Campbell gave him a little advice the same evening for without further ado he was ready early on Monday morning to start with the others.

Our guide, having seen us safely to the appointed destination, took his departure for Red Lake with his wife and child, seated in his well-earned cart drawn by the horse which is now his property.

With much regret I bade farewell to Mrs. Campbell and the children who took the stage from Fort Abercrombie to St. Cloud from where they will travel by railway to St. Paul and Montreal to embark from there for Scotland. We hope there will be time for visiting in Canada, especially with my own family there. It would be a great pleasure for me to take Mrs. Campbell to Lakefield and Rice Lake to introduce her to my mother and sisters but I must trust to letters for this.

Now that I have unloaded the cargo there is little for me to do but wait in camp for orders from Fort Garry. We have heard that the steamer "International" will arrive before long from there and also that Mr. McDonald is on his way here from Qu'Appelle. The Collector of Customs, in accepting my invoice, was very nice about it and wrote me to go ahead to St. Paul if I liked. Later I received a letter from him in which he has promised to comply with my request that an Inspector be sent up and we are expecting him on the first boat coming up from Pembina.

A week after we arrived Mr. McDonald came into camp with his train, which he had brought from Qu'Appelle by a more western route than ours. He passed to the west of the Turtle Mountains and was equally fortunate in eluding Riel's men for, starting later with farther to go, his train did not come into sight until after the disappointed enemy had turned back, thereby failing to capture either of us. As my Senior Officer, Mr. McDonald has assumed charge of both outfits and the responsibilities that at times have weighed heavily on my shoulders for well-nigh a month of travelling and camping since we left Fort Ellice.

We had not long to wait before the "International" puffed its way up the Red River on what may be the most eventful trip in the lifetime of the inland steamer, for among its passengers was the last of the Governors of Rupert's Land, William Mactavish, now on his way to England.

When I went on board and called upon him he received me with the kindness and courtesy so often extended to those in the Company's service, though it was apparent that he was suffering much from illness. He too, I believe, felt that it was the last occasion on which we might meet and asked me if I would like to go to Canada to see my mother.

"You can come with me and the Company will pay your expenses while Mr. McDonald and William Clarke take your train through to St. Paul," he added after a moment's reflection on seeing my hesitation. The prospect was most attractive but a matter for serious consideration on my part.

Mr. Campbell is expecting me to return to Swan River and I would prefer to see him before going on leave and there will be expenses other than what can be charged to the Company. If I go home now the question of my leaving the service will be sure to arise and I would rather stay here until I know how things are to be settled and under what circumstances the fur trade will be carried on. I am determined to see the present situation through. And so I thanked him warmly and offered my explanation.

"I have come across the line with all this property and without reporting at Pembina, and have been awaiting the arrival of an Inspector from there whom the Collector of Customs has promised to send by this boat to obtain my formal entry."

This is only another instance of the greatness of the retiring Governor of Rupert's Land and it is a great pity that in taking over the administration of the vast area entrusted to his care the Canadian Government has chosen to ignore him and all the valuable information and advice he so willingly would have given. There is a possibility that he may not leave St. Paul directly and that I may reach that city before he departs, in which case I may be able to reconsider his kind offer.

The Inspector has arrived by the same boat and has treated me very courteously instead of considering me a smuggler. He has looked through the furs which I unloaded from the carts; there were also those brought by Mr. McDonald for him to inspect. Mr. William Clarke came up in charge of the furs that were loaded at Fort Garry.

These formed the major part of the cargo, two hundred and forty seven packs in all, being the furs that Riel confiscated on November 10th when he took possession of Fort Garry and which he has released on payment by the Company of some eight thousand pounds in war supplies and provisions for his army. Mr. Clarke has joined me in camp and the "International" has returned to the north.

# SIXTEEN

## *A Trip to St. Paul*

ALL the furs that have come up on the "International" must be loaded on carts for the journey to St. Cloud and as Mr. Clarke is also my senior I am practically out of a job while the work of assembling more carts and men is being completed.

The Northern Pacific Railway is being constructed between the Great Lakes and the Red River and will, it is hoped, reach Pembina next year. At present the end of the line is on this side of the Mississippi from where a party of their engineers has come to visit us. From them we have heard that there is a band of elk some twenty miles to the south and across the Buffalo River.

Mr. Clarke was greatly interested from hearing me tell of hunting them in the Riding Mountains with Thomas Spence who is now with us. It was largely due to his skill as a hunter that we had obtained enough elk to prevent our running out of food at our Post there, and having to close it before the spring trade was over as in previous years. Clarke became most anxious to go out on an elk hunt though there is no immediate necessity to get any for food, but having been largely responsible for arousing his desire I felt I should try to satisfy it.

He was extremely pleased when I suggested taking Spence and a cart driver, with four saddle horses and four of the best buffalo-runners which I had brought from Fort Pelly, and going after the elk. Young McKinley came with us riding one of the runners, carefully selected from among the horses I knew so well, in the hope that each rider might have the animal best suited to him.

However, Clarke was not satisfied with the one I chose for him although I knew it to be the best in the band and would have kept it for myself had I not wished him to have our fastest runner. He preferred the one I was going to ride which I gave him, though I knew it does not possess the staying qualities for a long hunt. From his knowledge of hunting buffalo, Clarke wanted the swiftest horse that could keep up to these long-winded, slow-to-start animals for thirty minutes. Even the best runner cannot stay with buffalo at top speed for more than fifty minutes but with elk it is different, for they can outrun the fastest horse for eight to ten miles when they give out. They then make for the nearest bluff, or any shelter, and throw themselves down trying to hide like an ostrich hiding his head in the sand.

It was afternoon when we started for that part of the country where the elk had been seen, with the intention of making our camp in the vicinity and going out on a hunt next day. When about fifteen miles from Georgetown we stopped for the night. Breakfast was over when Spence came to me.

"We cannot hunt today," he said.

"And why not?" I asked.

"Today is Sunday" was the reply I knew, on reflection, to be right. I thought it was Saturday or I would not have set out until Monday, well knowing the halfbreeds' strict religious belief in never running buffalo on the Sabbath. Though this may be partly superstition, years ago a hunter was killed by his gun bursting when he was running buffalo on Sunday.

Wishing to respect Spence's religious scruples I reassured him, "We will move on a few miles and if we sight the band of elk we will go into camp and run them next day."

We broke camp and had not gone more than a few yards with Spence well in the lead when suddenly he galloped down the nearest ridge and back to his running horse, hastily changed his saddle to it and brought our runners up to us.

"Quick" he said, "Change saddles. I go after elk."

He had forgotten his resolution not to break the Sabbath. The sight of those elk was too strong a temptation with visions of fresh meat after living for months on pemmican and little else. Leaving the cart driver to follow our trail with the camp outfit and spare horses, we all went after the elk. We rode at a slow gallop for about an hour when we saw that the elk were getting winded and making for a bluff. Clarke's horse was also tiring noticeably which made me insist that we change saddles, and I gave him my horse saying to him that I did not care about killing an elk and would ride slowly while he followed Spence.

By the time I caught up with them they had overtaken the band, Clarke and Spence each killing two, while McKinley had shot one. This made me want to get one for myself after riding ten miles and, leaving the others to take care of the meat, I pursued the lagging quarry. It was not long before I came upon one and shot it, but only took the tongue which I tied to my saddle.

To rest my horse and cool it by degrees I walked it slowly a little further before returning to where I supposed my elk lay. To my amazement it jumped up and ran off.

"Well," I thought, "I have your tongue, which is all I want."

To my great surprise a little further on I came on my dead elk. I was now in a strange country at some distance from camp with a very tired horse. On carefully surveying my surroundings I saw a spiral of smoke some miles away which I took to be from our camp but on going towards it I realized after a few miles that I was heading in the wrong direction.

By this time it was getting dark and there was no fuel with which to cook the tongue. Though very hungry I could not eat it raw. I was able to tether my horse and unsaddling it I lay down for what sleep I might get. Altogether it was a most uncomfortable night and as I lay awake throughout I reflected at length upon Spence's objection to hunting on Sunday, concluding that it was well-founded and that I was suffering a just and well-deserved punishment for my transgression. Henceforth I shall hunt on the other days of the week only.

At daybreak I followed my trail, backtracking until I located the Buffalo River and followed its waters flowing down to Georgetown. At three o'clock that afternoon I arrived to find that Clarke had sent an Indian out to look for me. He, too, followed my tracks which brought him to the elk I had left, minus the tongue. This he brought into camp early the same evening.

Before long the combined cargoes of the Swan River Districts with what other furs had arrived or collected at Fort Garry, all duly itemized and recorded in the books of the Customs Officials, were loaded in carts and our train moved out from camp towards St. Cloud. Little more than a passenger in this long train, I enjoyed the easiest time I have had for years.

My attention was given to looking after Mrs. McDonald and the children, sometimes driving her wagon and at others playing with the kiddies, but more often riding ahead or afield to shoot game for our provisions. We travelled through the same country, but by a more northern route than the one by which I came with Mr. Bannatyne almost four years ago, and again for a time I revelled in a carefree life in an enchanted land until we came into camp at St. Cloud on the banks of the Mississippi where it is joined by the Sauk River.

Here is the end of railway transportation from St. Paul and here is where our entire cargo has to be unloaded from the carts and into the cars for shipment to the city. My work began again in earnest, setting up camp for our men, whose numbers have been increased considerably by the amalgamation at Georgetown. The same train which took our freight had as passengers Mr. McDonald and his family, accompanied by Mr. Clarke.

This has left me again in charge of our camp, now a much larger one in an unfamiliar setting. My instructions are to establish order and when all necessary arrangements have been completed, to proceed to St. Paul. One of my first duties was to pay the men and in so doing I ran short of money. St. Cloud has grown much larger than when I was here four years ago and is now a very nice thriving town. I went to one of the leading firms which without hesitation advanced me five hundred dollars so there is no doubt that the Company's credit is as good as ever.

It is a few days later and I find myself once again in St. Paul where Clarke and I are thoroughly enjoying this lively city after years of comparative isolation. We are staying at the Merchant's Hotel which as usual at this time of year is alive with Red River freighters and Hudson's Bay Company's officers. Old friends of both sides of the border meet here on their travels and the old families of St. Paul are as hospitable as ever.

My first duty was to report to Mr. Kittson who did not recognize me at first. Not only have I grown to full stature of over six feet but in travelling almost continuously since the beginning of February I have become very sunburned and must have presented a sorry looking sight with my badly worn clothes. The fatigue of many weary miles must have shown in my face, adding their weight to my twenty-two years and diminishing my resemblance to the carefree youth of eighteen he remembered in another June of past years.

We talked of our harvest of furs now on the way to London, by Mississippi riverboat to LaCrosse, Wisconsin, thence by the Chicago North-Western to Chicago, from where the Michigan Central and New York Central take them to New York to be placed aboard an ocean steamer. Mr. Kittson supplied me with what money I needed, for the Company gives us unlimited credit, directing me to stay at the Merchant's Hotel and enjoy the life of the city until he has the freight ready to send to St. Cloud for us to take north.

It has been necessary for me to purchase a complete new wardrobe, as my trunk is at Fort Ellice where I left it last fall. I was so much on the trail between there and Riding Mountain and the surrounding country that I had no need of it between visits. Clarke and I have been visiting the stores and, as in St. Cloud, we have received marked attention from all the head men of business. The photographer we visited thought I was so sunburned that he could not take my likeness but I thought my mother would like one, good or bad, if only to see that I have not changed very much since I left home.

My one disappointment is that Governor Mactavish has left St. Paul before my arrival thus preventing any opportunity for me to accompany him, though I would not like to ask leave to go to

Canada without first asking Mr. Campbell. Nor could I afford the money for I would not think of drawing that put aside for my mother, not even to go home. While I have been here I have spent a good deal but all this I will get back in time, for the Company pays all our expenses and has given me ten pounds sterling for incidentals such as fares. I expect Governor Mactavish put in a good word for us with the Company's Agent, Mr. Kittson, which accounts for the good reception given us by leading merchants.

All too quickly the days have been passing by for Clarke and myself. I felt this morning that we were really beginning to enjoy ourselves when to my surprise Mr. Kittson sent for me as he promised to do when our freight is ready. But surely it is too soon for this.

On my arrival at the Hudson's Bay Company's office their agent informed me that he had received a wire from the Mayor of St. Cloud to say that pandemonium reigns in their streets. The town has fallen into the hands of our men, some of them from our northern wilderness, who are enjoying city life in their own way – which unfortunately does not comply with the law and order of St. Cloud. My instructions are to take this afternoon's train back there and make sure that all is as it should be in regard to our camp.

It is Monday, the 20th of June, and I have just received a letter from my mother, written on the fifteen of this month, which I must answer before leaving St. Paul, if only a few lines to let her know I am well, though unable to come to Canada either to see her or to seek other employment. As to my leaving the Hudson's Bay Company, this will depend on how things are settled and under what rules and regulations the fur trade will be carried on. I will stand by the old ship to the last. She has weathered many a storm and though there are breakers ahead just now, she may yet reach port safely. Things look dark indeed at present but we know that the darkest hour is before the dawn and a bright day may be in store for us. I would not leave the country nor the service while things are in the present unsettled state. I would serve in a volunteer company or work for the Hudson's Bay

Company for a year *gratis* to see those rebels expelled from the Settlement. We do not expect our Company to dissolve, but it will require to be re-organized. My chance of an appointment in a new Company will be as good as most other clerks.

I would prefer, of course, to remain in the service, but at the same time I am not the least uneasy about my chance of making a living here or in Rupert's Land, for I could do well here were I out of employment. Many are leaving every day to work on the Northern Pacific Railway and as I know the whole staff of officers I believe I could get some appointment.

Yesterday Hardisty and his family arrived from Montreal on their way to Fort Garry; they probably will accompany me to Fort Abercrombie and may go this afternoon with me to St. Cloud. We may travel together until I branch westward from Fort Abercrombie to go straight home by Devil's Lake to Fort Ellice. Hardisty says that the best days of the Hudson's Bay Company are yet to come.

Word has just come in that the rebels have seized the steamboat and stopped the Company's business at Fort Garry, but we cannot be sure that this is true. If our freight is ready to go by this afternoon's train we could leave St. Cloud tomorrow, in which event Clarke will come with me today but in any case I must rejoin my Brigade now. Our carts will be loaded with bonded goods and as I am to be in charge of the Swan River Brigade I must send a man to pass the Custom House at Pembina as required, or go there myself.

Fort Garry is the proper address for all inland letters but if replies from Canada are sent to Abercrombie I will get them before leaving there as I must travel slowly with the carts. Letters to Willie will go as usual but mail from here is quicker and safer and I must relay the news from him in a letter just received, though there is very little time to finish my business here. I expect my family will have heard of the birth of a son to Harriet and Willie. He is to be called after me so I must take him up a present. So far they are all well, safe and happy.

Friends and relatives in Canada are eager to meet those

returning from Rupert's Land but I fear that Mrs. Hargrave will be disappointed in not seeing Governor Mactavish as he told me he was not going by the route through Canada. Major Boulton has met my mother, I am pleased to say, although I did not see him myself when at Portage la Prairie for he was then in prison. I spent the day with the Reverend Henry George where the prisoner had been staying and where I learned that he was very much liked by all, even at Fort Garry. There will be more news to share if I see Willie at Fort Ellice when I arrive with my Brigade.

Unfortunately my photographs are not ready but I may be able to send one to my mother from St. Cloud. Yesterday I called on Curry as requested or I would have missed seeing him. He seems to be a good sort of a fellow.

It was as I feared: the chief offenders of the peace in St. Cloud were our own Swan River men, Indians and Scotch halfbreeds who have never before seen a railroad nor a town of this size. It has been an easy matter to restore order, the first step being to remove our camp farther out along the trail we must follow as soon as our freight and passengers arrive from St. Paul. The citizens of St. Cloud are not used to as much horse-racing as takes place around Fort Garry in summer, and is enjoyed when visitors and settlers are all of Rupert's Land. While our men raced their horses through the streets of St. Cloud the usual traffic suffered, but far worse was the discovery that the long bridge across the Mississippi. only recently built, was a wonderful racetrack.

The large CAUTION and NO FASTER THAN A WALK means nothing to those who enjoy the bliss of ignorance in the form of illiteracy. They galloped under these conspicuous signs at either end and when the long span swayed with their motion their delight was all the more. The Chief of Police attempted to stop them, but not knowing any law but that of the Hudson's Bay Company they took him prisoner! The Mayor then wired Mr. Kittson and here I am, with my holiday cut short while my friends continue to enjoy the city of St. Paul which has grown and improved so much in the years following civil war.

I am keeping the men busy, repairing carts and making sure all is done in preparation for our departure, as soon as we can transfer the freight from the train to our Brigade.

This did not take long, and towards the end of June McKinley and I rode out along the trail across Minnesota beside our carts loaded with goods for our winter trade. Mr. McDonald and Mr. Richard Hardisty with their families have taken the stage which makes a weekly trip between St. Cloud and Fort Abercrombie. With them are Miss McDougall and Mr. Clarke, all enjoying the comparative luxury of the coach which will take them to their destination in three days, while we must travel more slowly with the carts.

It is Sunday, July 3rd, and I am at Fort Abercrombie where I found two letters to greet me: one from my sister Mary and the other an official despatch instructing me to send my Brigade on to Fort Ellice from here, while I go on horseback to Georgetown. Accordingly, I will see men and carts again take the trail this evening after supper with McKinley in charge, and then start north on the fifty-mile ride to the Post at the mouth of the Buffalo, where I expect to be for some time. I am heartily sick of travelling overland and shall try to go down to Fort Garry in the steamboat which will make the trip to Fort Ellice a much shorter ride from there.

A few minutes ago a party arrived at this Fort from Red River Settlement, having come up on the steamboat as far as George-town. Among others are Bishop Taché, a Custom House Officer and the Archdeacon of Assiniboine. The Bishop told me that all the disturbance around Fort Garry is likely to come to an end soon.

But the news that has been brought to me by another of the party is less reassuring. Willie has had a row with his men at Fort Pitt and would have been killed with an axe if someone had not caught the man's arm. My brother is now on his way to Norway House where he will receive an appointment to some other District, for he is not to return to the Saskatchewan District from where the ruling Chief Factor, Christie, goes home in disgust.

Dr. Cowan left Fort Garry at the end of May with his family, going by Lake Winnipeg to Hudson's Bay on his way to England. Two weeks to the day after seeing Governor Mactavish off on the boat to the south, his doctor, equally discouraged, went down the Red River also bound for the Old Land.

The letter from Mary was written ten days ago in her amusing way of telling the news from home that is most cheerful and welcome at this time of uncertainty. Our mother's health is so much improved that we may look forward to many years of a good life for her, though now not far off the proverbial three-score-years-and-ten. I am also glad to hear that Mrs. Campbell visited them in Lakefield and that they seem to like her. When I get to Georgetown, or home, whenever and wherever that may be, I shall answer Mary's letter at length but meantime will mail a few lines of acknowledgement from here. The likenesses I was not able to get before leaving St. Paul I have since received and have one ready to mail to Annie at Rice Lake, with a letter I have written to her to go by the next post south.

Towards the end of my second week at Georgetown a letter came to me from Mr. John McTavish who has succeeded to the charge of the Company's affairs following the departure of Governor Mactavish and Dr. Cowan. My instructions were to come to Fort Garry, stopping at Scratching River to deliver a message to a loyal French halfbreed there, Pierre Delorame. There was no explanation as to why I am to enter the Fort where Riel still rules, as far as I know, and whose soldiers I took good care to avoid three months ago.

Early on Monday morning, the 18th of July, I rode down the left bank of the Red River on the trail that runs from loop to loop of the stream. During the night a thunderstorm had cleared the sultry July air and refreshed the parched prairies that lay on either side as I cantered away from Georgetown, but by noon the overhead sun again beat down fiercely from a cloudless sky and it was intensely hot.

That evening I put my two saddle horses on the "International" at Frog Point and found, on its crowded decks, several old friends. One of these is William Drever of Red River who is bound for Winnipeg though he is a man whose movements are marked by the enemy because of his efforts during the past year to aid the settlers and the help he gave some of Riel's prisoners to escape. He has been able to inform me of recent developments but cannot vouch for the reception either of us may be accorded upon our arrival.

The last passengers to come aboard were two horsemen who had exhausted themselves and their steeds to reach the boat before it left its moorings at Frog Point. One of these, I have learned today through Mr. Drever, is Captain Butler, also on his way to Red River. He is travelling in the capacity of intelligence officer in advance of Wolseley's expedition with the object of acquiring first-hand information regarding the true state of affairs at Fort Garry.

On Wednesday morning I left the "International" at Pembina, taking my carts and horses as far as Scratching River. That night I stayed with Delorame to whom I delivered the message from the Company's Officer at Fort Garry which was sent to me at George-town. Delorame's loyal sympathies are representative of this area from where valuable aid was given Commissioner Smith in the furtherance of his duties while a virtual prisoner of Riel. Early next morning, on July 21st, I rode on with my two horses to Fort Garry.

Taking the precaution of coming down on the St. Boniface side of the river I called at the home of Mrs. MacKay's brother and was overjoyed to find Mrs. MacKay and the children who had come down from Swan River with Mr. MacKay. He, however, was at the Fort. I rode on and met him on his way home. He has been await-ing my arrival with the intention of persuading me to abandon all attempts to enter the Fort as Riel has made the Company's people prisoners, and I would of a certainty share the same fate. He urged me to come down with him to "Seven Oaks," the home of the Inksters, as that morning the "International" had been con-fiscated by *"le Président"* and none of the officers allowed to land.

"If you order me not to go to the Fort," I replied, "of course I will obey."

He reluctantly admitted that he now had no jurisdiction over me as Mr. John McTavish, head officer at Fort Garry, has borrowed me to send me to Georgetown. This is the first I have heard of being assigned to duties outside of the Swan River District.

"I have promised Mr. McTavish to let you stay in his District until fall," he added, "so you are now under his orders."

When he saw that I was determined to go in he let me give him my light horse to take back with him. I rode the other one to where I forded the Red River and crossed the common to the front gate of the Fort which was open. The guards all knew me as I entered and said nothing to me.

It was not yet noon for I had made a very early start that morning from Scratching River, and this thirty-five mile ride of one horseman was of little concern compared to the arrival of the "International" and Riel's determination to know who had come by it. As I rode toward the Fort I had seen the river-boat at rest by its moorings and wondered what had become of Captain Butler and William Drever.

# SEVENTEEN

## *Prisoner of Louis Riel at Fort Garry*

FOUR armed guards gathered round me and I was told I would be allowed to spend an hour in the Fort under their escort. In this way I entered the Bachelors' Hall where I found the people in a great state of excitement, the Company's Officers all collected there and smoking cigars as if they were in their own tents on the prairie. One, a Mr. McFarlane, just arrived on the boat from St. Cloud, was taken into custody, and like myself is now among the rest of the prisoners.

In a few minutes from the time I entered the Fort, Mr. McTavish came to greet me but was just then sent for by *"le Président."* He soon returned to say that he had been told by Riel that the boat would be released on condition that she left immediately for Georgetown.

"You must start for Georgetown in twenty-four hours, if possible. I will keep the steamer waiting until you can be ready but be ready as soon as you can," were the instructions he gave me.

If I were to be in charge of Georgetown, there were matters to be discussed and arranged, but I had little doubt but that I could be ready at the appointed time for the boat to leave and assured Mr. McTavish accordingly. But when that time came the boat was not ready. The days have passed and there is no word of it leaving other than it is expected to leave early on Monday morning.

It is not clear to me how Mr. McTavish has been able to effect my release on condition that I take the "International" and return to the United States. Riel does not know that I was ordered to come here to receive instructions regarding my new appointment and that his disposition of myself coincides happily

197

with the Company's interests in despatching a new clerk to Georgetown.

Meantime I am enjoying myself very well in the incongruous role of prisoner-guest. The officers are not molested in any way. We have the freedom of the Fort but are not allowed outside its walls, nor can I complain of any lack of courtesy on the part of my self-imposed host. There is no trade so there is no work of any kind going on in the office, which means that the clerks have nothing to do but to spend their time playing cards and billiards, reading, writing letters and looking forward to the arrival of the troops under Colonel Wolseley.

The Fort is a queer looking place – like a garrison indeed: cannon facing you at every turn, ball and shell lying about like stones and the Governor's lawn, that was always so well kept, now turned into a corral for Riel's horses in front of the residence. Ever since the clerks at a distance heard that Riel had taken possession of the Fort, we have wondered how the Company's people could bear to remain and witness all that took place.

At first sight I was shocked to see the disorder: rooms were untidy, corridors littered and unswept, but before I was here two days I became used to it and now feel just as much at home as ever, though we have not our old rooms. These were used as a guard house last winter and are not ready to be returned to our men who quarter all over, the single ones crowding themselves into the hospital. Clarke and I are in the druggist store where all the medicines are kept, and which smells so strongly of drugs that we can hardly shut the windows.

The married clerks have been permitted to retain their own quarters, while the single ones have the use of the Governor's dining room to replace their confiscated mess room. Bachelors' Hall has been converted into the prison where I am at present. Riel is occupying the residence of Dr. Cowan.

When Governor Mactavish and Dr. Cowan left in May, J. H. McTavish, as the Officer in charge of Red River District, moved into the Governor's House. The Provisional Government occupy the Officer's House and buildings, the former being now Government House, a grand establishment. Riel has retained our Officers' Mess as his Council Chamber and uses the Company's office as a commissariat for his rebel retinue.

The PG's occupy stables, horse park, etc., and we are obliged to keep our horses at a livery stable in town or in the Fort among the guns. Clarke and I took one of the ammunition wagons and emptied the things out to make a grain store of it. We tie our horses to the wagon and feed them out of the boxes for ammunition. I think the PG's consider us pretty cheeky.

As to what happened to Captain Butler, I only know what I have heard and seen within the Fort as Riel's prisoner. It has been said that two passengers came down from Georgetown and instead of waiting until the boat landed they jumped off when, in round-ing the land to turn into the Assiniboine, the Captain backs the "International" into the Red.

In so doing he came so near the north bank that it was a fairly easy matter for the two men to go ashore there. One is a man belonging to Red River who was in gaol last winter and who was let out. A body of guards was sent out and he was taken prisoner, but the other man could not be found. This led Riel's men to believe he was some sort of spy and that they were justified in seizing his companion with the intention of keeping him until his fellow traveller turned up. In the meantime they prevented the Company from discharging the cargo for fear that he might be hiding somewhere on the boat.

By Friday it became known that he is a Captain Butler, sent to ascertain the resources of the country as to provisions, etc. He is of the Sixty-Ninth Regiment from Canada and had been so worked upon by his Red River companion on the boat that he expected to be taken prisoner. To avoid any danger of this he started for the Lower Fort without any intention of visiting the Upper Fort at all, and would have gone on to Fort Alexander in the belief that Riel was going to resist the expected troops if John McTavish had not gone down to persuade him to come up here.

On Saturday Captain Butler dined with us. We were a queer set of officers to represent the Hudson's Bay Company at its seat

199

of government: John McTavish, the Gentleman-in-Charge, and all the rest of the clerks less like commissioned clerks than a whole band of Apprentice Clerks without one Commissioned Officer, but we were all the more jolly for that. Captain Butler interviewed *"le Président,"* or rather, *"le Président"* sought the interview, after which our visitor went his way in peace. How much of the safety accorded his coming and going was due to the letter he carried with him from Bishop Taché I do not know, other than that the letter was given him by the prelate in St. Paul.

William Drever was set free by Friday and I have learned from him how Captain Butler eluded the guards sent out for him and who took my friend prisoner. Butler was seen on the "International," as it passed Pembina, by the guards stationed there who sent two messengers on fast horses to notify Riel of the mysterious stranger. Before the boat docked at Fort Garry, Riel, attended by O'Donohue, Lepine and a strong body of guards, was on the landing to take him as their prisoner.

But the wanted man was nowhere on board, though Riel put his guards on the boat to search for him, whereupon Captain Aymond sent for the American Consul, who told Riel that he must keep off the "International" as it is under American registration and flying the American flag. Riel withdrew his guards at once.

In the meantime Captain Butler was making his way on foot in the darkness along the road running north from the village of Winnipeg. He arrived at the Lower Fort early next morning.

Unlike my fellow clerks I am not being detained long enough to become weary of the enforced idleness, but confess to thoroughly enjoying this opportunity to see for myself the Red River rebellion from within the Fort, and to learn about it from my senior clerks.

Over a year ago, on March 8th of 1869, the British Government concluded negotiations with the Hudson's Bay Company in London whereby the latter has relinquished its title to Rupert's Land except for five hundred acres to be selected at each Trading Post, amounting to some forty-five thousand acres in all, and one-twentieth of the land of the Fertile Belt (defined as south of the North Saskatchewan River, east of the Rocky Mountains and west of the Lake of the Woods and the waters connecting it with Lake Winnipeg), two sections to be selected in each township as the land is surveyed, when it is to be deeded back to the Company.

Thus, for a consideration of three hundred thousand pounds sterling, paid to the Directors, an empire of more than two million square miles, (exclusive of the above deductions retained by the Company) has changed ownership. Canada has purchased this territory directly from the Hudson's Bay Company, but the terms have been arranged by its London officials through the Imperial Government in conference with the Canadian delegates, Sir George Carter and Mr. William McDougall, and without the knowledge or consent of the Hudson's Bay Company's officers in Rupert's Land.

It was also agreed to confirm to the settlers occupying land in the Red River Settlement the titles to all homesteads and all lands sold by the Company in accordance with the grant by Lord Selkirk. Furthermore, it was agreed to provide for the endowment of the different educational institutions and the churches, as the Company had done.

The first intimation the Red River settlers had of the purchase of their country by Canada was in the early summer of 1868 when there arrived in Winnipeg, by way of Fort William and Rainy Lake, a corps of engineers in charge of a Mr. Snow who began to locate and construct a wagon road from St. Boniface to the northwest angle of the Lake of the Woods, to be known as the Dawson Route. In 1869, surveyors were running boundary lines of townships through the homesteads of settlers along the rivers south to the International Boundary, north to Lake Winnipeg and west to Portage la Prairie. Some of the farms are long and narrow, like lanes running back from the rivers and the halfbreeds, seeing lines surveyed across their property, thought their lands were being confiscated.

There has been great distress in this area where grain has not been grown for two years. Flour is ten cents a pound or in the currency of Rupert's Land, five pence, while pork is a shilling a pound. The summers of 1867 and 1868 saw every affliction that adverse conditions can impose, reminding the Selkirk Settlers, who came over fifty years ago, of their early hardships. The hordes of grasshoppers I encountered in Qu'Appelle were here also. The eggs they left in the soil hatched to plague the farms the following year. When we put a pan of dirt under a stove in the Swan River District I saw them hatch out in wintertime.

The buffalo hunts have failed to such an extent that it is feared these animals are being rapidly annihilated. Moreover, the catches of fish have been negligible and the rabbits and other game, formerly so plentiful, have been scarce. The only sure source of food is in Minnesota, from where it must be transported in Red River carts in summer and on sleds in winter.

It was anticipated that the building of the long hoped-for road to the Lake of the Woods would provide employment for the needy, while establishing the much desired all-Canadian route for freight and passengers now coming by way of St. Paul, and which will come by a proposed route from Duluth, unless our own road is completed. This is being surveyed through the French settlement on the east side of Red River to another French settlement thirty miles east at Oak Point.

Unfortunately this first undertaking by the Canadian Government in the form of a public highway did not furnish the employment expected for the settlers, but did provide work for a number, needy or otherwise, who were brought in from Canada by Mr. Snow and the surveyors. To make matters worse many of these were Orangemen, while the natives employed were chiefly Catholics who claim that they have been discriminated against in favour of outsiders. This resentment created constant friction which terminated in fights when the workers returned to Winnipeg.

One of the principal agitators was poor Thomas Scott who was executed.

It was hard enough for the Dominion of Canada's government, itself only three years old, to assume the administration of a vast, little-known empire without some misunderstanding and mistakes, but the possibilities were unnecessarily increased by misrepresentations in the *Nor' Wester,* a paper published by Dr. Schultz, and other writings appearing in Toronto newspapers. There have been misrepresentations of the Company and uncomplimentary allusions to it, and those connected with it, which have been resented by the old settlers and their families. One of the chief offenders was Charles Mair whose articles published in the *Toronto Globe* contained disparaging remarks about the native ladies.

He was attached to the Superintendent of the Dawson road and was said to be a close friend of the new Governor to whom he would serve as secretary. One lady, singled out for his criticism, is no other than Mrs. Bannatyne, wife of Winnipeg's leading merchant and daughter of Andrew McDermott, one of the most highly respected of Lord Selkirk's settlers. One of her sisters is the wife of Governor Mactavish and another is Mrs. Andrew Strang.

These ladies have graduated with honours from St. Croix Ladies' School which is presided over by an English lady with a competent corps of assistants, all under the supervision of the Bishop of Rupert's Land. When the papers with the offensive articles reached Winnipeg, Mrs. Bannatyne encountered the author on the Post Office steps and expressed her disapproval by applying her riding crop vigorously to his unfortunate person.

The people of Red River naturally take exception to a stranger from Canada criticizing the ladies of the land, who in my opinion are well qualified to take their place in the best society in any country. When I heard that Mrs. Archibald McDonald, the wife of my first *bourgeois* at Qu'Appelle, was going to visit in Montreal I wrote to my mother in Lakefield asking her to invite Mrs. McDonald to spend a week with her at "Westove," for while living at the same post I had received much kindness and pleasure in her society.

It so happened that my letter reached my mother in Brockville where she was visiting the Hargraves and where Mrs. McDonald arrived to stay with her cousin, the wife of Chief Factor Christie. My mother who called to see Mrs. McDonald, subsequently wrote to me that she had never met a more brilliant conversationalist and congratulated me on being stationed where the châtelaine of the Post was so charming a person. My sister wrote in no less glowing terms of Mrs. Christie whom she met on the same occasion. I think my mother and sister quite as competent to judge the native ladies as Charles Mair.

Another cause of ill-feeling has been the ambiguous and indiscriminate use of the word "native," often in a sense too limited and disparaging by newcomers little qualified to judge. Chief Factors and Chief Traders, when their days of active service were done, have settled in the Red River District, in the heart of which the village of Winnipeg is now growing and thriving. They and their descendants have prospered and, upholding their best traditions, have exerted a great influence for good in the land they love for its wondrous beauty of lakes and plains and value for its potential wealth.

It is true that by tracing the family trees of many of the native sons and daughters one at length might arrive in the shade of Pocahontas, or another member of the First Families of America, yet the ties with the Homeland have been strengthened thereby rather than relaxed, for with that high regard for education characteristic of our Scottish forbears, the youth of this country have been educated in schools and colleges in Red River and in Great Britain.

Consequently the natives, both English and French, though not resenting these newcomers from the newly formed Dominion, wonder why it is that they, having been received and entertained and having associated with the best families in England, Scotland and the United States and with members of the Imperial Parliament and the House of Lords, should be slighted by Canadians who are coming to rule them.

The transfer of Rupert's Land to the Dominion of Canada was to take place formally on last December 1st, 1869. Some time previous to this date Mr. William McDougall was appointed to be Lieutenant-Governor of the new territory and proceeded with his staff to Red River by way of St. Paul, arriving at Pembina in October. It was getting late that month when he continued down the river in anticipation of the Queen's Proclamation that would place in his hands the administration of the country he was entering. Before he had gone very far, however, Louis Riel's men blockaded the road and refused to allow the intended Governor to continue his journey to Fort Garry.

During November, while Mr. McDougall remained on the American side of the border at Pembina, Riel and his followers installed themselves in possession of Fort Garry. They took the Company's employees prisoner but did not molest them other than to confine them within the walls of the Fort. Riel summoned a Convention at which he presided and passed a Bill of Rights, establishing himself as the head, or President, of a Provisional Government.

On December 1st McDougall ill-advisedly issued from Pembina a Proclamation to the effect that the transfer had taken place. Riel, acting on the assumption that he was not living in Canadian territory as yet, disregarded the notice. The Canadians, under the leadership of Dr. Schultz, congregated at his combined business and dwelling place in Winnipeg and took up arms to support the entry of Mr. McDougall into the country he had been sent to govern. Riel promised them there would be an amicable settlement between himself and the prospective Governor whereupon they trustfully laid aside their weapons and were taken prisoner by the rebel leader on December 7th.

The prisoners, including the Company's employees, were not ill-treated and the Canadians given the same food as the Hudson's Bay people, nor have there been any restrictions regarding food and luxuries sent in by their families and friends. Dr. Schultz, Charles Mair and Thomas Scott were more closely guarded, but the first two escaped while the tragic fate of the third has been told.

Major Boulton went to live at Portage la Prairie where in February he organized an expedition of about sixty men and proceeded to walk with them in the dead of winter to Fort Garry with the object of freeing the prisoners. They were a disorganized mob armed with shotguns and anything they could acquire. They arrived in a blizzard and encamped in the Kildonan Church below St. John's from where they demanded that Riel release the prisoners or they would do so by force. They had been joined by Dr. Schultz and others with an ancient cannon mounted on an ox-sled drawn by four oxen. Their numbers had grown to several hundreds and Riel sent a messenger with word that he would comply with their demands.

In the meantime it so happened that a half-witted French-Canadian youth, Alex Parisien, was on his way home from wood-cutting at Fort Garry when, in passing the encampment at Kildonan, he was taken for a spy. He managed to escape from his captors in the morning and was fleeing across the river to his home when he met John Hugh Sutherland urging his horse over the frozen surface as fast as was safe to bring the news of the promised release of the prisoners. This word had just been brought from Riel by his father, John Sutherland, who was largely instrumental in obtaining the promise of their freedom. Parisien confused the approaching rider with his pursuers and shot him twice, wounding him so badly that he died next morning. In the struggle following, Parisien received fatal injuries. Young Sutherland was the second son of one of the oldest and most respected of the families of the Selkirk settlers and there never has been a more lamented death in Red River.

Satisfied that they had succeeded in the purpose for which they had come, Major Boulton and his force started home but instead of going through Winnipeg they detoured north and when opposite Fort Garry, Riel's men rode out and gathered them in without resistance, for meantime *"le Président"* had heard of the tragedy at Kildonan. He chose to regard Boulton as responsible for the first bloodshed and condemned him to be shot at noon on the day following Sutherland's funeral. It was only the persistent intervention of Donald A. Smith, Archdeacon McLean, and finally the mother of Sutherland, brought from her home where she was ill in bed, that saved Major Boulton from the fate that was meted to Scott a few days later.

Donald Smith was here from December 27th to March 18th as a

Commissioner for the Canadian Government, and also as the one in whom is vested the highest authority assigned in Canada by the Hudson's Bay Company. He lived in Government House which Governor Mactavish had been forced to share with Dr. Cowan and his family when Riel seized the latter's home for his own use. Though a virtual prisoner he managed to acquire knowledge of the situation and to call a Convention from the different parishes, thereby arranging for the appointment of two delegates to Ottawa and thus saving the country from civil war. Following the shooting of Scott he refused to treat with the man who had perpetrated the crime over his strongest possible protests and left the Fort two weeks later.

Hitherto Riel was not a criminal, but had always been a law-abiding subject under the Company's officers, who for years have ruled the country without friction and without force under Governor Mactavish, who was also the representative of the British Government. His Council consisted of fifteen members selected to be his advisers from all groups of the populace including the French halfbreeds, and such leading men as the Bishop of St. Boniface, the Bishop of Rupert's Land and other competent persons. With their aid Governor Mactavish has been governing the country to the satisfaction of the settlers regardless of race or creed. Unfortunately, at the time that the reins of control should have changed hands smoothly the Governor of the old régime was dying, Bishop Taché was attending a Vatican Council in Rome and two much-needed Councillors, Breland and Amlin, were wintering in the West.

Governor Mactavish has been censored for allowing Riel to enter the Fort, but had he been in good health he was without the power to resist for there is no military or police force stationed in the country with which to uphold authority.

Herein lies the weakness, or possibly the strength, of the Company's administration. The English halfbreeds would not have been willing to take up arms against their French halfbreed neighbours, with whom they have lived in peace and who, like themselves, have supported the rule of the Hudson's Bay Company through the advisers selected from among them by the Governor.

The Company and its officers have been accused of being in sympathy with Riel. Such is not the case. I have never heard an officer, or any employee of the Company, French or English, who did not condemn Riel. Mr. John H. McTavish, accused by all the Canadian party of being a Riel sympathizer, is the only Catholic, and speaks French. The fact is that not only did he plead with Riel to save the life of Major Boulton after Donald Smith and others had failed but he and his wife have done everything possible for the comfort of the Canadian prisoners. I, too, being a prisoner with the officers, know that Mr. McTavish is loyal.

If the Canadian Government, instead of appointing a Lieutenant-Governor with a ready-made cabinet, had recognized the natives, both English and French, both would have given their loyal support. Moreover, had they recognized the Company's officers and asked their assistance, there would have been no rebellion. Former rulers and their subjects have been ignored in Ottawa though there are here able men like John Norquay, Sutherland, John Inkster and his son Colin, Patrick Boreland and James McKay all of whom would prove their worth as legislators if elected by the people.

In fact, there are men in every parish well qualified to assist in government by reason of their education and business integrity. There are not any better men in the Dominion than the Selkirk settlers and their descendants. But the misguided politicians of the new Dominion have exemplified, for history's possible benefit, another case of trying to govern a people without their consent.

As a British subject and a Canadian by birth, also a Hudson's Bay officer, I have resented the French halfbreeds' activities in regard to the rebellion and have done my humble part to protect the Company's property and to assist in leaving the country those whom it was not wished that Riel should detain.

Today is Sunday, July 24th, and those clerks who are my seniors and who have suffered a long period of confinement cannot conceal some dissatisfaction and envy that I have received an appointment that coincides with my deportation as an undesirable citizen who has exported a valuable amount of furs without Riel's permission. When it became known this afternoon that I am to leave on the "International" tomorrow morning I stressed the fact I am merely being borrowed, as our garden tools at home are borrowed sometimes by the neighbours, and that I shall soon be returned to Swan River District. But at times the garden tools are not returned, and I wonder if I shall be!

Time has passed pleasantly for me while a prisoner. I have enjoyed meeting old friends and making the acquaintance of clerks from inland and the Bay whom I have never seen before and may never see again. In this country people part to meet no more. They may live for years in the same place and in a few weeks a change of appointments will separate a whole staff of officers.

My own saddle horse has been confiscated, my faithful companion of three years over many miles of trail. When I say mine I mean the one I have ridden and which Mr. MacKay kindly let me take when I left his District. Mr. McTavish has arranged for a horse and spring wagon for me to take off the boat at Frog Point. I asked him if he could not persuade Riel to let me have my own horse but he assures me that I shall find plenty of good saddle horses at Georgetown where they have been sent, including the Governor's carriage team, Polly and Pet, in order that they might not fall into Riel's possession.

"The two horses you brought," Mr. McTavish continued, "will become the property of the Company when the war is over and will be sent back to Fort Ellice with the Swan River Brigade in September. You will get them back when you return there in October."

All day Monday the boat remained at its moorings, but that evening I had an interview with "*le Président*" Louis Riel. I was introduced to him by Mr. McTavish and found him to be extremely polite. He is a fine looking fellow speaking broken English, but I fear he will not live in such style when the troops come in.

The Provisional Government has sent a party to meet the new Lieutenant-Governor and to accompany him to the Fort. There is hope that a better understanding may prevail over the causes of the Rebellion. Certainly, while a prisoner, I have learned of many extenuating circumstances, not the least of which is the length of time required for any communication to span the hundreds of miles between Ottawa and the Red River Settlement. Commissioner Smith's efforts to guide the agitation into safe and peaceful channels failed to prevent the murder of Scott but did succeed in leaving a strong faith in his sound judgment and wise policies based on his simple rule: "Put yourself in their place."

# EIGHTEEN

---

## *Appointment at Georgetown, 1870*

IT is now Tuesday morning, July 26th, on board the "International" which only started today at five o'clock. I am attempting to write under full steam, something I am not used to and find difficult but I trust my family will excuse all errors. I was overjoyed to find their letters awaiting me at my prison, and also a long letter from Mrs. Campbell, who wrote to me from Montreal that she was much pleased with her visit to Lakefield. I am sorry indeed that the Campbells are leaving this country, but even were they here I might never see them again. Little did I think when I passed Georgetown four years ago that I would one day be the officer in charge there, but "such is life in the Hudson's Bay Company."

I will copy a paragraph or two from public despatches on the subject of my removal, but of course they become strictly private now:

*Wm. MacKay, Esq:*

*I find that the Company's business requires that I should send Mr. Traill up to Georgetown for a time, a month or two at least, permanently if approved of by the President of the Council. I trust you will find it convenient to spare him from Swan River. Were the case not an urgent one I would not take it upon myself to make the change but I consider it indispensable.*

J. H. McTavish

The next is from the same person to the clerk at present in charge of Georgetown, who has been reported at headquarters as allowing his men to make too free with the Company's Gentlemen in passing. He says:

*Mr. A. Purcepont:*

*I have been hearing queer stories lately regarding the conduct of the Company's establishment at Georgetown. The place is too small to have more than one master and of far too much importance to have no master at all. As everyone passing the place is at a loss to know as to whether you or Reid [his cook] is the person in charge I have decided upon sending a person to take charge regarding whose position there will be no mistake.*

*Mr. Walter Traill has been appointed to take charge of the Company's business at Georgetown so you will please deliver up the keys of the establishment to him as it is desirable that he should assume charge immediately after he arrives.*

J. H. McTavish

Armed with this document I am on my way to Georgetown. I need only say that the change is an agreeable one to me, being an advantageous one. I suppose we shall reach Pembina tonight where we shall have to stay for an hour or so to take on some cows.

July 27th. Reached Pembina at eleven o'clock last night and started again early this morning. I got a couple of cows for my establishment, also a buggy. We stopped for a few minutes at the military fort to clear the cargo at the Custom House where I saw the Commanding Officer of the United States Forces. We sailed yesterday under the Union Jack and this day we crossed the lines and hoisted the Stars and Stripes and now we have the Hudson's Bay flag flying.

The boat is now under full steam and a strong wind blowing at the same time which accounts for my letters being so difficult to read that I cannot read them myself. I am acting as clerk for the trip and have to write whenever the boat stops for wood, for I cannot manage to write well enough for business purposes while travelling.

The weather is now fine and cool, the river pretty and the company on board select. Steamboat travelling is very pleasant after overland travelling. We have every comfort and luxury here that money will buy. The Captain, Chief Engineer, and Mate are all good fellows, so we have a jolly time.

In the end I brought my own horse with me, the one I had in Swan River. I have also my dog Bob. He has followed me in all my travels. We started together from Riding Mountain on February 4th and since then we have been travelling constantly. I think by the time I reach my destination I shall have travelled by every possible means of locomotion.

I started with a horse and carriole, I then went to Red River with a train of dogs and a carriole. Next I walked on snowshoes. I then started with carts on horseback, then with a buggy. I then drove an ox-wagon for a day. I then travelled in the cars and now I am on the steamer.

It will soon be six months since I left home. A servant has been sent with me to care for the animals and sundry things I am taking up. I am rather in a hurry to be at the place to receive Governor Archibald when he arrives from Canada. I have been promised a clerk from York Factory if any come this year, but at any rate I will have someone.

We hear all sorts of rumours that this time the English will rise and prevent the Lieutenant-Governor from entering the country. It is most amusing to hear the English halfbreeds talk about what they will do when the troops come in. They seem to think that they will then have nothing to do but say "Hang this one" and he will be executed immediately, though they made no effort to help the Company when they saw that their goods were being plundered.

This they did not mind for they thought: "When the Company is no more we will have the fur trade in our own hands." The stupid brutes. They have been fed and clothed by the Company all their lives and now they are beggars because the Company is not employing them. I am not surprised, however, that outsiders think that the Hudson's Bay people are in with the rebels, for every horse the French guards are seen riding has HB on its blankets and saddle, as also have the wagons and buggies they are using.

July 28th. We are drawing near Frog Point where the steamer stops—as the river is too low for it to go further. I will have to take my horse and buggy off the boat there and drive the thirty nine miles to Georgetown.

I shall be able to write more about that Post when I get there. It is a freight depot where all the goods are reshipped from the wagon trains to the steamer when higher water permits it to go up that far. The Company has a large claim of twenty thousand acres in Minnesota and Dakota States and wants me to open a sales shop and establish a farm.

By insisting on my deportation, Riel has unconsciously assisted the Company's business, but my appointment is not a permanent one until approved by the Governor and Council.

While I was enjoying St. Paul, heedless of the official deliberations concerning my future which were taking place in the annual June meeting, it was decided by the Governor-in-Council that Mr. MacKay should succeed Mr. Campbell as Officer-in-Charge of the Swan River District, the latter having arrived at the time of honourable retirement. Mr. MacKay will therefore be transferred to Fort Pelly and somewhat to my surprise I find that I have been appointed to the charge of Fort Ellice, though with one exception I am the Junior Clerk in the District and this Post is the most important one, next to Fort Pelly, and includes the supervision of Riding Mountain.

If I don't return there my place will most likely be filled by Willie who I am sure will be glad of the change. I shall be sorry to leave Swan River although I would prefer Georgetown in spite of many things I shall miss. But I am going to keep dogs in winter so on the whole shall be able to pass the time pleasantly. There are no Indians and no halfbreeds there, and no Red River carts, thank goodness. I would like to have brought down some of the Sioux beadwork which the women do very nicely, but they have been so badly off for silks and quills that I was never able to see very much of it.

Georgetown is, I believe, a good place for farming. In Red River there are no crops at all. Between the grasshoppers and the

Provisional Government, farming is not going to be a paying thing this year, and I hope the crops in Canada turn out as well as is expected.

Farming here and in Canada are two different things. I shall try it at Georgetown if I am there next summer, and may do a good deal of it for the Company. They already have some fine farm horses there. Were I to leave the service I might farm for myself but not in Canada, nor anywhere as long as I have a good place in the Company.

I would indeed like to see them all at home and to ride the young horse of which my sister writes, for I like nothing better than a good horse. I hardly think I shall wait for the increase of my own to pay my expenses home, though if I could afford to go I may not be able to leave. The Northern Pacific is to be completed from Duluth to Georgetown by the 1st of July next year, 1871, and I can then run down to Canada and back in a week, and for half the money, if I am able to take time to go by Lake Superior.

On looking back over the past months I realize that on the whole I spent a pretty jolly winter after I left Riding Mountain, while those at home in Canada, judging from their letters, have been anxious about all that may have been happening to me. I must reassure them that in addition to my personal safety, I have not fallen into bad habits. There is no need to be alarmed that a few bottles of wine, champagne and brandy will make our heads ache, for the Company's liquor is all imported from London and is so good that it has no headaches bottled up in it.

Nor is there any need to fear that I may become a Scot for I am now more likely to become a Yankee since I am going to live in Yankeeland, and besides, I am very fond of some of my fellow clerks and they are nearly all Scotch. McDonald, who came down to St. Paul with me, is certainly a good fellow.

In future I hope to be a better correspondent. I can at least write often, if not long letters, as the stage coach carrying mail runs into Georgetown from St. Paul three times a week. I must draw this to a close now, as the boat rocks so that I can hardly write and we are near Frog Point.

215

Georgetown is, as Mr. McTavish informed me, and as I have learned during my first week here, well stocked with many head of horses. Its warehouses are overflowing with the north-bound freight, which has been accumulating here since last November, when Riel blockaded the country to which it is consigned, and the warehouses are much in need of repair.

When I arrived on the evening of July 28th I at once delivered to Mr. Purcepont the letter I bore from Mr. McTavish appointing me to the charge of this Post. At the same time I offered him the opportunity of staying here as my second if he did not care to return to Fort Garry, but he chose the latter course. An hour later, having gathered up his belongings, he took his departure with the mail clerk on his way to the boat at Frog Point. I have just heard that on arriving at Fort Garry he promptly joined Riel's staff.

It was with no little discouragement that I viewed the dilapidated Post with no one to show me where things are among the hundreds of tons of freight which have been unloaded here from the carts from St. Cloud, to go down the river by boat. As this is the point of transfer, there is ample accommodation for ordinary traffic but the cargoes have been piling up and now the head of navigation is forty miles farther down the river.

General Wheaton of the United States Army arrived on his way to Pembina with a train of twenty-five teams and wagons loaded with lumber for the erection of a military Post there. I thought of the Fort I had established at Riding Mountain for someone else to live in, and wondered how I could improve this one, and who would reap the benefit of my work. Alone once more, I contemplated my desolate surroundings with something akin to resentment as the wagon train crossed the ferry to the west side.

Then I became aware of someone beside me.

He was one of the Negro drivers who either had lingered behind or returned. Arrayed in a ragged red flannel shirt, high rubber boots and what remained of a large straw hat, he was not a very prepossessing figure. But the crownless brim was swept to the ground with a deferential bow as he made his request:

"Say, Boss, can you give me a job?"

It had been a long day and I was not in a very amiable state of mind. Visiting my discouragement upon the innocent man, I returned an abrupt "No."

He remained as though absorbed in thought while we viewed the uncared for buildings with whitewash scaling off, broken windows and once painted roofs now almost bare of paint. There was something appealing in his attitude of concern which matched my own, or was he weary of driving mules, or merely loath to travel farther from his native Alabama?

"What can you do?" I asked more kindly.

"Say, Boss, I can whitewash." His enthusiasm was encouraging and I was grateful.

"Then you are just the man I am looking for."

We searched among the congestion of supplies awaiting delivery and found several barrels of lime and some red ochre, then some oil for mixing the latter and some window glass. But no whitewash brushes could we see anywhere. For these we have sent to Alexandria by the mail carrier. While awaiting them Ike is busy replacing broken window panes and repairing buildings, which will improve what accommodation we have to offer visitors who pass this way. The first boat to follow the one which brought me here will arrive at Frog Point with its passengers in a few days.

It was not long after writing the above that mail and passengers arrived. During late summer and autumn when the water is low, travellers must make their way from the landing at Frog Point to the end of the stage line at Fort Abercrombie, a distance of over ninety miles.

Among the passengers was Archdeacon Cowles who came up from Red River expecting to meet Bishop Taché. He fears there is going to be more trouble at Fort Garry, as the long-expected troops have not arrived.

The mail has brought me a telegram from the Hudson's Bay House in London ordering me to forward the freight which has collected here to Fort Garry, not knowing of the situation there. The one who might help me is in New York and I don't know what to do, as I have two thousand bales of the Company's goods for which I am responsible and which I must not allow to fall into the hands of the Provisional Government.

The telegram is accompanied by a cable, also from the London House with orders for me to convey a despatch to Frog Point where the steamer is now lying some forty miles away. There I must ride tonight.

To brighten the foreboding news from the Settlement of this final threat to Hudson's Bay property, I turned to my private letters only to receive the crushing blow of word of my brother's death. If I had reached Pembina five minutes earlier last week I would have then received my mother's letter with its awful tidings of the tragedy that took place on July 7th. As it was, her letter went down to Fort Garry and has reached me only just now.

Oh, my dear Mother, how I feel for you and what would I not give to be near you. I have no heart to write, but I cannot let the mail go out without a few lines to enclose with all the money I have that can be used. Fortunately I have some Canadian dollars for which I exchanged gold on the way up, meaning to send them to my sister. Were I to send Hudson's Bay notes they would not pass. I have urged my mother to apply to me for what may be needed as I can send money by express. I am so glad that the Stricklands are near to assist her. I cannot bear to write to my brother's widow, Lilly, and the children, but send my sympathy for my mother to give them with my love to my sisters Kate, Mary, Annie and all at home. I feel too horrified to write on the subject but will be back from Frog Point in four days and will write more then.

However, I must tell my mother that I have heard from Hudson's Bay that Willie is at Carlton House and will most likely fill my appointment at Fort Ellice. He and all his were quite well, so there is no need to worry on their account, nor on mine, for I am under the immediate protection of a military Fort so am also out of danger. It is not from any lack of affection that Willie and I do not write to each other as much as formerly now that he has a little son and a wife to look after and to look after him. I write so many official letters that I seldom write a private one except to my mother and then not as often as I ought. August 9th will be my twenty-third birthday but men age quickly in a country like this and I feel much older.

# NINETEEN

---

## *Riel Evacuates Fort Garry*

BEFORE the end of August a messenger from Fort Garry brought my first despatch from Governor Smith. Not being familiar with his handwriting it conveyed as much information as Chinese characters and required a whole night's study to convert the greater part of it into English which I managed to do by patience and perseverance. His official communication confirms that he is now the head of the Company's affairs in Canada and that the title, Governor of Rupert's Land, has been abolished with the title of the realm itself. He informs me that the troops have arrived and the blockade is broken.

On August 24th Colonel Garnet Wolseley reached Fort Garry with two battalions by the difficult water route of Lake Superior, Rainy Lake, Lake of the Woods, Winnipeg River and the southern end of Lake Winnipeg, a history-making achievement that took three months. He ascended the Red River to enter our western stronghold with less opposition than was given the rebel nine months previously for Riel had fled across the Assiniboine and, according to rumour, has found refuge in St. Boniface or St. Norbert. There does not seem any real desire on the part of the Canadian Government to take him prisoner for it would not appear difficult to do so.

Governor Smith was with Colonel Wolseley to witness the melting away of *"le Président"* and his "government" and the Union Jack again flying over the Fort with the Hudson's Bay flag bearing the Company's coat-of-arms.

After leaving his prison in March the Commissioner had made his way south by dog teams to reach Montreal from where he made a rapid trip by way of Fort William and Rainy Lake to Norway House. There he presided over the Northern Council in June, the last assembly to meet under the old order. Its most important business was to represent the claims of the wintering partners to a share of the purchase price paid to the Company by the Canadian Government. Among lesser matters discussed was my appointment to Fort Ellice and I eagerly await the outcome.

It was on July 23rd that Captain Butler dined with us in Fort Garry from where he made his way to meet the approaching expedition. A month and a day after he was our guest the faithful Intelligence Officer, still well in the van of the army, returned with Colonel Wolseley.

Meanwhile I had returned to Georgetown to prepare for the traffic that would flow into Red River Settlement as soon as it was freed from the "little Napoléon." My instructions are to forward all freight at Georgetown to Frog Point by teams. Fortunately I met George Weston, and engaged him to remain at the upper Post. The tons of freight that had been accumulating since last November were soon ready to send down as soon as it was safe to do so.

Directly I heard that Her Majesty's troops had arrived we began to load the carts. Leaving George Weston to forward the trains to me, I came down to Frog Point where I have been unloading the carts. The "International" had all of our cargo she could take on her first trip down after Riel left.

On its return trip the boat brought up Chief Factor Robert Campbell, who stayed with me while I again put on board as much of our freight as possible. He remained two days in order that I could go up with him as far as Georgetown. He was much interested to hear that I had been in friendly conversation with one of Riel's men, who had been sent out to confiscate the Swan River furs, and that I had learned from him that he and his companions had returned several days later and followed our trail to the boundary where they had turned back.

My former *bourgeois* was as usual very kind but told me he was very surprised to hear of my change and wrote immediately to Governor Smith to have me sent back to the Swan River as soon as possible, and to Mr. Christie countermanding MacKay's request for Willie to take charge of Fort Ellice. He does not want my brother there because he has too many relations at that Post. I thought at first he was only joking when he spoke of my going back there.

"Who are you going to put at Riding Mountain?" I asked.

"Who are you going to put there?" he responded. "You will have Mr. Andy and a postmaster and if you like to put one of them at Riding Mountain you can keep the other at Fort Ellice."

Mr. Campbell spoke so decidedly that I think there is little doubt about my returning there. He spent a night with me at Georgetown before going on to Fort Abercrombie to catch the stage for St. Cloud. However, I have heard nothing yet from Fort Garry regarding my appointment other than that Governor Smith told Captain Aymond that "Mr. Traill would remain at Georgetown until the business is over." That is as much as to say "then he will leave." Now that I have everything in such nice order I shall be sorry to go.

When the whitewash brushes arrived from Alexandria, Ike went to work. He has painted the roofs red, whitewashed the buildings and mended the broken windows. In fact, he has painted the whole town and wrought such a miracle of transformation that what was our most disreputable Post is now very attractive in its setting between the Buffalo and Red Rivers.

I hope to know soon where I shall spend the coming winter. If I stay here I have to build a Post at Frog Point. I shall call it Fort Mactavish in memory of our late Governor who lived only a few hours after he returned to England. Four months ago I bade him farewell at Georgetown, hoping to overtake him in St. Paul, but I was not to see him again. So much for plans! I must be ready to go anywhere.

The next boat brought up two army officers with the Express to go from Frog Point to Fort Abercrombie. I had horses ready and we left at two o'clock for Georgetown, where we stopped for dinner and fresh horses. Ike is a good cook and capable of providing an excellent meal on short notice which he did on this occasion. I drove on to Fort Abercrombie which we reached at eight o'clock next morning having covered a distance of ninety-five miles from Frog Point.

One of the officers was Colonel McNeill who knows Colonel Chamberlain and speaks very highly of him. Mrs. Chamberlain is my cousin Agnes, whose husband has very kindly sent me a letter of introduction to Governor Archibald, for which I am most grateful. Though I may never see him this is of great importance to me at this time of some uncertainty. It is always good to have more than one string to a bow in a country like this.

On my return to Georgetown I found the mail had piled up. My horse was saddled at nine o'clock next morning to take me to Frog Point, but it was after dark before I could leave. Letters, letters, letters, until I wished there were mail only once or twice a year as in Swan River. I am writing on board the "International," most of my time being spent at Frog Point from where I go home only for a few hours, sometimes for a day or two, but always to find a pile of letters and documents to be answered.

I am now staying at Frog Point to receive and reship the northern outfits that are being hurried in from London to be forwarded to Fort Garry before the close of navigation. The steamer leaves tonight for Red River and I must go down with my horse on board for a few miles to finish the Customs House papers and ride up by moonlight.

In another month or two I hope to be less worried with work and then I shall try to make up for lost time in writing to my mother the letters I should like to have sent her in this time of affliction.

It is September 16th and I have just received her letter of the 19th of August. I must steal a few minutes to answer it and to assure her that my silence has been due to the bustle in which I live and not to any want of affection.

Aunt Gwillym (née Sarah Strickland) is ever kind to my mother I see and hope that Kate will accept her invitation and go home to England. I will furnish her with all I can to help her dress, etc.

223

I think the change will do her good as they have had a disagreeable and unhealthy summer.

Well, we have had the same. People rave about the climate of Minnesota but so far I have not seen much to enjoy. The mosquitoes began on the 10th of May and have continued ever since. The weather is warm and wet, the most disagreeable summer I have known since I left home. I long for the beautiful clear cold weather that we have in Hudson's Bay.

The Northern Pacific is constructing its line west from Brainerd to the Red River at a great rate and people are flocking in just as fast. The railroad will be here next July when, if I am here and can spare the money, I shall go down to Canada as I am sure of getting a free ticket from some of the railway officials. But if I am in Swan River I must try to go down to Montreal on Hudson's Bay Company's service or pay my own expenses. And now the boat is just starting and I must have her bill of lading ready.

Railway surveys are being made through Dakota to the Missouri River and the engineers under General Thomas Rosser have established a supply station and headquarters south of Georgetown where I have met them in passing and on their visits to my Post. I have become acquainted with all the officials who are chiefly eastern men and have been offered a good situation with an engineering party: one hundred dollars per month and all expenses paid, permanent employment and little to do. I could have got nearly double those wages but of course I could not leave the Hudson's Bay service before June 1st, even if I would then, which is doubtful. So far I like our Company best but if at any future time I should require a situation I have acquaintances who will do something for me. Six months ago none of us thought we would have employment under the present Hudson's Bay Company but now we see that they are only beginning to develop the country instead of departing from where they have ruled and where the people have shown their faith in us.

On September 16th I received a whole packet of letters from Fort Ellice with two written by my mother in March and April. It is strange to read old letters, written when everything looked so dark before us, the past, the present and the future then unknown, but now so different from what we expected.

Newpapers arrive regularly but I do not get time to read them though I take one of the St. Paul papers and receive *The Globe.* I see that Napoléon has surrendered; the war in Europe has indeed been a dreadful slaughter. One can hardly call it by any other name.

A letter came from Willie in the above mail. He wrote from Carlton but at that time had not heard of my being here. I have not heard from Mrs. Hargrave for many months. I fear she has forgotten me. I find it difficult to write when I am so very busy. I have not written to any of my fellow officers inland since I left Fort Garry and only brief notes to my family.

Towards the end of September I returned to Georgetown one evening after seeing off the last boat for the month with the intention of staying up for a day or so. The next morning a party of ladies and gentlemen on their way from Canada to Red River arrived: Mr. and Mrs. Begg of Winnipeg, Mrs. Howard, the wife of one of the military officers there and Miss McTavish from Grafton, Canada, John McTavish's youngest sister. When they said they intended going to Frog Point to wait for the boat I could do no less than accompany them. Before we left, a clerk by the name of McLenaghen arrived from Fort William on his way to Fort Garry. He also would have to wait for the boat so we made a jolly party.

We had no more than set out when we met Colonel Jarvis and Captain Herchmer, both of the Canadian Rifles, on their way to Canada. They were furnished with letters of introduction from Governor Smith who requested me to "send these gentlemen on to Fort Abercrombie." I returned with them to give an order for three fresh horses (from here) and to spend some time in conversation before seeing them off, well-mounted, for Fort Abercrombie.

My horse was as eager to overtake the ones from which he had parted as I was to rejoin my new friends. I arrived at Frog Point to find them ready for supper. The ladies had taken possession of my office, which I had made by piling up cases of merchandise to make a house over which I had spread an oilcloth. With sugar kegs for seats and part of a threshing machine for a table we made the place very comfortable. At least the ladies insisted they found it so after being cramped up in a tent. They stayed for three days and as the boat did not come, they would wait no longer but started by land for their destination.

They had only just left when Judge Johnstone from Montreal arrived on his way to Fort Garry. He brought letters of introduction from the Hudson's Bay House in Montreal, so I did my best to entertain him while he was waiting for the boat. This was indeed a pleasure as he is one of the jolliest old fellows I ever met. I felt quite sorry to take leave of him to attend to the loading of the boat.

The same evening I returned to Georgetown, having been away for the past week waiting for and loading the steamer. This time I hoped to remain for a few days but find that it is absolutely necessary that I go down to Pembina on Hudson's Bay Company's service and that I must start tomorrow morning. I shall drive down and return on the boat that left today.

Our new Governor's letters to me have been very kind in expressing great satisfaction at the way in which I have managed the business here and treated the government and military officers who came my way. He particularly requested me to give him my opinion on the affairs of this Post regarding the transport of goods and travellers. This I have done. Once steamboat navigation is closed for the winter there is no communication between Fort Abercrombie and Fort Garry except a weekly mail carried by buckboard or dogteams to Pembina.

A week later I am back again at Georgetown. I started on the 5th of October to drive to Pembina and overtook Mr. and Mrs. Taylor on the way, so we travelled together. I went down on special business to the Custom House and could stay only one night. William H. Watt, who wintered with Willie at Fort Pitt, is now in charge of Pembina Post and is a really good fellow. I spent the night with him and was sorry I could not stay longer but as we are neighbours, and the distance is not great, I shall take many a run down during the winter. We called upon the officers of the Volunteer Company that is quartered nearby. I had also the pleasure of meeting Mr. O'Donohue riding to church upon a "stolen horse." He has since taken his departure for parts unknown and has just passed here but did not honour me with a call.

On October 4th, mail from Swan River brought more letters but none from Willie or Harriet. Her father wrote that some time ago she went up to Carlton. He tells me that he did not send my clothes down because he was expecting me back this fall. I don't see how that is to be managed though I feel homesick for old friends up there and at times I wish to be back in Swan River again.

Willie was appointed by Council to the charge of Fort Albert, a small wintering post between Carlton and Cumberland but he may not winter there. The whole minutes of Council have been reversed. I have given up thinking that I will be sent back to Fort Ellice. Governor Smith has written to me several times without hinting at such a thing so I am to suppose that he intends to keep me here. I don't know who will take my place at Fort Ellice. I suppose Mr. MacKay will have to remain there, it is no sinecure for any person.

It is October 19th and I have just returned to Georgetown after seeing the "International" off on her last trip for the season. I shall now have less to do and be able to stay here the whole time instead of running between the two places, but I am, if anything, more out of society than I would be at Fort Ellice. I never knew how fond I was of inland life until now.

However, I expect to go down to Fort Garry in a few weeks. I have asked for leave but am not sure I can go down if my request is granted, as I have to go in the opposite direction to Alexandria or St. Cloud to meet the Government stores directly they arrive.

The affairs of Manitoba are rather unsettled though there has been a marked improvement, I hear, since Governor Archibald arrived. The state of civilization, however, is not high. The Canadian troops and voyagers, I believe, are but little better than Riel and his crew. One or two of the halfbreeds have been killed or else frightened to death by the volunteers. I wish they had a military Governor and martial law for a year or two. Canada will never govern the country without a strong force inland. It is to be hoped that the Government will guard against filling its offices with Canadian adventurers. That is the rock that they will split upon again if they are not careful, for a new country attracts mischief-makers and law-breakers.

At last, on November 30th, I have heard from Mr. McTavish that I am not to return to Fort Ellice this winter. He has ordered my things sent down from there. I have every reason to be pleased with the change as I like my new Post very well. My work is more to my taste than trading with Indians. I keep eight men and a clerk, a carpenter and a good many men cutting wood for the steamboat. All this and sundry other things keep me fairly busy although there is no longer the necessity of working night and day as when loading cargoes.

There is no cause for me to wonder what I shall do this winter as my work is pretty well laid out for me. My instructions from Fort Garry are to provide material for a freight depot at Frog Point in the spring. We have been favoured by good weather and preparations for a building by the steamboat landing have been going forward. Already I have built a shack there, having arranged for the pre-emption of one hundred and sixty acres and their survey when the land office is opened at Pembina. Lumber will be shipped for our new Post from the end of the St. Paul and Pacific Railway at Benson.

We have had beautiful autumn weather, since the end of September. I never saw a finer fall in Canada. The climate is more moderate than in Swan River and the golden days of Indian Summer have continued well into November.

A letter from my mother written on November 13th has reached me seventeen days later with one from her dated October 31st. My family have been putting R.R. on their letters with the result that they are put in the through mails to Pembina which causes a delay of sixteen days. Worse still, mail addressed in care of the Hudson's Bay Company via Pembina is forwarded to Fort Garry and cannot be opened here. My proper address is Georgetown, Minnesota, via St. Paul and Fort Abercrombie. I enlisted Mr. Kittson's help in getting the postmaster in St. Paul to send my mail directly to me from there instead of up to Pembina and this has had the desired effect.

In replying to my mother by return mail I am pleased to be able to report that I have recently heard from Mr. Watt that the smallpox is out of Carlton and that Willie and his family are alright. The Government has sent out medical aid and medicine for the relief of the Indians in the Saskatchewan District. It is to be hoped that Willie's trials are at an end for they have had a terrible summer. I have had a long account of the sufferings of the Indians and freemen around Fort Ellice, from Matheson, who is in charge of that Post. He does not like it and says I am lucky to be here. Andy is very much pleased with being changed from acting as second in command at Fort Ellice to the Post I built at Riding Mountain, which he likes very much. I wonder where I shall be next year. The whole Swan River District has been turned bottom-side up and it is just possible that I may be sent back there when winter is over.

During the coming months I hope to have more leisure. I feel that I have been neglecting my mother by not writing more frequently but I have had to write my business letters while talking to or listening to some wagon master or servant. I have had so little time to myself that I have gone out shooting after a hard day or night's work to rest myself. I have not answered Mrs. Campbell's letter nor Kate's.

I hope my sister will try to go home to England this winter or next summer. It would be a pity for her to lose such a good chance as the offer which Aunt Sarah has made.

229

"Dear old Aunt Moodie is well," I hear from my mother, who has not been well herself, but who, I trust and hope is better now and when writing will give my love to Aunt Moodie, Mrs. Tully, and Walter, also my kinds regards to Captain Boulton on seeing him, as he is now in Lakefield. I feel as if we are old friends although we have never met.

Since being here I have seen more of the outside world than the inland clerks. The other day I saw young Harrison from Belleville who passed on his return from Fort Garry to Canada. We had a long chat over old times and old acquaintances. One of the steamboat hands I saw at Frog Point knew Arthur Dupont who was then at Michipicoten, but perhaps he has been changed like myself.

Before long, I suppose we shall have cold and snow and the whole country, from Fort Abercrombie to Pembina will be a howling wilderness. The population from Otter Tail Lake north to the International Boundary is only a hundred and eighty-eighth part of a white person to the square mile and to make this average it is necessary to include Joe Peron, offspring of a Digger Indian and a Mexican cowherd, and his family consisting of a Grosventre wife and half a score of the fruits of the union. Not the least in importance are his train dogs with which he drove Donald A. Smith, Governor of the Hudson's Bay Company, on his first trip to Fort Garry in the capacity of Commissioner from the Canadian Government last December.

Joe also started north from Fort Abercrombie last April with another passenger, Mr. J. J. Hill, who is agent for the St. Paul and Pacific Railway to Benson, and also their agent for the Red River Settlement. At Kelly Point there arose a difference of opinion as to whether Joe and his dogs or Mr. Hill should have the first choice of the food at breakfast. The matter was settled by Mr. Hill ordering Joe to take the back trail, which he did, making a hasty and somewhat disorderly retreat at the point of his erstwhile passenger's six-shooter. Mr. Hill finished his journey of some thirty miles to Pembina on snowshoes and without food.

Now that navigation is closed I must furnish transportation for any freight, or persons, the Company may want forwarded. I also have instructions to open a sales shop at Georgetown for which I am to make requisition on Mr. Kittson in St. Paul for goods. He is the General Manager of the Steamboat Company and Wagon Transfer to Fort Garry and a man who is universally respected by freighters and his fellow officers in the Hudson's Bay Company.

As Officer-in-Charge of the Red River American Hudson's Bay Company's business I am grateful to him for unstinted assistance and timely advice, both of us serving, as we do, under Mr. McTavish, the Officer-in-Charge of the Red River District. Our acquaintance and business relation that began with me as a boy in St. Paul over four years ago is becoming a warm friendship.

As the connecting link between that city and Fort Garry I am placed in a very responsible position, far more than is warranted by my length of service. Our trade in the Red River District has been demoralized during Riel's administration and must be revived. There is much work to be done which falls heavily on Mr. McTavish as Officer-in-Charge although he can count on the loyal support of his Post Managers, including myself.

Our new Governor, Donald A. Smith, has remained at Fort Garry but as yet I have not met him, though I have been in almost daily correspondence with him. Today, November 30th, I have sent a pair of horses and a wagon down to bring him up whenever he can come. He has been greatly concerned regarding the transportation business and among other matters the importance of establishing a Post at Frog Point, the head of navigation in low water.

Evidently, thanks to following his advice, his confidence in me has not been misplaced, though I have been left to my own devices in many respects. His letters expressing much satisfaction with my management of the Company's business have been an encouragement throughout our busiest season.

"You will have great responsibility and will make mistakes, as we all do, but remember that the Company will always sustain you," he advises, "but always carry out any contract you make, either verbally or in writing because your word must be the Company's bond, and in dealing with others, if in doubt, put yourself in the other person's place. If you think you would not consider a transaction to be just, you know then that you are wrong."

It is in accordance with this rule that I must endeavour to conduct my Post, or Posts, in relation to the early settlement of the Red River Valley. It is an excellent rule to observe in private life and in the administration of the Company's business.

The long hours and hard work of recent months decided me at one time to leave the Company's service in the spring and accept the situation with the Northern Pacific Railway at one hundred dollars per month unless the Company could hold out a stronger inducement for me to remain than seventy-five pounds per annum. I doubt if I could bring myself to serve under the officials of another company merely for the sake of money. I have such a contempt for the money-craving spirit one sees at times that I would rather be poor all my life than gain riches as I see some men do.

Our Governor is a good friend to me and I think will do all he can for me in the way of an advance in my salary. Mr. McTavish, who has always been my friend, is the kindest of *bourgeois* and will do likewise. I fear my family has been cherishing false hopes that they will see me this winter, but I cannot spare the time to go down to Canada, even if I had the means, which I have not. If, as I hope, I get my hundred pounds next year I will promise to go home for at least a few days.

The Hudson's Bay Company is now in a better position than ever to carry on the fur trade and to develop the resources of the Northwest. Free trade is a mere bubble that will burst and vanish into thin air directly the law, which prohibits the trade of spirits to the Indians, comes into force. The Company can, by re-organizing their system and whole staff of officers, control in general the trade and make more money than ever they have done before, or they can continue to keep up their present establishments which would bring the whole of their operations to a stop soon. But I think there is little fear of this happening. Governor Smith appears to be a thorough man of business and will, I believe, make the necessary changes.

232

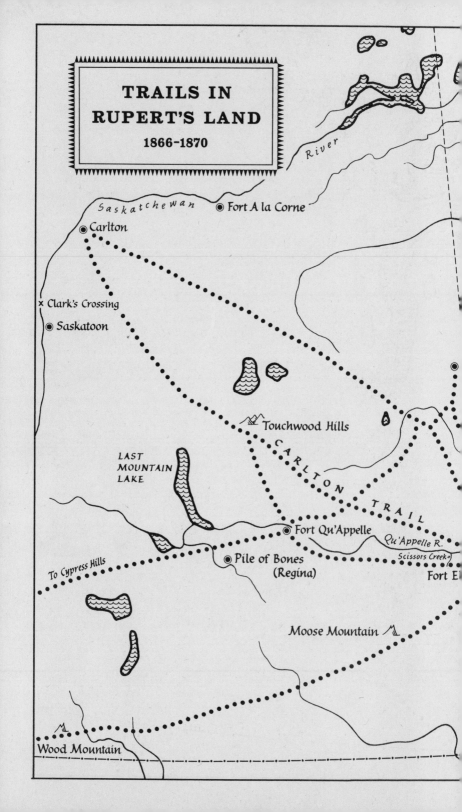

TRAILS IN
RUPERT'S LAND
1866-1870

Saskatchewan River

◉ Fort A la Corne

◉ Carlton

× Clark's Crossing
◉ Saskatoon

Touchwood Hills

LAST
MOUNTAIN
LAKE

CARLTON TRAIL

◉ Fort Qu'Appelle
Qu'Appelle R.
Scissors Creek

To Cypress Hills

◉ Pile of Bones
(Regina)

Fort El

Moose Mountain

Wood Mountain